WITHDRAWN

MULTIVALENCE

The Moral Quality
of Form in the Modern Novel

MULTIVALENCE

The Moral Quality
of Form in the Modern Novel

Alan Warren Friedman

LIBRARY
BRYAN COLLEGE
DAYTON, TENN. 37321

Louisiana State University Press

Baton Rouge and London

82149

Copyright © 1978 by Louisiana State University Press
All rights reserved
Manufactured in the United States of America

Design: Patricia Douglas Crowder
Typeface: VIP Melior
Composition: The Composing Room of Michigan, Inc.
Printing: Thomson-Shore, Inc.
Binding: John Dekker & Sons, Inc.

LIBRARY OF CONGRESS CATALOGING IN PUBLICATION DATA

Friedman, Alan Warren.
   Multivalence.

   Bibliography: p.
   Includes index.
   1.   English fiction—20th century—History and
criticism.   2.   American fiction—20th century—
History and criticism.   3.   Point of view
(Literature)   I.   Title.   II.   Title: Moral
quality of form in the modern novel.
PR888.P57F7   823'.03   78-17485
ISBN 0-8071-0399-3

For my grandparents (Fannie and Jacob)
my parents (Anne and Lee)
my sisters (Elaine and Sharon)
my children (Eric, Scot, Lorraine)

Contents

H. J. Muller The admission of relativity and multivalence does not make value illusory or judgment futile.

George Boas Even in the field of the terminal values of form, a work of art is multivalent.

Preface

The present study derives in part from an earlier book of mine, *Lawrence Durrell and "The Alexandria Quartet": Art for Love's Sake* (1970). The bulk of that book is a novel-by-novel examination of Durrell's quartet—a construct whose distinctive parts overlap and interweave to form a fictional continuum—and then an overview of that multiple novel as a unity; for the intention was to see both the trees and x the woods. In referring to the quartet's appended Work-points, Durrell indicates that the quartet's events could have been examined through any number of additional perspectives without altering the novel's essential structure. It could never, he correctly maintains, have become a *roman fleuve*; for quite clearly he was not writing that type of multivolume novel. The question then became, "What kind of multivolume novel *was* he writing?"—a question that I hope was answered in the concluding chapter of my book.

But other questions remained beyond that book's scope. For one thing, Durrell, though idiosyncratic, is not unique. Many other twentieth-century authors write multivolume novels quite different from Durrell's, and yet they too are usually not *roman fleuves*. For another, it seemed to me that, to some degree, inherent in all extended novels is a kind of narrative I call "multivalent"; that is, such fiction dramatizes multiple, conflicting perspectives and, like Durrell's quartet, often provides little overt evidence for ascertaining precisely the author's sympathies and ethical predilections. Finally, something of a quantum leap into "modern" fiction seems to have occurred, since early multivolume novels tend to be univalent—focusing on one protagonist throughout and employing a single narrative voice—while most written in the twentieth century are multivalent.

These notions, in turn, crystallized for me the problem that remained for those of us who, while profoundly influenced by Wayne C. Booth's brilliantly perceived and argued *Rhetoric of Fiction* (1961), were yet unhappy over his rigid, even reactionary, response to the moral relativity he finds pervading what has come to be known as the modern and the postmodern novel. Consequently, this present study, whose debt to Booth should be obvious throughout, is also in part an attempt at rebuttal, an attempt to advance the basis of critical discussion from the rather sterile univocal / ambivalent dichotomy, to the

synthesizing multivalent, a term denying neither thesis
nor antithesis but affirming the organic validity of both.
At the same time, it seeks to define a major literary phenomenon: the modern multivolume novel.

Perhaps the keystone of the present book is the appended "Galaxy of Multivolume Narrators," the idea for
which derives in part from Booth's "Gallery of Unreliable
Narrators and Reflectors." It gives shape to the book as a
whole, for the scheme of the chapters roughly parallels
that of the first two sections of the "Galaxy." Chapter One
surveys the vast range of multivalent fiction and explains
the book's focus on its peculiarly modern exploitation in
the form of multivolume novels. Chapter Two examines
the varieties of narration undertaken by named characters, Chapter Three the two other main narrative modes:
multifarious and third-person-subjective. Chapters Four
and Five, on Conrad and Faulkner respectively, consider
fiction of the greatest narrative complexity, fiction which
brilliantly interweaves all three major narrative forms.
Sections III and IV of the "Galaxy" cite works outside the
basic framework of my approach; they serve as counterpointing and workpoints—for this study and perhaps for
others as well.

My intention in choosing the works for close consideration in the chapters that follow was to select only
multivolume novels written in this century. For while
multivalence occurs in fiction before 1900, it seems to me
peculiarly modern in its twentieth-century multivolume
form, a form which, I argue, has attained the status of a
major genre. For ease of direct accessibility and to avoid
problems created by translation, I also preferred to treat
only novels written in English, though including works
from both sides of the Atlantic. In addition, I have generally not dealt with works still in progress (J. D. Salinger's
Glass family saga, Simon Raven's *Alms for Oblivion*,
Brian W. Aldiss' Horatio Stubbs quartet), preferring to see
these complete before attempting to take their measure.

xii And finally, I concentrated primarily on novels that seemed capable of bearing the weight of my approach; that is, they had to be sufficiently interesting and successful both to warrant such consideration and, in a sense, not to need it. I saw no point in resurrecting the trivial just to make a case, in investing in an edifice destined to fall.

My intentions, however, often altered under the pressure of actually writing this book, for the process created a fittingly multivalent tension between a priori hypotheses and actual critical conclusions, Fortunately, hypothesis usually yielded, though not always without a fight. Thus novels other than multivolume, twentieth century, written in English, complete, and major are sometimes alluded to not just for contrast but as examples in their own right intended to strengthen and advance the argument. I can only hope that, in the context, they have succeeded in justifying their otherwise intrusive presence, for like a modern novelist I have found it impossible to do other than allow the creatures of my imagination opportunity to make their own way.

Acknowledgments

I wish to express my gratitude to the National Endowment for the Humanities for granting me a fellowship for 1970–1971 and to the University of Texas at Austin for a supplementary grant from its Research Institute along with a year's leave of absence. This support afforded me the time that made completion of this study possible. Finally, I wish to express thanks for the friendship and professional assistance—

xiv critical in the best sense of that term—that I received from Bettie P. Cook, David J. DeLaura, James Gindin, John Halperin, David Hayman, R. James Kaufmann, Gordon Mills, Christopher Ricks, Charles Rossman, Warwick P. Wadlington, and Max Westbrook. It is people of their caliber who render the humanities among the noblest and most interesting of human endeavors.

As indicated below, portions of this book have been previously published in somewhat different form and are reprinted by permission:

"Faulkner's Snopes Trilogy: Omniscience as Impressionism," *Delta* (France), III (November, 1976), 125–51.

"Conrad's Picaresque Narrator: Marlow's Journey from 'Youth' through *Chance*," in *Joseph Conrad: Theory and World Fiction*, ed. W. T. Zyla and Wendell M. Aycock (Lubbock: Texas Tech University Press, 1974), 17–39.

"The Modern Multivalent Novel: Form and Function," in *The Theory of the Novel: New Essays*, ed. John Halperin (New York: Oxford University Press, 1974), 121–40.

"Joyce Cary's Cubistic Morality," *Contemporary Literature*, XIV (Winter, 1973, © by the Regents of the University of Wisconsin), 78–96.

I wish to acknowledge the following for their kind permission to quote extensively from published works:

Doubleday and Company for Joseph Conrad, "Youth" and "Heart of Darkness" in *Great Short Works of Joseph Conrad*, copyright 1966 by Doubleday and Company, and *Chance*, copyright 1968 by Doubleday and Company.

Grove Press for Henry Miller, *Tropic of Cancer*, copyright © 1961 by Grove Press.

Random House, Inc. for William Faulkner, *The Hamlet*, copyright 1931 and 1958 by William Faulkner, 1932 and 1959 by Curtis Publishing Company, 1936 by Charles Scribner's Sons, 1964 by Estelle Faulkner and Jill Faulkner Summers; *The Town*, copyright 1957 by William

Faulkner, 1957 by Curtis Publishing Company; *The Man-* xv
sion, copyright 1955 and 1959 by William Faulkner; and
for Dorothy Richardson, *Pilgrimage*, copyright 1967 by
Random House, Inc.

University Press of Virginia for Frederick L. Gwynn
and Joseph L. Blotner (eds.), *Faulkner in the University*,
copyright © 1959 by University of Virginia Press.

List of Abbreviations

The following abbreviations designate works by these authors in these editions:

Joyce Cary

PG *Prisoner of Grace*. London: Michael Joseph, 1952.

EL *Except the Lord*. London: Michael Joseph, 1953.

NHM *Not Honour More*. London: Michael Joseph, 1955.

PR *Writers at Work: The "Paris Review" Interviews*. London: Secker & Warburg, 1958.

Joseph Conrad

Y *Youth* in *Great Short Works of Joseph Conrad*. New York: Harper & Row, 1966.

HD *Heart of Darkness* in *Great Short Works of Joseph Conrad*. New York: Harper & Row, 1966.

LJ *Lord Jim*. New York: Holt, Rinehart, 1963.

C *Chance*. New York: Norton, 1968.

William Faulkner

H *The Hamlet*. New York: Vintage Books, 1940.

T *The Town*. New York: Vintage Books, 1961.

M *The Mansion*. New York: Vintage Books, 1965.

List of Abbreviations

F in U *Faulkner in the University*, ed. Frederick L. Gwynn and Joseph L. Blotner. Charlottesville: University of Virginia Press, 1959.

Ford Madox Ford

SDN *Some Do Not.* New York: Alfred A. Knopf, 1961.
LP *The Last Post.* New York: Alfred A. Knopf, 1961.

Wyndham Lewis

Chi *The Human Age, Book One: Childermass.* London: Methuen, 1956.

Henry Miller

BHM *The Best of Henry Miller*, ed. Lawrence Durrell. London: Heinemann, 1960.
BS *Black Spring.* New York: Grove Press, 1963.
CE *The Cosmological Eye.* Norfolk, Conn.: New Directions, 1939.
DP *A Devil in Paradise.* New York: Signet, 1956.
SW *Sunday after the War.* Norfolk, Conn.: New Directions, 1944.
T Can *Tropic of Cancer.* New York: Grove Press, 1961.
T Cap *Tropic of Capricorn.* New York: Grove Press, 1961.
WH *The Wisdom of the Heart.* Norfolk, Conn.: New Directions, 1941.
WS *The World of Sex.* New York: Grove Press, 1965.

Dorothy Richardson

P *Pilgrimage.* 4 vols. London: J. M. Dent & Sons, 1967.

Evelyn Waugh

MA *Men at Arms.* Harmondsworth, Middlesex: Penguin, 1952.
OG *Officers and Gentlemen.* Harmondsworth, Middlesex: Penguin, 1955.
US *Unconditional Surrender.* Harmondsworth, Middlesex: Penguin, 1961.

MULTIVALENCE:
The Moral Quality
of Form in the Modern Novel

Ronald Paulson[1] Either skepticism or a kind of
happy comic acceptance may
be the result of the spectrum
of discrepant perspectives.

Marcel Proust The great men of letters have
never created more than a sin-
gle work, or rather have never done more than refract
through various mediums an
identical beauty which they
bring into the world.

1
Multivalence:
Form and Function

One of the notable phe-
nomena of twentieth-century fiction is the extent to which
it has become extended. E. M. Forster gave the term novel
one meaning when he defined it as a prose work in fiction

---

1 "The Pictorial Circuit and Related Structures in 18th-Century England," in
The Varied Pattern: Studies in the 18th Century, ed. Peter Hughes and David
Williams (Toronto: A. M. Hakkert, Ltd., 1971), 182. Epigraphs to Chapters Two
and Five are also taken from this essay.

2 of a certain extent. But many novels have moved beyond the finitude of "certain" to occupy the amplitude of "indefinite." For since the novel has become psychological and open, the novelist who would terminate the stream of his fiction finds that it has no necessary ending, that it goes on multiplying perspectives and possibilities—often into several or many volumes.

This is not to say that twentieth-century novels are simply longer than their predecessors—for certainly Samuel Richardson, Henry Fielding, and Anthony Trollope, for instance, had no qualms about extensive verbiage. The later novelists, in fact, tend to write shorter novels, but once having written them they frequently find the job less than complete—and so write them again from a somewhat different angle or vision, and sometimes again and again. The result is the modern multivalent novel—a work of fiction whose hallmarks, as I hope to demonstrate in this chapter, are its expressing an overt consciousness of itself as artifact and its juxtaposing of different ethical perspectives.

In a sense, the very elaboration of a novel into several volumes is an ineffaceable act of self-consciousness (and therefore an assertion of multiple perspectives)—far more than the perhaps largely accidental or passive initial creative action. Just as no artist attains full expression through a single achievement—no matter how singular or sublime—so too no single work fully expresses itself by itself. More likely it will attain the status of an historical oddity, a chance happening—like Henry Roth's brilliant but largely neglected novel *Call It Sleep*. Every artistic expression—a Michaelangelo statue, a Shakespearean play, a Beethoven symphony, a Picasso painting—asserts the fullest sense of itself by defining a place and role for itself within an entire corpus. And the multivolume novel—almost invariably self-conscious and pluralistic because simultaneously both a series of discrete parts and a unity—necessarily creates and defines a context, a pat-

tern, for itself. The separate volumes must stand on their
own, and yet their interrelated existences require of us a
comparatist's eye and judgment. The whole becomes the
sum not only of the parts but also of something more: the
interconnectedness between and through the several volumes. For the temporally linear act of reading, like
Proust's madeleine cake, creates responses that ripple
outward both with and against the conventional current
of time—and never more so than in the multivolume
novel with its self-contained dramas that are yet acts
within a larger play. On the grandest scale one might,
with Balzac, call that play the human comedy and write a
hundred of its countless acts.

The term *multivalence* derives from chemistry, where it
denominates those atoms capable of combining with
other atoms in multiple combinations; univalent atoms
possess a single combining characteristic; and the word
ambivalent has the same etymological root. Univalence
in fiction is essentially what we mean when we speak of
authorial intrusiveness, or any other device by which a
single, unambivalent narrative stance dominates, and
thus embodies the values of the book. Narrative ambivalence occurs when several perspectives merge, creating
moral confusion. The multiple perspectives on moral reality offered by multivalent art transcend both the sanctity accorded univalence and the frenzied ambivalence of
such writers as William Burroughs.

My interest in the concept of multivalence primarily
concerns its manifestation in novels I call "multivolume," yet the two terms are not coextensive. In their
simplest form, multivolume novels offer linear sequels in
the episodic fashion of the picaresque or the chronicle
form of the *roman fleuve*. They may differ in setting and
mood, but structurally and morally they are often identical. In C. P. Snow's eleven-volume novel *Strangers and
Brothers*, we participate in a sequence of events in much

4 the same way as we do in *Robinson Crusoe* or de Sade's
Justine and *Juliette* or Scott's Waverley novels: a series of
adventures or misadventures confronts the protagonist
(the passive is the proper mood, for the protagonist,
though energetic *within* the actions, is generally passive
between them: they befall him). Each episode contains
rising action, climax, denouement, and perhaps moral,
but little of significance is sufficiently well learned to ensure that the same or similar incidents will not recur to be
confronted again as if for the first time. Thus, de Sade's
Justine endures an almost endless series of similar experiences in no significant order; Juliette repeats the process in mirror image. Snow's *Strangers and Brothers*
seems anachronistic in its technique because it is
"closed" (i.e., moving chronologically from early life to
marriage or death, the terminal conditions that reverse
the expanding action of most pre-twentieth-century
novels), although it is stretched to great length.[2] With
such fiction as *Strangers and Brothers*, then, multivalence
means little more than multivolume: Lewis Eliot differs
from novel to novel not because he is perceived differently but only because he ages.

    Multivalence is a double-focused term: it applies both
to multiple ways of viewing and to multiple ways of
being seen. Aesthetically, the term implies deliberate
counterpointing on the author's part, a demonstrating of
concern for moral issues even when answers to them may
be beyond him, or anyone. Multivalent fiction differs
from the simple deployment of opposing moral stands
that occurs typically in Westerns and detective stories, for
the classic "good guy versus bad guy" arrangement offers
us no alternatives, only a vicarious involvement with one
side against the other. But Westerns like Walter Van Til-
burg Clark's *The Ox-Bow Incident* and detective fiction
like Conrad's *The Secret Agent* distribute virtue and vice

---

2 For a discussion of closed and open novels, see Alan Friedman, *The Turn
of the Novel* (New York: Oxford University Press, 1966), 15–37, 179–88.

in radically different terms, in ways that require us to give
consideration to different moral possibilities, that require
not mere identification with the personified forces of
truth and goodness, but a fundamental inquiry into their
very nature.

Thus, even a narrator like Snow's Lewis Eliot—who
himself raises many of these issues—partakes of multivalence because, though a traditionally continuous character, he views his world with unique perspective at each of
the eleven stages of his life. Dickens' Pip and Conrad's
Marlow look back on earlier versions of themselves—and
contrast themselves as they had thought they were, themselves as they now think they "really" were, and (implicitly) themselves as *we* now find them to be. Ford
Madox Ford's Dowell in *The Good Soldier* and Durrell's
Darley in *The Alexandria Quartet,* having been forced to
reexperience themselves through others' eyes, proceed to
revivify and contradict what had previously seemed fixed
and immutably past in their lives—and in the process
they inevitably reveal more aspects of themselves than
they know. Self-dramatized voices like James's narrator
in *The Aspern Papers,* Cary's monologists, many of Nabokov's (in *The Real Life of Sebastian Knight, Lolita, Pale
Fire*) are not actually seeking truth (as they claim), but
rather to impose their own limited visions upon the recal-
citrant world about them. They too display conflicting
realities about themselves, for we are aware of the distance between what they say and what they do, how they
act and how they think they are acting.

Thus, many single-volume novels and single-volume
parts of larger works may be dynamically multivalent. In
various ways, they depict conflicting voices of significant
scope and self-assuredness. A novel like *The Sound and
the Fury* or *Absalom, Absalom!* or *As I Lay Dying,* for
example, offers a series of partial views of events; and
each view is both compelling and undercut to a large extent. In *Tristram Shandy* and *The Good Soldier* the narra-

6 tive voice—a self-conscious subjective protagonist—is divided against his ostensible narrative purpose; in such works the monologue form is multivalent because of the strongly felt presence of an implied author who is at a distance from his narrator. A similar effect results from a form I call third-person-subjective; in such works as *The Beast in the Jungle, The Secret Agent, A Portrait of the Artist,* an anonymous and undramatized though intensely personal narrator is ironically at odds with his narrated material. Most unclassifiable (because broader than any possible categorization) are novels, like *Moby-Dick* and *Ulysses,* employing a full spectrum of narrative perspectives and techniques—from the highly subjective ("Call me Ishmael," the "Proteus" chapter of *Ulysses*) to the objectification of the playlet in *Moby-Dick* and "Ithaca" in *Ulysses.*

Though employing different narrative techniques, multivalent works like Cary's trilogies, Faulkner's *The Sound and the Fury, Absalom, Absalom!,* and *As I Lay Dying,* Woolf's *To the Lighthouse* and *Mrs. Dalloway* all offer a multiplicity of unique perspectives. Each perspective is self-conscious and inadequate, but a still possible way of envisaging a reality that remains in flux even while one seeks to perceive and define it. Such works as these, then, for all their internalizing, emphasize the seen as much as the seer—and it is only a remarkable world (remarkable in its reality) that can sustain such a variety of conflicting approaches. The technically least interesting modern novels are either multivalent only in the simplest of ways (like *Strangers and Brothers*) or else only apparently multivalent (Graham Greene's *The End of the Affair*[3]). To a great extent, the morally and aesthetically richest are, as I discuss below, multivalent in both senses of the term.

Granted that single-volume novels can be multivalent, of what importance is the idea of the multivolume work?

---

3 See pp. 12–13 below for a discussion of this novel's central problem.

Fiction employing multiple perspectives—as well as narrative self-consciousness, unreliability, and reflexivity—has of course predominated since Flaubert and James. But as I seek to demonstrate, the very *function* of multivolume novels as a genre seems to have become the deploying of multivalent techniques and stances, and in ways often strikingly new and different from most previous fiction. Throughout this study, I will be discussing and applying both terms—multivalence and multivolume—with the intention both of elucidating meaning and validating linkage.

In considering multivolume novels as a group, we may discern certain patterns even in their lengths. Most double-volume novels offer one of two kinds of reexperiencing perspectives: a self-contained series of adventures befalls a protagonist, followed by (1) a subsequent and consequent self-contained series, or (2) a second and structurally equal protagonist experiencing an analogous series. The first form generally employs protagonist narration—as in Samuel Butler's *Erewhon*, John Braine's *Room at the Top* and *Life at the Top*, Durrell's *The Revolt of Aphrodite*—although Cervantes employs a dramatized narrator of constantly shifting dimensions and Lewis Carroll's Alice books use third-person-subjective. The second variety varies from the dual protagonist narration of de Sade's *Justine* and *Juliette*, to the third-person-subjective of Bunyan's *Pilgrim's Progress* (within the dream frame), to Twain's shift from the one type of narration to the other in *Tom Sawyer* and *Huckleberry Finn*.

The triple-volume novel also occurs in two main forms: (1) the triple perspective, as in Beckett's and Cary's multiplistically narrated trilogies (and such single-volume analogues as Gertrude Stein's *Three Lives* and John Dos Passos' *Three Soldiers*), predicated upon a prismatic, pluralistic conception of reality; and (2) the *Bildungsroman*—Dreiser's Frank Cowperwood series, Farrell's *Studs Lonigan* and *Bernard Carr*, Henry Miller's trilogies,

8 Leslie P. Hartley's *Eustace and Hilda*, Evelyn Waugh's *Sword of Honour*—tauter forms of the *roman fleuve* that more extended works generally become.

The tetralogy or quartet generally focuses on a complexly evolving central consciousness—whether it employs protagonist narration as in Durrell's *Alexandria Quartet* (and Swift's *Gulliver's Travels*), third-person-subjective as in Ford's *Parade's End*, or some combination of the two as in Conrad's Marlovian narratives. Regardless of technique, all of these counterpoint the central consciousness with contrasting perspectives: with the various spokesmen for the alien cultures encountered in *Gulliver's Travels*; with the frame narrators and the ostensible central characters in Conrad; with the multiple internal monologues in the last book of *Parade's End*; with Balthazar the character and *Mountolive* the book in *The Alexandria Quartet*.

Beyond four, the *roman fleuve* and *Bildungsroman* predominate, and their endlessly extendable structure imposes no necessary limit, makes little formal distinction among five- or six-volume series (Trollope's Barsetshire and Palliser novels, Farrell's Danny O'Neill series), the dozen or so volumes in Galsworthy's Forsyte chronicles, Anthony Powell's *A Dance to the Music of Time*, Sinclair's Lanny Budd series, Snow's *Strangers and Brothers*, the fifteen volumes of Henry Williamson's *A Chronicle of Ancient Sunlight*, the twenty-seven volumes of Jules Romains' *Men of Good Will*, or even the nearly one hundred volumes of Balzac's *Human Comedy*. The significant distinction concerns that between one running story (Farrell, Galsworthy) and many stories connected under a looser rubric (Scott, Balzac). Only a few multivolume novels seem capable of this sort of length without assuming the form of the *roman fleuve*: Proust's seven-volume *Remembrance of Things Past*, Faulkner's fourteen-volume Yoknapatawpha cycle, Salinger's incomplete Glass family saga. These last cited are all com-

plexly dynamic in their unfoldings, for Proust, Faulkner, 9
and Salinger brilliantly create the rich patterning of a
highly wrought short story where the very lengths of their
works would seem to demand the easy temporality of the
roman fleuve.

That there are multiple ways of viewing the multivalent novel does not, of course, invalidate any one of them.
To focus on one while affirming the validity of others is
not only to acknowledge multivalence but to practice it as
well. Games of this sort are, after all, fun to play, and
perhaps also potentially meaningful—provided of course
one doesn't lose a sense of perspective and assume that
categorization alone represents some ultimate purpose.
By themselves, such groupings can make no moral or
aesthetic distinctions. Besides, categorization according
to narrative mode necessarily ignores all sorts of matters
of at least equal significance—tone, for example, and
method of character revelation and style. What I am after,
then, in the appended "Galaxy of Multivolume Narration,"[4] is not rules but tools, an apparatus for doing a
specific job in one of the many possible ways that it might
be done.

My concern with multivalence derives to a large extent
from the fact that Booth's discussion of ambivalence in
The Rhetoric of Fiction leads him into a classical contradiction. Through brilliant practical criticism, he
sweeps away the significance of all such critical distinctions, as, say, "telling" and "showing," by demonstrating
that successful novels transcend all abstract criteria. But
he then goes on to proclaim his own: that novels fail to
the extent that they are morally ambivalent.[5] As another
Alan Friedman puts it,

4 As indicated in the Preface, this "Galaxy of Multivolume Narration" plays
off "Gallery of Unreliable Narrators and Reflectors" in Wayne C. Booth's *The
Rhetoric of Fiction* (Chicago and London: University of Chicago Press, 1961),
432–34.
5 " . . . an author has an obligation to be as clear about his moral position as
he possibly can be" (*Rhetoric of Fiction*, 389). This idea, which lies behind

10   One wonders whether in fact Booth is—as he supposes—
raising fundamental issues about judgment, clarity, and responsibility in the novel, or whether he is not looking for the
old judgment, clarity, and responsibility in the newer form,
worriedly searching in the newer pattern of the novel for the
specific ethical process embodied in the older pattern. The
antinomies of ambiguous and even rationally contradictory
ethics in modern fiction are themselves, strictly speaking, a
"judgment"—a judgment that implicitly asserts that it alone
can help man be fully man.[6]

Antinomies imply multivalence, not an amoral relativism
but a *multi*-moral, pluralistic flux in which disparate and
irreconcilable voices all claim (with varying degrees of
legitimacy) to speak with the rights and perquisites of authorial privilege.

At least at first, the result is uneasiness for the unsus-
pecting reader. Writing of *Don Quixote*, the archetypal
modern multivolume novel, Dorothy Van Ghent says:

> It would seem that "great books" . . . have a very special am-
> biguity distinguishing them from lesser works. In the case of
> Cervantes' great novel, this quality seems to lie in the con-
> stant reversibility of perspective between deeply distant ex-
> tremes. . . . What the reader's attention is directed to is not
> one aspect (moral or practical) of action, but the action itself,
> the adventure itself, as an event with many aspects. It is
> rather difficult for the rationalizing, moralizing intellect to
> think in this fashion. We feel the need of singling out some
> aspect as predominant and as definitive of worth-while val-
> ues.[7]

Booth, a "rationalizing, moralizing intellect" if ever there
was one, would seem to require Cervantes to affirm his

Booth's critical discussions throughout the book (see especially pp. 346–74,
378–96), seems innocuous and unassailable. But by "clear" Booth implies both
"simple" and "good," and thus confuses aesthetic criteria with philosophical
and ethical ones. Both extremes of narration are equally anomalous: for those
who proclaim showing at the cost of telling, the *reductio ad absurdum* novel is
the play, but for Booth—who effectively scores points off such proclaimers—it
is, equally absurdly, the sermon.

6 Friedman, *Turn of the Novel*, 185.
7 Dorothy Van Ghent, *The English Novel: Form and Function* (New York:
Harper Torchbooks, 1953), 18–19.

hero's moral stance while on his quest and deny it when he is on his deathbed—or vice versa. But surely Van Ghent is right to suggest that it is a mark of Cervantes' achievement, not his failing, that we feel a double pull: that the good Don's moral posture is simultaneously compelling *and* inadequate at *both* stages of his life. To a large extent, the brilliance of the achievement lies in our being made to recognize that this is one of those frequent times when opposing moral appeals are equally valid and therefore both irreconcilable and viable. Booth would seem to ask more of Cervantes than we are capable of ourselves, in our lives; but then Booth, unlike Cervantes and most great artists, is not only dogmatic but comfortably so.

It might be useful at this point to make clear my understanding of the word *moral*. In the representation of plural perspectives on the morality of some person, action, or thing, it does not necessarily follow—as Booth would seem to have it—that one view or value scheme must be self-evidently good or good as measured against some absolute standard, while all the others are bad. This is only one possibility and, while successfully exploited in such works as Browning's *The Ring and the Book*, it is the least likely in serious modern fiction. The two more common possibilities are that among the several perspectives one emerges as morally superior to the rest or else that they are all equally good or equally bad. An example of the former is the emergence of Ratliff as something of a moral spokesman in Faulkner's Snopes trilogy. Joyce Cary's two trilogies offer examples of the latter: despite sharply conflicting ethical positions, the first trilogy's narrators are all trustworthy and good, those of the second trilogy are the opposite.

Clearly, Cary and Faulkner are writers who care deeply about moral matters, writers who are not playing games by withholding "truth" from us and thus trivializing what their work has us take seriously. Rather, unlike Browning in *The Ring and the Book*, they lack clear-cut

12 answers to many problems they perceive and portray. We need to separate an author's ethical concern from his ability to articulate an ethical position, and to recognize that we may and commonly do have the one without the other—and in highly successful works. "Modern" artists often strike us as arrogant, as, in Joyce's terms, Gods of creation indifferently paring their fingernails while we, unaided, wrestle with their enigmatic creations. But even writers like Joyce often provide necessary judgment (Stephen is treated harshly in *Ulysses*, Bloom with boundless sympathy), and the other side of arrogance is humility—a recognition that there can no longer be any automatic claim to higher authority or any assurance that our judgments, even in the best of circumstances and with the best of intentions, will be infallible.

By itself, the term *multivalent* confers no special distinction. To apply it to a novel is to say little, if anything, of that novel's aesthetic or moral quality or significance. It is always a serious mistake, as Robert Scholes and Robert Kellogg indicate, to treat descriptive terms (novel, epic, tragedy) as if they were evaluative.[8] And just as technique is unavoidable in any mode of expression, it is, as Booth reminds us, nothing by itself. There are bad multivalent novels as well as good. For example, Graham Greene's *The End of the Affair*, unlike such religious novels as Joyce Cary's *Except the Lord* and *The Captive and the Free*, is essentially a religious statement disguised as a novel. Another way of saying this is that multivalence is reduced to a trick in this novel: the several apparently conflicting perspectives lead to univocality, not only a deus ex machina but God himself. Where Cary offers contradictory but equally possible human interpretations of reality, Greene's central incident (like the falling door which may or may not have killed his protagonist,

---

8 Robert Scholes and Robert Kellogg, *The Nature of Narrative* (New York: Oxford University Press, 1966), 8.

Maurice Bendrix) makes an extraterrestrial appeal that points us back to the pre-novel didacticism of Bunyan's *Pilgrim's Progress*. According to Bendrix, the door blown in by the exploding rocket caught and held just above him (though, oddly, he is bruised as if the door *had* actually landed on him). According to Sarah Miles, his mistress, the door did fall and kill him—and his being alive must be a miracle. She renounces her love for him because, on seeing him dead, she had promised God she would do so if Bendrix were restored to life. The rest of the novel demonstrates that her interpretation is correct, alas—for it not only destroys the characters, it destroys them *as* characters. Greene's problem here is that he fails to make dogma dramatic; Sarah and Maurice die for us just when his thesis demands that they begin to live. *The End of the Affair* returns us to the world of Browning's *The Ring and the Book*, a world in which infallible spokesmen pronounce divine Truth—but without the poem's sustaining dramatic power.

The term *multivalence* has value, then, within a sharply defined conceptual framework, and only to the extent that it provides us with critical handles on an important modern literary phenomenon. Of course it is the fiction and not the categories that matters, just as analyses employing categories must, if they can, stand on their own merit. In Scholes's important distinction, criticism enables us not to "know" but to "know about." Scholes adds: "All interpretive criticism amounts to this. That is the limitation of such criticism. . . . It clarifies, at the expense of reducing the experience of fiction, through which we 'know' a work, to a discussion through which we 'know about' it. Thus its only use is to prepare us to encounter or re-encounter the primary material, the work itself."[9] The terms and categories applied to the multivalent novel are

9 Robert Scholes, *The Fabulators* (New York: Oxford University Press, 1967), 141.

14 not fixed and immutable, but part of the ongoing process
of our continuing response to the demands such works
make upon us.

Morality is, as Booth maintains, the sticking point in
modern fiction; but only novelists who practice a relatively unself-conscious art—and, like Lawrence and
Kerouac and Snow, risk appearing anachronistic—seek
in their writings an ethic equivalent to pre-Darwinian an-
thropology, pre-Einsteinian physics, pre-Freudian psy-
chology. Despite an apparently quite different thrust, the
multivalent novel also seeks to determine where truth
lies, but at the same time it acknowledges that that is
exactly what "truth" often does. It thus derives much of
its dynamic tension from an anti-absolutist ethical commitment, one too self-confronting to permit any denial of
the inductive immediacy of the human moment.

In fiction, morality of purpose and action is inextricably linked with manner of revelation. Conrad's complex
narrative structure in *Lord Jim* aims at one crucial effect:
sympathetic involvement with Jim's plight before we
learn the morally damning fact of the *Patna*'s failure to
sink. Had we come to know Jim in a more straightforward
manner, we would likely dismiss him as beneath contempt. Conrad's narrative structure does not negate the
moral reality, but it creates a context denying us the lux-
ury of a single-faceted response towards Jim: we condemn *and* sympathize, loathe and admire, reject and
identify with. The union of morality and structure is also
Frank Kermode's concern when he defends the presentation of horror and depravity in William Golding's *Pincher
Martin*: "What makes all this bearable and Golding a
major novelist is the total technical control: nightmare,
hysteria, every kind of beastliness and depravity are
given the virtue of form." Kermode adds that "Golding's
novels are simple in so far as they deal in the primordial
patterns of human experience and in so far as they have
skeletons of parable. On these simple bones the flesh of

narrative can take extremely complex forms. This makes
for difficulty, but of the most acceptable kind, the difficulty that attends the expression of what is profoundly
simple."[10] This may serve as something of a rationale for
what I am trying to do here. For defining and codifying
basic patterns of narrative revelation should facilitate our
apprehending the moral center of multivalent fiction—
and the ways in which teller and tale interact.

The "Galaxy of Modern Multivolume Narration" aims,
then, to categorize novels in which narrative perspective
is not simply a donnée but a central aspect of the ongoing
and unfolding process of the novel we are reading. The
two main principles for inclusion are general quality in
the work and its organic use of narration as a technique
for affording multiple perspectives on the world it depicts. With these in mind, I exclude a variety of multivolume works: the essentially two-dimensional detective
series; children's literature even when it has pretensions
to something else (A. A. Milne's Winnie-the-Pooh series,
C. S. Lewis' *Chronicles of Narnia*, L. Frank Baum's *Oz*
series, Henry Williamson's *Animal Saga*—though I in-
clude writers, like Carroll, Twain, Tolkien, whose works
look both to the world of childhood experience *and* quite
beyond it, and thus become multivalent in outlook as
well as form); the exotic but hollow (Edgar Rice Burroughs'
Tarzan, C. S. Forester's Hornblower, H. Rider Haggard's
Allan Quartermain); and situation comedies (P. G. Wode-
house's Jeeves, Durrell's Antrobus series).

In general, the modernity of multivalent fiction results
from a double self-consciousness: that of an engaging and
multiply viewed narrator or implied author, and that of
the novel itself seemingly obsessed with its own identity
as a work of art and its relationship to those who experience it. In "modern" fiction, this awareness is often embodied in the form of a self-dramatized narrator whose

10 "William Golding," in *On Contemporary Literature*, ed. Richard Kostelanetz (New York: Avon, 1969), 378, 381.

16 focus is the telling as much as the tale: Sterne's *Tristram
Shandy*, *Moby-Dick*'s Ishmael, Pip in *Great Expectations*,
Conrad's Marlow, Dowell in *The Good Soldier*, Ratliff in
Faulkner's Snopes trilogy, Cary's and Beckett's triple narrators, Darley in Durrell's *Alexandria Quartet*. Each of
these is an impressionistic explorer/creator of the physical and moral realm he seeks to define, express, and
judge. "Modern" in this sense is conceived not as a temporal designation but as a quality that has been called
psychological, open, indeterminate, and that often manifests itself through self-consciousness in narration. Such
an approach conceives of an artistic creation as process,
still in motion even when complete, a finished edifice
with all the scaffolding of its construction not only still in
place but permanently so. Thus, the planned formless-
ness of a work like *Tristram Shandy*, which not only de-
velops forward in time but opens outward and backwards
as well, embodies a modernity (a quality term) that reduces the socially constricted worlds of novelists like
John Braine and Alan Sillitoe to the merely contemporary
(a temporal term). For the novels of the latter function in
aesthetically narrow ways: as urban versions of the simple picaresque, lacking the moral and structural reverberations of the complex picaresque like *Don Quixote* and
Huckleberry Finn.

My approach makes certain other assumptions. It
maintains, for instance, the essential interrelatedness, the
unity, of certain sequences—Salinger's Glass stories,
Faulkner's Yoknapatawpha novels, Conrad's Marlovian
tales, all of Thomas Wolfe's novels, Joyce's *Portrait* and
Ulysses, Huxley's *Brave New World* series—that may
otherwise seem conceptually disparate. The very placing
of these works into categories borders on critical arrogance, an implicit assumption that they can be thus defined and categorized, though not of course circumscribed.
Further, it may represent debatable literary judgment—
for example, to classify Salinger's Glass stories as pro-

tagonist narration is to assert that they are all narrated by 17
Buddy Glass and that he is their protagonist. This seems
to be both defensible and responsible, but it is by no
means universally accepted. To list Durrell's *Quartet* as
employing participant narration plus third-person-subjective is to argue that *Mountolive* is narrated not objectively
(the common assumption) but from the perspective of its
title character.[11] Similarly, to say that *Portrait* and *Ulysses*
together constitute a single multivalent novel is to imply
that *Ulysses* concerns itself with affording another way of
viewing Stephen Dedalus. It does so, of course, although
other things—for example, and extraordinarily vital and
complex depiction of its title character—are more central.

Such an approach, then, necessarily imposes something of itself upon these works, but it also opens up
additional perspectives on them. The categories may be
said to distort only if one views them as Platonic univer-
sals; what they can provide is one of many possible ways
of looking at a blackbird. It should not be assumed that
they are intended to do more, or that they could. In fact,
even within these terms, the implicit hard-and-fast distinctions represent a further distortion: in actuality, the
categories fade into each other like adjacent colors in a
rainbow, each of them only subtly different from the next.

With such reservations very much in mind, then, I am
suggesting that the modern multivalent novel (whether
multi- or single-volume) may usefully be categorized according to three main narrative modes: (1) multifarious
narration, (2) participant narration, and (3) third-person-
subjective. There are, in addition, variations on each of
these, as well as hybrids resulting from combinations of
any two or all three of these basic forms.

Multifarious narration is a term conceived to replace

11 This is the argument that I do in fact make in my *Lawrence Durrell and
"The Alexandria Quartet": Art for Love's Sake* (Norman: University of Oklahoma Press, 1970), 126–32.

18 the imprecision of *omniscience*. In the early days of novel criticism, the universe must still have seemed a permanent and harmoniously ordered continuum in which God was the Artist of Nature and man strove to emulate him in the available media. How else account for the use of *omniscient* to designate the most common mode of narrative revelation? One may well believe, further, that arrogance breeds absurdity—as in the subsequent appearance of the oxymoron *limited omniscience*. The need for refinement is great, but meaningful discrimination lies, rather, in such a direction as Booth's delineating of narrators in such terms as distance, irony, degree of dramatization, reliability, and so on.[12] It lies, too, in the utter abandonment of *omniscience* as a defining term. Scholes and Kellogg acknowledge the irrelevant world view implicit in the term: " 'Omniscience' itself is . . . a definition based on the presumed analogy between the novelist as creator and the Creator of the cosmos, an omniscient God. . . . But a narrator in fiction is imbedded in a time-bound artifact. He does not 'know' simultaneously but consecutively." (There are exceptions—*Tom Jones* has already happened for Fielding's narrator; thus he *knows* spatially though he must *speak* temporally—but they are rarer than is commonly assumed). And they offer us *multifarious narrator* in its stead, a term properly implying that even the most objective and removed commentator "is not everywhere at once but now here, now there, now lookng into this mind or that, now moving on to other vantage points. He is time-bound and space-bound as God is not."[13]

The multifarious narrator, by definition limited in significant ways, is most at home in certain novelistic modes: in the chronicle rather than the picaresque, in the wide-ranging panoramic rather than the intensely per-

12 Booth, *Rhetoric of Fiction*, 150–65. See also Norman Friedman, "Point of View in Fiction: The Development of a Critical Concept," *PMLA*, LXX (December, 1955), 1160–84.
13 Scholes and Kellogg, *Nature of Narrative*, 272–73.

sonal, in the realistic and naturalistic rather than the impressionistic. This is not to say that the multifarious narrator embodies an aesthetically or morally inferior mode, but rather that the effects aimed at and the conventions employed are strikingly different from those of other types of narrators. The multifarious narrator is often not terribly profound, but he must be skillfully various, light on his metaphorical (because only partially dramatized) feet. He is called upon, like an adroit and active puppet-master, to display and manipulate a variety of figures in succession, often several at a time—with something of a stage role for himself often included along with the rest. And when this approach affords us several views of events and people, then multifariousness becomes multivalence.

Earlier multivolume novels rely mainly on multifarious narration. The narrative voices employed by Scott, Thackeray, and Trollope (like those of Fielding and Jane Austen) are all physically distant from the action they narrate—and often intellectually and morally distant as well. They make little pretense of an independent reality for the characters and actions they unfold. Thus they can claim kinship with storytellers in the oral tradition—for whom interaction with an actual audience plays an important part in the telling—and also with the modern self-conscious narrator, for whom the process of interacting with a created and creative consciousness constitutes part of the aesthetic product. Multifarious narration in the hands of implied authors like those of Cervantes, Fielding, and Thackeray is, in fact, a progenitor of self-consciousness in the modern novel.

My second category, participant narration, replaces the more general term *first-person narration*. Novels in this group occupy an aesthetic gamut from Proust's *Remembrance of Things Past* to Snow's *Strangers and Brothers*. In one sense, such works are full-scale expansions on the hints of dramatized narrators contained in multifarious narration. Proust's focus is not the chronological aging of the protagonist / narrator, but the complex and circuitous interacting of such a figure with time and memory. The process is more circular than linear, as the taste of madeleine cake summons up remembrances of things past and the narrator journeys backward and downward rather than temporally forward. Yet the linear is never lost; we are carried into the future as well because we follow not only the actions of the past but also the mind of the protagonist / narrator as it seeks to recapture and depict, and therefore create, the past in the image of the present.

In contrast, Snow's *Strangers and Brothers* offers little introspection. In the process of aging, Lewis Eliot undergoes a variety of experiences; though he tries not only to live them but to make sense of them, surfaces and externals remain his focus of concern. By the end, his broad, humane outlook implies, for all its chaotic disparateness, a life well and fully lived, an overall, self-validating pattern. We are not in the realm of Proustian reverberations, where the single momentary sense impression can expand to encompass a world, but in one where such impressions are continually subsumed by the continuum of temporal events. Yet fundamental similarities do exist between the two. As Ian Donaldson notes in discussing Sterne and Samuel Richardson, life constantly intrudes on "present-tense narration." [14] The past ceases to be object and becomes process, fully alive to the exigencies of later (narrative present, reader present) thoughts and needs. In this conception of time nothing has ever purely and simply *happened*, for the past remains *happening*, never finished or behind us. (Thus Pursewarden, a minor character and a suicide in the first book of Durrell's *Quartet*, can become increasingly dominant, articulate, and vital throughout the rest of it.) The past lives in and

14 Ian Donaldson, "The Clockwork Novel: Three Notes on an Eighteenth Century Analogy," *Review of English Studies*, XXI (February, 1970), 14–22.

through Marcel and Lewis Eliot in the continuing present as surely as they emerge from it to speak to us. One immediate consequence is that protagonist narrators—characters who both narrate and are the focus of the tales they tell—are often types of the self-conscious speaker who, as Booth puts it, "intrudes into his novel to comment on himself as writer, and on his book, not simply as a series of events with moral implications, but as a created literary product."[15] This is true for Tristram Shandy, Ford's Dowell, Beckett's and Cary's monologists, Durrell's Darley, and many others.

Dorothy Richardson's *Pilgrimage* bears marked resemblance to Proust's extended protagonist narration, for it too is an impressionistic portrayal of an evolving interpreting consciousness grappling simultaneously with external and internal realities. But Richardson's intensely intimate narrative—like that of multivolume novels by Romain Rolland, Farrell, and Hartley, as well as James's *Ambassadors*, Joyce's *Portrait* and much of *Ulysses*, and Alain Robbe-Grillet's *Jealousy*—represents a third category, for it is cast in the form of third-person rather than first, a perspective that James calls "the indirect vision," and that I call third-person-subjective.[16] Far from being omniscient or even multifarious, such a narrator as Richardson's anonymous and disembodied voice is myopic: "he" sees and feels with the eyes and senses of a single character, confining "himself" (with more or less consistency) to an individual perspective. In comparison to the multifarious narrator, the third-person-subjective voice has a more narrowly defined but more penetrating role to play. He never dramatizes himself (and thus can be spoken of as "he" only for the sake of convenience) but, rather, articulates the "internalizations" of one or more

15 See Booth, *Rhetoric of Fiction*, 205–218.
16 David Hayman and Eric S. Rabkin use this same term in discussing narrative techniques in their excellent anthology, *Form in Fiction: An Introduction to the Analysis of Narrative Prose* (New York: St. Martin's Press, 1974), 24–27.

22 central characters. The technique is inherently dualistic, for it places us within the protagonist while implying an external perspective from which to view the dramatized myopia. And the dualism can be doubled (Uwe Johnson's *Two Views*, David Lodge's *The British Museum Is Falling Down*), tripled (Gertrude Stein's *Three Lives*), or multiplied without theoretical limit (Woolf's *Mrs. Dalloway*, Ford's *Parade's End*).

The convention behind this narrative mode is that voice and order have been given not to the protagonist but to his thoughts and feelings, and that we can experience them directly and coherently, without such intermediary devices as participant narration employs: Pamela's and Clarissa's letters, Tristram Shandy's circuitous and frenzied writings, Gulley Jimson's "honorary secretary," Humbert Humbert's imagined jury, and the like—and without the apparent narrative chaos of such confused self-confessors as Ford's Dowell and Durrell's Darley.[17] Further, no immediacy or intensity need be lost—we are as close to Joyce's Stephen, Dorothy Richardson's Miriam, Saul Bellow's protagonists as we could or should be. Thus, despite the formal dissimilarity, Richardson's narrative voice is far closer to Proust's than to, say, Thackeray's arbitrarily shifting narrative perspective. For third-person-subjective has the force though not the form of protagonist narration, and both are equally congenial to impressionistic and stream-of-consciousness fictions.

Third-person-subjective is extremely flexible and effective in the novel of personal saga and it has long been widely employed. From the novel's early days, writers as aesthetically and morally different as Cervantes and Bunyan have found advantage in being able to present their protagonists personally but non-obtrusively (they often intrude as implied authors, but that is a matter of author-

17 I say "*apparent* narrative chaos" because authorial control is structuring it. See Van Ghent's discussion of Sterne's false "authorial distress" (p. 88).

ial predilection rather than narrative necessity). Structurally, then, third-person-subjective represents something of a mean between the relatively wide-ranging multifarious narrator who, remaining limited in depth-knowledge, shifts perspective, tone, and distance as it suits his purposes, and the intense univocality inherent in protagonist narration.

The personal modes—participant narration and third-person-subjective—are often compounded in a "multiples" form that contrasts with the concept of time as meaningful change, and instead emphasizes a kind of "frozen reality" through contrasting perspectives. Cary's trilogies, Faulkner's *Sound and the Fury, Absalom, Absalom!, As I Lay Dying*, Beckett's trilogy, all counterpoint multiple participant narrators to create an essentially atemporal focusing on individual uniqueness. Similarly, novels like Woolf's *To the Lighthouse*, Forster's *Passage to India*, Lowry's *Under the Volcano*, though they all employ multifarious narration as their outermost frame of reference, gain their power from a third-person-subjective dramatizing of several intensely visualized consciousnesses.

Finally, there are what might be called hybrids occurring in a wide variety of permutations and combinations: multifarious plus participant narration (R. H. Mottram's *Spanish Farm Trilogy*, Huxley's *Brave New World* sequence, Georges Duhamel's *Pasquier Chronicles*); participant narration plus third-person-subjective (*The Alexandria Quartet*); multifarious narration plus third-person-subjective (Lawrence's *Rainbow* and *Women in Love*, Wolfe's novels, Waugh's *Sword of Honour*); and even all three together, multifarious plus participant narration plus third-person-subjective (Joyce's *Portrait* and *Ulysses*, Conrad's Marlovian works, Faulkner's Yoknapatawpha cycle). For a fuller citing of examples, as well as additional variations on the multivalent form, see the appended "Galaxy," sections II and IV.

24   Of the earlier analogues of the twentieth-century extended novel, only the single-volume ones are "modern."
With rare exception, the multivolume novels (section III
of the "Galaxy") are morally and structurally univocal,
and thus raise quite different questions about form and
voice. Such works commonly assume one of two main
forms: (1) chronicle or *roman fleuve* (Scott, Cooper,
Thackeray, Trollope, Disraeli), or (2) counterpointed: variations on a theme or subject—the "further adventures
of . . ." or " . . . revisited" (Cervantes, Bunyan, Defoe, Carroll, Twain, Butler). Both types persist in the twentieth
century—(1) Galsworthy, Powell, Snow; (2) Braine,
Huxley—though more complexly multivalent forms have
come to characterize the modern multivolume novel. The
"Galaxy" includes relatively unself-conscious and
morally univalent multivolume novels (Dreiser, Farrell,
Snow, Braine)—partly to set off the more "modern" fiction, partly because the very extendedness of certain
novels (regardless of intention) often *does* create something akin to multivalence. In Braine's *Room at the Top*,
for example, the moral worthlessness of Joe Lampton's
ambition is clear enough, but he is still portrayed sympathetically. Only in the sequel, *Life at the Top*, do we see
Lampton, having attained everything and nothing, reveal
his utter hollowness. (This is not to argue that we *need*
the sequel, or that it is a good book; on the contrary, it
lacks its predecessor's driving energy—because it depicts
Lampton as static, no longer in motion—and tells us little
we could not have inferred from *Room*.) The two taken
together, then, do constitute a multivalent novel because
the sequel offers a differently distanced (in this case, less
sympathetic) perspective on Braine's protagonist. Thus,
while Braine has not shifted his moral perspective between the two books, he has done something potentially
more interesting: he has *seemed* to do so. Unfortunately,
Braine's stylistic infelicities vitiate the significance of the

shift—which, though undeniably present, may well be largely unintended anyway.

To varying degrees, then, every multivalent novel partakes of two determining characteristics: (1) a self-conscious awareness of itself as artifact, as product, and (2) a counterpointing of conflicting ethical stances, a process in which one or more protagonists participates or serves as object. The gamut of possibilities for both types is virtually as extensive as the art of fiction. Self-conscious structuring ranges from Tristram Shandy's mock powerlessness as imposer of aesthetic order ("Ask my pen,—it governs me,—I govern not it"), to the ironic distancing of Conrad's narrator in *The Secret Agent,* from Dos Passos' intricately wrought "objective" devices like the "camera eye" and newsreel and biography in *U.S.A.* and *Midcentury,* to the mutually revelatory but similarly partial views of self and others revealed by the several narrators in Cary's trilogies and Durrell's *Quartet.* We are conscious of structure as process in such works because one or more narrators or narrative voices seem self-consciously determined that we should be.

Opposing moral perspectives may be dramatized through a fairly simple reversal of aesthetic and human norms (Wilde's *Picture of Dorian Gray*), through a reexperiencing—with enhanced understanding—of a still-alive past (*Great Expectations, The Good Soldier,* Proust's *Remembrance,* Durrell's *Quartet*), through morally diverse and spatially overlapping perspectives (de Sade's *Justine* and *Juliette, To the Lighthouse,* much of Faulkner, Cary's trilogies, Joyce's *Portrait* and *Ulysses*), or through the unfolding antics of a single protagonist divided against himself (Henry Miller's Henry Miller, Farrell's Studs Lonigan, Nabokov's Humbert Humbert). And of course many multivalent novels—among them the best and most interesting—employ more than one multivalent technique.

26   As a further structural refinement, such novels contain one or more protagonists who function as subject of an ethical quest and are therefore minimally distanced from the implied author (Defoe's Robinson Crusoe, Galsworthy's Forsytes, Tolkien's ring fellows, Snow's Lewis Eliot, Powell's Nicholas Jenkins, Harry Kemelman's Rabbi); or who function as object in novels emphasizing their indeterminate quality (Melville's Confidence Man, Claude Houghton's Jonathan Scrivener, Lowry's Consul, Beckett's Watt); or, most often, who function as a self-conscious and complexly perceived combination of the two (Swift's Gulliver, Ford's Dowell and Tietjens, Joyce's Stephen and Leopold Bloom, the six monologists in Cary's trilogies). In some of the most interesting and highly wrought multivalent fictions, an ostensible subject—sometimes without knowing it, sometimes discovering it only in the process of portraying himself—becomes object as well (Conrad's Marlow, Faulkner's Gavin Stevens, Salinger's Buddy Glass). Nicholas Urfe, the protagonist / narrator of John Fowles's *The Magus*, is designated "the searcher" early in the book, but he then becomes the object (he uses the word *victim*) of perhaps the most elaborately staged questing in all of modern fiction. The results here are oddly negative, for all the trappings strip away Urfe's own masks and defenses, allowing in the end far less confidence about his actual identity—for him and for us—than at the beginning. Since so much of the emphasis is on the protagonist as self-conscious and inadequate narrator, all such characters appear in what might be called psycho-aesthetic novels—fictions whose paradigm is the modern artist gamely struggling with the intractable materials bequeathed him: himself and the world about him.

The genre is further complicated by the multiple possibilities for resolving the moral conflicts that arise. The simplest (and least "modern") is to appoint a definitive moral spokesman, like the older and wiser Pip in *Great Expectations* or the Pope in Browning's *Ring and the Book*. More problematical approaches deploy participant narrators—Ishmael in *Moby-Dick*, Conrad's Marlow, Shreve and Quentin in *Absalom, Absalom!*—offering their only partially acceptable attempts at resolutions, or ironic commentators like those in *The Secret Agent* or *Passage to India* or *Under the Volcano* offering theirs. Or else a confused protagonist / narrator will wind up mired deeper in confusion than ever (Gulliver, Tristram Shandy, Ford's Dowell, Humbert Humbert), or actually attain something resembling a moral resolution (like Henry Miller's Henry Miller, Durrell's Darley, Braine's Joe Lampton)—though only a temporary and partial one because it remains in flux. Or such works may reflect a stripping away, a negating of the central perspective, and an affirming (if at all) only by implication (*The Beast in the Jungle*, *The Aspern Papers*, *The Picture of Dorian Gray*, *Lolita*), or their partially self-validating resolutions may remain counterpoised against each other, none of them ever simply acceptable or rejectable (*Parade's End*, *To the Lighthouse*, Cary's trilogies, Durrell's *Quartet*), though various characters may express full satisfaction with what has been attained: "I have had my vision," says Lily Briscoe in *To the Lighthouse*, thus terminating the novel (though not necessarily the story).

What all multivalent fiction requires is readers willing themselves to participate in the creative and ethical processes involved in the rendering, willing to hold aesthetic and moral prejudices in abeyance long enough to experience opposing appeals and to confront their irreconcilability honestly and directly. Thus, despite Booth's call for moral neatness, the multivalent novel usually expects us to participate sympathetically, in turn, with each of several perspectives. Albert Guerard rightly tells us that *Lord Jim* is a different book from first reading to second (as we

28 are different readers),[18] but this phenomenon is far from unique. For multivalent novels typically shift their focus and apparent purposes (and thus their "facts") even as they reveal themselves to us. The ceaseless becoming of such works determines the marvelously varied continuum of challenges we are made to experience through them.

I would add only that the novel is, of course, the most malleable of art forms. And nowhere is it more various than in the broad scope of extended multivalent fictions. As a genre, the multivolume novel is a sprawling mode of artistic expression that, especially in its modern manifestations, has lent itself to a fascinating and seemingly endless variety of narrative types and forms. Despite the novel's doomwatchers, this form deserves treatment in its own right and on its own terms, not only as the powerful and exciting means of artistic and moral expression that it has been for twentieth-century writers and readers, but also because it may well be the best humanistic device we have for spanning the worlds before and beyond: the premodern locus in linear time and an already emerging future predicated upon the oxymoron of post-McLuhan literateness.

18 Albert Guerard, *Conrad the Novelist* (New York: Atheneum, 1967), 153–55 ff.

Ronald Paulson As Partridge shows when, at a performance of *Hamlet*, he cannot distinguish the ghost until he sees Hamlet-Garrick's response to it, the response may define the object.

Emerson (quoted by Miller as epigraph to *Tropic of Cancer*) "These novels will give way, by and by, to diaries or autobiographies—captivating books, if only a man knew how to choose among what he calls his experiences that which is really his experience, and how to record truth truly."

David Hume (quoted by Ronald Paulson) "Beauty is no quality in things themselves: It exists merely in the mind which contemplates them; and each mind perceives a different beauty.... One person may even perceive deformity, where another is sensible of beauty;... To see the real beauty, or real deformity, is as fruitless an enquiry, as to pretend to ascertain the real sweet or real bitter."

2

Personal Narrators Playing God and Man

All art is self-projection and self-manipulation—none more so than the solipsistic art of the confession or of autobiography, the most striking, immediate, and pervasive form of first-person narration. A strong-willed persona asserts a world that seems to exist only to flesh out and contextualize his own image and viewpoint, his own sense of selfhood. Typically, the implied author articulates a version of himself to serve a

30 double function: to narrate the process by which his youthful self becomes the narrator and also to comment on whatever physical, intellectual, emotional, and moral distance separates the two selves or aspects of self at key points along the way. What matters above all is what the protagonist sees and experiences, what he learns or fails to learn, the lesson he has to teach or even the vision he feels impelled to impose upon us.

The first part of this chapter, "Henry Miller's Henry Miller," discusses the self-manipulation occurring in a fiction that, both internally and in its author's extrinsic commentary, defines itself as autobiography, and thus in a way that relates it complexly to an asserted vision of truth and reality. The rest of this chapter considers two variant forms, two other distancing techniques in participant-narrated fiction. "The Minor Voice Speaks" focuses on fiction in which the protagonist / narrator is, in effect, bifurcated: the narrator remains dominant as artist and shaper but becomes a subordinate character in the tale he relates. In "Joyce Cary's Cubistic Morality," the narrative voice is qualified in yet a third way: by being teamed with and paralleled to co-equals, and thus having to oppose two antithetical views to assert itself. In different ways, all three kinds of personal narrators presume the complete validity of their own narratives and yet, by the nature of the structures containing them, they exist in a framework that questions and qualifies them. We finally affirm the perspective and vision of such narrators only to the extent that they succeed in taking us beyond a skepticism aroused by their ordeals of contradiction, for these occur where, because of the self-assuredness the narrators project, we might least have expected them.

I
Henry Miller's Henry Miller

Autobiographical self-projections, whether avowedly fictional or not, assume various tones and forms. The speaking voice relates to the implicit author along a spectrum of possibilities ranging from identity to antithesis. In instances of identity, the work claims literal reality as its basis, like Augustine's and Rousseau's confessions, Cellini's and Franklin's autobiographies. Where narrator and implied author are clearly distinct, the work proclaims itself as fiction—*Fanny Hill, Moll Flanders, Great Expectations*—although many affinities still exist between the two personae despite the fairly common difference in gender. Structurally and tonally most interesting are fictions which, like Proust's *Remembrance*, fuse literal and imaginative realities into an inseparable unity by confounding our attempt either to equate implied author and narrator or else to distinguish them completely from each other. Proust's fictive world, for example, subsumes people and places he has experienced directly in a way that at times suggests a *roman à clef*, and its presiding genius bears and shares his name. In his Preface to *A Moveable Feast*, Hemingway says, "If the reader prefers, this book may be regarded as fiction. But there is always the chance that such a book of fiction may throw some light on what has been written as fact."[1] Similarly, Norman Mailer subtitles *Armies of the Night*, his firsthand account of antiwar protests in Washington, "History as a Novel / The Novel as History," and like Henry Adams in the autobiographical *Education*, refers to himself always in the third person. With such writers, we enter the realm of memoir / confession / autobiography as nonfictional novel, a mode that forces us to define our own uncertain relationship to outspoken yet protean narrators who appear as both artisans and artifacts.

The range of possible relationships between narrator and evolving self, like those between implied author and narrator, is also extensive. The narrator may be totally self-approving of his younger self from the first, like Cellini or Franklin or Frank Harris in *My Life and Loves*,

1 Ernest Hemingway, "Preface," *A Moveable Feast*. New York: Bantam, 1965.

32 condemnatory of a younger self that is, however, educable and therefore perhaps salvageable (St. Augustine, Dante in *The Divine Comedy*, Pip in *Great Expectations*, Henry Adams in his *Education*), or relatively neutral, portraying himself as, in one mood, Hamlet does his father: "He was a man, take him for all in all." Thus Rousseau proclaims: "This is my work, these were my thoughts, and thus was I. I have freely told both the good and the bad, have hid nothing wicked, added nothing good.... I have exposed myself as I was, contemptible and vile some times; at others, good, generous, and sublime."[2] In the same spirit, Mark Twain had his autobiography suppressed until after his death so that he need hold nothing back.

The plot structure of such narratives is developmental, the dramatized process usually defined as maturation or education, as an awakening or reawakening, as a movement from darkness to light; and the purpose of the work is to serve as exemplum. The reader is usually expected to feel superior—as the narrator himself does except when he identifies completely with his younger self from the first—to the ignorant, misguided, or lost protagonist he encounters at the start, to participate vicariously in the journey from innocence to experience (often via revelation or conversion), and finally to feel impelled to take a similar journey or to be left among the uninitiated. As in Whitman's "Crossing Brooklyn Ferry," we look back on a figure portrayed as inferior to us (if only because past), observe the process of his moving up to and even beyond us, and then often find that *we* are being looked back on. Whitman's persona speaks, first, of being on the ferryboat with "the hundreds and hundreds that cross returning home," and he addresses "the others that are to follow me," those "that shall cross from shore to shore years

2 Jean-Jacques Rousseau, *The Confessions*, revised and completed by A. S. B. Glover (New York: Heritage Press, 1955), 3–4.

hence." But then the present, and we, are caught and
passed:

> It avails not, time nor place—distance avails not,
> I am with you, you men and women of a generation, or
>   ever so many generations hence,
> Just as you feel when you look on the river and sky,
>   so I felt...
> These and all else were to me the same as they are to you .....

The poem invites us to participate if we would in the
poet's double journey, not only the spatial one *on* the
ferry, but also the temporal one that transcends the physical and enables us to look back upon an event that is
simultaneously present and past. We experience such literature, as we do certain heightened moments of our own
lives, as both participant and observer, as in effect both
spontaneous artist and removed analyst.

Henry Miller's Henry Miller has affinities with all the
self-portrayers mentioned above. As in true autobiography, but also as in Dante and Proust, Miller confers his
own name on the protagonist / narrator who appears in
most of what he writes. Relatively late in his career, Miller says: "There was just one book I always wanted to
write.... Even had I lost the notes, it would not have mat-
tered: everything that ever happened to me had been
burned into my brain. The writing of this one and only
work has been going on for many, many years—the
greater part of it in my head.... How the final edifice
will shape itself I still do not know" (WS, 87). The single
work that is the Miller canon is both autobiography and
fiction, both an accurate representation of the life whose
outlines and details it dramatizes and an imaginative
structuring by a detached implied author playing god (in
his constructing) and playing equally human games of
rhetorical strategy (in denying that he is playing god). An
author named Henry Miller both shapes and identifies
with a narrator of the same name; the narrator turns the

34 same trick on the character who similarly bears his name. Fiction and nonfiction, reliable and unreliable narration, identification and irony—the categories and terms break down for a writer who both proclaims and denies distance between implied author and narrator and between narrator and protagonist. No wonder Miller's writings have eluded our classificatory instincts: their basic thrust is a full-scale attack on such instincts. We thought we knew about protagonist / narrators: their lives were wrong from the start (like Augustine and Dante), and they would teach us the lessons they have learned; or they were always in the right (Cellini, Franklin, Frank Harris), and, like Shelley's Ozymandias, they would have us look on their works and despair; or they proclaimed a fidelity to truth (Rousseau, Twain, Malcolm X), and let the chips fall where they might. Miller of course embraces all three approaches—denouncing his early life in America, asserting his consistently valid vision, and yet proclaiming his utter fidelity to truth—and so leaves us with a chaos of categories comparable to that he finds in his world: "There was never any time when I was living *one* life, the life of a husband, a lover, a friend. Wherever I was, whatever I was engaged in, I was leading multiple lives. Thus whatever it is that I choose to regard as *my* story is lost, drowned, indissolubly fused with the lives, the drama, the stories of others" (*BS*, 25). Not only does such an artist refuse to do our job for us, he denies the terms and validity of our attempting to do so. Like Miller, and Whitman before him, we must ourselves play democratic bard in order to reinvent and repeople a world whose verities such writers seem constantly to deny. We must turn, with Whitman, and look back on ourselves looking back at him, and create, with Miller, the single organic work which we would do well to call "song of myselves."[3]

3 Miller refers to Whitman as "that one lone figure which America has produced in the course of her brief life. . . . Whatever there is of value in America Whitman has expressed, and there is nothing more to be said" (*T Can*, 239–40).

Following Whitman—who speaks of being vast and 35
containing multitudes—Miller carves out a complex relationship to the protagonist speaking for him, for they both
blithely emit contrarieties without pause or concern. Miller's narrator maintains that everything is true "about this
universe of ours" (*DP*, 56), even the most outrageous and
deliberate lies (*T Cap*, 13, 190; *WH*, 25); that art can reveal the truth of life (*BMH*, 282, 283), yet that no one can
tell the truth;[4] that art is at odds with life (*T Can*, 2; *BMH*,
130), "only a make-shift, a substitute for the real thing"
(*CE*, 5), but that it can lead you to life (*CE*, 5; *WH*, 24); that
the artistic process has greater importance than "what
one has to tell" (*WH*, 20), yet through art one can transcend, even destroy, art (*T Can*, 11; *CE*, 5, 7) in order to
reenter life. Miller proclaims that only the natural, the
spontaneous (like him), has value: "What is not in the
open street is false, derived, that is to say, *literature*. I was
born in the street and raised in the street.... To be born in
the street means to wander all your life, to be free" (*BS*,
1–3). As a logical extension of this view, Miller de-
nounces all efforts to distinguish his life from his writings, to view them as other than coextensive and inspired
by a single source. The central paradox lies, perhaps, in
what Miller presumes and asserts here: that his writing
accurately and directly reflects his life, that while he has
lived willfully, self-assertively, the writing results from
the opposite, a passivity, a Keatsean "negative capabil-
ity," and thus is not literature (which is bad) but by-
product; not Wordsworthian "experience recollected in
tranquility," but a direct and immediate access to unre-
flected experience.

Miller maintains that no thought or consideration determines his writing, that everything flows as from "a

---

4 Benjamin DeMott quotes Miller as saying, "I struggled in the beginning. I
said I was going to write the truth, so help me God. And I thought I was. I found
I couldn't. Nobody can write the absolute truth," in "Henry Miller: Rebel-
Clown at Eighty," *Saturday Review* (December 11, 1971), 32.

36 writing machine. The last screw has been added. The thing flows. Between me and the machine there is no estrangement. I am the machine" (*T Can*, 28). And he never revises, never alters what he writes, for "I detest the eraser" (*BS*, 55); he has, he says "made a silent compact with myself not to change a line of what I write. I am not interested in perfecting my thoughts, nor my actions. Beside the perfection of Turgenev I put the perfection of Dostoevski. . . . Here, then, in one and the same medium, we have two kinds of perfection. But in Van Gogh's letters there is a perfection beyond either of these. It is the triumph of the individual over art" (*T Can*, 11).

Miller's books do seem to reflect a dislike for erasers, for they are commonly redundant, associational, anarchic—like several dozen random versions of cut-and-paste jobs done on one vast, flowing diary. The themes, the settings, the imagery are few, but the variations on them are infinite, or seemingly so. The artist endlessly shapes identical blocks—those not "gone, scattered, wasted in talk, action, reminiscence, dream" (*BS*, 25)—under the same inspiration, and the products vary only through accidents of time and sometimes place. Only the haphazardness of human nature and conditions, it seems, prevents the results from being mechanically identical.

Yet as with Thomas Wolfe, a writer with whom Miller has much in common, artifice and art coexist in the published books; for all their length and verbiage, Miller's works result as much from pruning as accretion. "My books," he says, "are purely autobiographical," implying that they are coextensive and of a piece with his life. But like a good modern craftsman he then speaks of technique: "In telling the story of my life I have frequently discarded the chronological sequence in favor of the circular or spiral form of progression" (*WS*, 83). Sometimes, in fact, his books will fail to appear because they are never satisfactorily realized. Benjamin DeMott refers, for example, to one work that Miller wrestled with for decades as "a catastrophically complicated, luckily abandoned book about D. H. Lawrence."[5] Miller himself speaks of elaborately reworking *The World of Sex* for a second edition: "As I reread the book I began making certain corrections; it became a game which I could not resist playing to the end. Every page of the original version I went over in pen and ink, hatching and criss-crossing until it looked like a Chinese puzzle. In the new edition a few photographic copies of these corrected pages have been inserted; the reader may judge for himself what a task I gave myself" (*BHM*, 355).

In a classic exchange, Edmund Wilson congratulates Miller for his brilliantly imaginative creation of character, setting, and theme in *Tropic of Cancer*—and an outraged Miller responds that he doesn't write fiction.

> Wilson praised Miller for his skillful ironic portrait of a particular kind of "vaporing" poseur, for making his hero really live, "and not merely in his vaporings or his poses. He gives us the genuine American bum come to lead the beautiful life in Paris; and he lays him away forever in his dope of Pernod and dreams." To all of this praise for irony, Miller replied, "The theme is myself, and the narrator, or the hero, as your critic [Wilson] puts it, is also myself.... If he means the narrator, then it is me.... I don't use 'heroes,' incidentally, nor do I write novels. I am the hero, and the book is myself."[6]

Both Wayne Booth and Philip Stevick cite this interchange as illustrating the contemporary critic's dilemma when considering the crucial question of distance between author and character, and they sympathize with Wilson for making a natural error. Stevick comments that "the immediate impasse in this exchange between novelist and critic is point of view. But dependent upon that central matter of technique is every other value in the novel. Presumably, if Edmund Wilson were to accept

---

5 *Ibid.*, 30.
6 Wayne C. Booth, *The Rhetoric of Fiction* (Chicago and London: University of Chicago Press, 1961), 367.

38 Henry Miller's own statement of intention, he would be obliged to find *Tropic of Cancer* not a detached and perceptive work at all but a banal and silly one. A whole history of the novel ... could be written around just such problems in the perception of point of view." [7] Aside from the sticky question of the effect avowed authorial intention can have on the validity of a work, the important consideration that Booth and Stevick fail to pursue is that, despite the protestations of Miller and his protagonist, Wilson is basically right. For the first-draft manuscript of *Tropic of Cancer* was three times the length of the published version, and three times Miller rewrote the book. About his Chronology, a supposedly factual account designed to settle many such difficulties, Miller has said, "There are times when I myself no longer know whether I said and did the things I report or whether I dreamed them up. Anyway, I always dream true. If I lie a bit now and then it is mainly in the interest of truth." [8]

The same attitude prevails throughout what Miller calls his "autobiographical romances." After vividly detailing an extensive series of sexual conquests, the protagonist of *Tropic of Capricorn* comments: "It was going on this way all the time, even though every word I say is a lie" (*T Cap*, 190). As Kingsley Widmer, in the best book to date on Miller, has noted, "it is unavoidable in discussing Miller's work to call the central figure Henry Miller, as does Henry Miller, though this is not a claim that the experiences are literal fact.... in all probability Miller's writings about Miller are not true, in several senses." [9] In another sense, of course, all of it *is* true, even the outrageous lies, because intensely experienced and proclaimed by both author and character.

For Miller, an artist despite himself, both form and sub-

---

7 Philip Stevick (ed.), *The Theory of the Novel* (New York: Free Press, 1967), 86.
8 Henry Miller, *Selected Prose*, I (London: Mac Gibbon and Kee, 1965), 13.
9 Kingsley Widmer, *Henry Miller* (New York: Twayne, 1963), 8.

stance follow function. The manic release of automatic
writing flows from the depression engendered by endless
rewriting; similarly, a nonstop exuberance for life
emerges from personal despair. For the half-hidden central plot of all of Miller's writing concerns the failure of
passion consequent to youthful love gone awry. The Miller we see, although obviously obsessed with the *idea* of
sex, is largely indifferent to it in reality. Taking a woman
to bed—although he does so at every opportunity—
seems always to be someone else's idea: the various
women who accost him in the streets or the cafes, the
blushing Hindu afraid to venture upstairs in a brothel
alone, the friend who offers him the loan of his own latest
bedmate. Miller's reaction to the latter is typical: "I didn't
know whether I wanted to or not," he says, but of course
he does (*T Can*, 291). It is free, it is convenient, and it
saves him the cost of a night's lodging.

Earlier in *Cancer*, he speaks of watching his friend Van
Norden "tackle" one of the inevitable nameless prosti-
tutes: "It seems to me that I'm looking at a machine whose
cogs have slipped. . . . I am sitting on a chair behind him,
watching their movements with a cool, scientific detachment. . . . It's like watching one of those crazy machines
which throw the newspaper out. . . . The machine seems
more sensible, crazy as it is, and more fascinating to
watch, than the human beings and the events which produced it. My interest in Van Norden and the girl is nil. . . .
As long as that spark of passion is missing there is no
human significance in the performance. The machine is
better to watch" (*T Can*, 143–44). Miller's own lack of
passion, the antithesis and source of his manic exuberance, ties in with his pivotal theme of "the misery and inspiration connected with the Dark Lady of passion. She is
partly the *femme fatale* of the romantic, an inverted traditional muse of the artist, the Eve-Lilith of primordial
knowledge, a witch-goddess of sexuality and power, and,
according to Miller's insistence, his second wife. Under

40 the names of Mona and Mara, she haunts most of Miller's
work; and she appears, at least briefly, in almost every
book he has written."[10]

Certainly her appearances are brief and intermittent, for
her story is as fragmented as everything else in Miller's
discontinuous narrative. Nonetheless, Miller's treatment
of her constantly emphasizes her emotional centrality to
his life and to his work. For one thing, the Mona / Mara
passages are remarkably free of both censorable language
and excremental references. Descriptions of Mona and of
scenes with her, unlike those of the other women in the
Tropics, never become flights of nihilistic, semiabstract
imagery indulged in for their own sake. Of the significance of Mona, the "Her" to whom *Capricorn* is dedicated, Miller writes: "Everything I endured was in the nature of a preparation for that moment when, putting on
my hat one evening, I walked out of the office, out of my
hitherto private life, and sought the woman who was to
liberate me from a living death" (*T Cap*, 64).

In *Cancer* she appears initially as a figure of almost
virginal purity, a kind of antiwhore who embodies love
rather than sex. Miller has been eagerly awaiting her return to Paris when "suddenly," he writes,

> I see a pale, heavy face and burning eyes—and the little vel-
> vet suit that I always adore because under the soft velvet
> there were always her warm breasts, the marble legs, cool,
> firm, muscular. She rises up out of a sea of faces and em-
> braces me, embraces me passionately.... I hear not a word
> because she is beautiful and I love her and now I am happy
> and willing to die. (*T Can*, 19)

Then in bed their intense passion finds expression, as do
Miller's tenderness and love—and a new emotion, fear.

> She lies down on the bed with her clothes on. Once, twice,
> three times, four times ... I'm afraid she'll go mad ... in bed,
> under the blankets, how good to feel her body again! But for
> how long? Will it last this time? Already I have a presenti-

10 *Ibid.*, 69.

ment that it won't. . . . Finally she drops off and I pull my arm
from under her. My eyes close. Her body is there beside
me . . . it will be there till morning surely. . . . My eyes are
closed. We breathe warmly into each other's mouth. Close
together, America three thousand miles away. I never want
to see it again. To have her here in bed with me, breathing on
me, her hair in my mouth—I count that something of a miracle. Nothing can happen now till morning. (*T Can*, 20)

But in the morning everything happens. They wake to
find each other crawling with bedbugs; Mona, wanting a
bath, food, and adequate clothing, loses her temper at
Miller's having forgotten to provide for money; and, although Miller does not detail the rest of the sequence of
events, by the next page Mona disappears from the
narrative—not to be even mentioned again for some 120
pages. Again he longs for her, wondering how different
life might be with "a young, restless creature by [his]
side"; but his image of her has altered drastically, and,
bitterly, he sees her as alien to his European world. If she
ever should return, he wryly speculates,

She'll probably tell me right away that it's unsanitary. That's
the first thing that strikes an American woman about
Europe—that it's unsanitary. Impossible for them to conceive of a paradise without modern plumbing. . . . She'll say
I've become a degenerate. I know her line from beginning to
end. She'll want to look for a studio with a garden
attached—and a bathtub to be sure. She wants to be poor in a
romantic way. I know her. But I'm prepared for her this time.
(*T Can*, 152)

Exactly what is good about being poor in an unromantic
way Miller never explains, but certainly he is correct
about being prepared for her—for he manages, at least for
the moment, to blot from his mind everything that belongs to the past, especially those few years when they
were together and life was, if not edenic, at least vital and
intense. Now when he thinks of her—and he is unable to
keep himself from doing so entirely—it is "not as of a
person in a definite aura of time and space, but separately,

42 detached, as though she had blown up into a great cloud-like form that blotted out the past." Regardless, he adds,

> I couldn't allow myself to think about her very long; if I had I would have jumped off the bridge. It's strange. I had become so reconciled to this life without her, and yet if I thought about her only for a minute it was enough to pierce the bone and marrow of my contentment and shove me back again into the agonizing gutter of my wretched past. (*T Can*, 177)

And yet, no matter what the reason, a man who willfully destroys his past, as Miller begins to realize, commits spiritual suicide: "It seems as if my own proper existence had come to an end somewhere, just where exactly I can't make out. I'm not an American any more, nor a New Yorker, and even less a European, or a Parisian. I haven't any allegiance, any responsibilities, any hatreds, any worries, any prejudices, any passion. I'm neither for nor against. I'm a neutral" (*T Can*, 153). But this statement serves first as manifesto and only subsequently as actual fact, for after the climactic moment when he recognizes the irrevocable loss of Mona, he gives way to a despairing loneliness so profound and so terrible that all else seems irrelevant. Yet in his hopelessness he comes full cycle, rediscovering his affinity with all the sordid and cancerous aspects of Paris, a city that "attracts the tortured, the hallucinated, the great maniacs of love," a Paris that "is like a whore. From a distance she seems ravishing, you can't wait until you have her in your arms. And five minutes later you feel empty, disgusted with yourself. You feel tricked" (*T Can*, 181, 209). Ultimately there are only the streets for refuge—the streets which, in the childhood reminiscence of *Black Spring*, define his freedom in America—for the streets take every man's torments, every man's raging despair that is so precious because it confirms his significance as an individual capable of suffering, and the streets make of it something neither for nor against, but simply neutral. Miller, as we see him at the end of *Cancer* and then again at the end of *Capricorn*, is a diminished figure wondering "in a vague way what had ever happened to [his] wife" (*T Can,* 318). "A vague way"—the phrase is revealing—for it suggests, and this is borne out in the later writings, that the failure of the relationship may well have resulted from Miller's intrinsic inadequacies. As Widmer has put it: "While his version of the Dark Lady myth aims to show Miller as the victim of love, he really presents himself as the victim of his own lovelessness."[11]

But Miller anticipates us in this as he does in everything else we might care to say about his writing. Early in *Capricorn* he says, "Things were wrong usually only when one cared too much. That impressed itself on me very early in life. . . . This caring too much—I remember that it only developed with me about the time I first fell in love. And even then I didn't care enough. If I had really cared I wouldn't be here now writing about it. . . . It was a bad experience because it taught me how to live a lie" (*T Cap,* 15). As much as such things ever can, this recapitulation explains Miller's self-projection in all he has written and been, for his assertion of himself as a writer who never revises is of a piece with his assertion that he cares for no one, for nothing.

Thus, the manic self-dramatization is a way of both confronting and avoiding, a way of defining oneself that denies momentary disasters of every kind and wills a reality that endures for poets and children. For a certain kind of writer, usually sophisticated Americans insecure in their sophistication, a public persona represents, in Ben Jonson's phrase about his son, "his best piece of poetry." Franklin's pious spouter of platitudes, Frost's kindly old country grandfather, Hemingway's supermacho Papa, Mailer's endlessly belligerent good bad boy—all represent imaginative constructs in a grand style. Miller, too, offers a self-dramatization above all,

11 *Ibid.,* 75.

44 himself as twentieth-century fulfillment of Whitman's
call for spontaneous democratic bard, a poet by instinct
rather than training now returned to the land where such
willful creation of self seems most possible and necessary. "The United States themselves are essentially the
greatest poem," Whitman writes. "Of all nations the
United States with veins full of poetical stuff most need
poets and will doubtless have the greatest and use them
the greatest." [12] But, as Anaïs Nin pointed out in *Cancer's*
original preface, Miller is no more an untutored, spontaneous genius than Whitman, and seeming naïvete is
willed and purposeful: "Here the symbols [of art] are laid
bare, presented almost as naively and unblushingly by
this over-civilized individual as by the well-rooted savage. It is no false primitivism which gives rise to this savage lyricism. It is not a retrogressive tendency, but a
swing forward into unbeaten areas" (*T Can*, Preface,
xxxii). What then, we might ask, is Miller up to?

Tropic of Cancer, Miller's first writing success after
several unpublished novels, may be read as a scatological
Down and Out in Paris and London, for both books concern the quest for food and shelter (among other things)
during the days and nights of the Parisian Depression—
only Orwell seeks even the most menial and degrading
work in order to survive at any cost. Miller, on the other
hand, becomes a parasite in order, as he maintains, to
survive on his own terms (that is, without working) but
also, despite his protestations, in order to make literature
of the experience. At the beginning of *Cancer*, Miller offers us a miniature portrait of the artist and his art.

> It is now the fall of my second year in Paris. I was sent here
> for a reason I have not yet been able to fathom.
>   I have no money, no resources, no hopes. I am the happiest
> man alive. A year ago, six months ago, I thought that I was an

12 Walt Whitman, "Preface, 1855," in *Complete Poetry and Selected Prose
by Walt Whitman*, ed. James E. Miller, Jr. (Boston: Houghton, Mifflin, 1959),
411–14.

artist. I no longer think about it, I *am*. Everything that was 45
literature has fallen from me. There are no more books to be
written, thank God.

This then? This is not a book. This is libel, slander, defa-
mation of character. This is not a book, in the ordinary sense
of the word. No, this is a prolonged insult, a gob of spit in the
face of Art, a kick in the pants to God, Man, Destiny, Time,
Love, Beauty . . . what you will. I am going to sing for you, a
little off key perhaps, but I will sing. (*T Can*, 1–2)

Art, then, becomes both art and non-art, for it is not only
formless and eclectic, negative and destructive, but it
serves for the artist both as an end in itself and also as a
means to life. Elsewhere, Miller writes that "art is only a
stepping-stone to reality. It is the vestibule in which we
undergo the rites of initiation. Man's task is to make of
himself a work of art. The creations which man makes
manifest have no validity in themselves; they serve to
awaken" (*SW*, 155). They can, in fact, serve as means for
passing beyond the immediate, beyond fiction and reality, beyond even truth and its antithesis: "For years I have
been trying to tell this story and always the question of
truth has weighed upon me like a nightmare. Time and
again I have related to others the circumstances of our
life, and I have always told the truth. But the truth can
also be a lie. The truth is not enough. Truth is only the
core of a totality which is inexhaustible" (*T Cap*, 333).
Further, "The sum of all knowledge is greater confusion. . . . Truth comes with surrender. And it's wordless"
(*DP*, 58). "I believe," he adds, "that one has to pass beyond the sphere and influence of art. . . . All art, I firmly
believe, will one day disappear. But the artist will remain,
and life itself will become not 'an art,' but *art*. . . . Once art
is really accepted it will cease to be. It is only a substitute,
a symbol-language, for something which can be seized directly" (*WH*, 24). Thus, the artist must cease "immolating
himself in his work," must cease creating out of a martyr-
dom "of sweat and agony. . . . We do not think of sweat
and tears in connection with the universe; we think of joy

46 and light, and above all of play" (*SW*, 156). Despite the evidence of his own experience, the artist assumes this art to be a spontaneous outpouring, an automatic byproduct of unrecollected and untranquilized emotion—because, at least in Miller's case, it serves the purposes of art and life, of narrators playing god and man. The paradox, the contradictoriness, becomes the point, the message as well as the medium for the persona projecting himself as *both* the literal and created embodiment of his author's psyche. Identification between the two is of course inexact, but the very dichotomy—in a form that seeks to deny that there is any—has much to teach us not only concerning protagonist narration but also about distancing techniques in fiction and elsewhere. Despite appearance and expectation, blatant self-assertion in the service of complex revelation about fiction, art, reality, life—or in Miller's terms, "God, Man, Destiny, Time, Love, Beauty . . . what you will"—may be not the most accessible or trustworthy mode of communication, but something approaching its opposite.

II
The Minor Voice Speaks

Participant narration is usually the business of the protagonist or of a group of central characters. But occasionally it is usurped by what might be called the minor voice, a character peripheral to the book's central action. When such a character does assert himself, when he steps out of the relative passivity of his assigned role to shape and form the actions of others, he usually acts upon them like a magnet on an electric current—distorting the flow by a powerful attraction. Thus Conrad's Marlow not only narrates but interacts with what interests him in the lives of Jim, Kurtz, and Powell to such an extent that, one could argue, he becomes a dominant influence on them and, subsequently, uses them to prefigure himself.

One of the most interesting features of Browning's *The Ring and the Book* is its giving voice to peripheral figures. "Half Rome," "The Other Half-Rome," and "Tertium Quid" propound their positions with the removedness of distance and noninvolvement; they are as easy to ignore as are "the people" in the sort of history that recounts the rise and fall of kings and statesmen. And yet such a dismissing distorts equally in both cases. For as Browning's minor voices imply, the larger events occur in a social and moral climate largely created by those we tend to overlook. Further, both the contradictoriness of their several points of view and the passion with which each asserts his own indicate that these characters are neither objective nor so far removed from the central events as they first seem. Each, in fact, occupies the center of a drama in which the events of Guido and Pompilia and Caponsacchi become subordinate to what is central to the speaker: the immediacy of his own life. This leads to an interesting and finely handled conflict between these figures and Browning's multifarious narrator, for while the former attempt to enlarge their minor roles, the latter works to keep them in their place—and ultimately succeeds by means of a number of devices: (1) quantification (they speak only three of the poem's twelve sections, whereas the central characters—if one includes the lawyers and the Pope—speak a total of seven), (2) placement (all of the characters are framed by the narrator of "The Ring and the Book" and "The Book and the Ring" sections, but the minor voices, declaiming in sections II–IV, also serve as prologue for the other participant speakers), and (3) subordination (the minor voices constantly allude to the central characters, but the reverse does not occur). Thus, the effect in the end is the opposite of that in Conrad's Marlovian tales, for Marlow, though beginning askew of the reality he relates, comes to occupy center stage.

Still, the presence of this conflict of roles distinguishes *The Ring and the Book* and Conrad's Marlovian tales from

48 other works in which the minor voice speaks not only to play games of subtle self-assertion, but to dramatize the central character from a particular angle: solely in terms of how he appears to others. This sort of narrative perspective—that of the largely effaced yet dramatized participant—is very tricky to handle. Browning and Conrad have both worked wonders with the narrative methods they employ, yet the type itself is really more natural than that in which the minor voice asserts himself sufficiently to narrate, yet lacks pretension to a central role in the action he narrates. Hence the rarity of this latter type.

A few interesting examples do exist, however—enough, perhaps, to suggest the possibilities of the form. Conrad's *Under Western Eyes*, Fitzgerald's *The Great Gatsby*, Houghton's *I Am Jonathan Scrivener*, Mann's *Doctor Faustus*, and Nabokov's *Pale Fire* are all dualistic in that their narrators present themselves as rational, truth-seeking "histors," [13] affirming objectivity, and yet, to varying degrees, are sucked into the emotional whirlpool created by the compelling and rather mysterious personalities of those who fascinate them and whom they choose for their protagonists. Conrad's teacher of languages, Fitzgerald's Nick Carroway, Houghton's James Wrexham, Mann's Serenus Zeitblom, Ph.D., and Nabokov's Charles Kinbote are all self-conscious and fully dramatized narrators, but they vary greatly in their relationship to the events they narrate. Conrad's teacher (as the title suggests) dominates the book's angle of vision, but

13 The *histor*, according to Scholes and Kellogg, "is the narrator as inquirer, constructing a narrative on the basis of such evidence as he has been able to accumulate. The *histor* is ... a projection of the author's empirical virtues. Since Herodotus and Thucydides the *histor* has been concerned to establish himself with the reader as a repository of fact, a tireless investigator and sorter, a sober and impartial judge—a man, in short, of authority, who is entitled not only to present the facts as he has established them but to comment on them, to draw parallels, to moralize, to generalize, to tell the reader what to think and even to suggest what he should do," in *The Nature of Narrative* (New York: Oxford University Press, 1966), 265–66.

he remains peripheral to its action. Zeitblom and Kinbote are similar to Ford's Dowell, Browning's and Cary's monologists, Nabokov's Humbert Humbert; imposers and poseurs, they intrude the frame of their narrative upon its ostensible subject matter. Their every utterance is simultaneously self-delusive and self-betraying, for they remain convinced that they seek only to portray their putative protagonists (Adrian Leverkuhn, John Shade), yet they demonstrate an obsession solely with self. *The Great Gatsby* and *I Am Jonathan Scrivener* remain most problematical. Nick Carroway is more involved than Conrad's teacher, but he still seems able to tell Gatsby's story without bias or intrusiveness; and yet Nick's exact role in the novel has become a matter of increasing conjecture—even to the point of its being argued that he himself is its center.

The largely unknown *I Am Jonathan Scrivener* is an odd sort of novel: a mystery that ends not with a solution but with ambiguity. Either the mystery is about to be solved (on the pages that would have followed had the novel been longer) or else no mystery ever really existed. The plot itself is minimal. James Wrexham, lacking ties, prospects, and measurable qualifications, impulsively accepts a position as secretary to the title character. He never meets his employer and he communicates with him only through a somewhat disapproving lawyer. The job consists of cataloging Scrivener's impressive but by no means overwhelming library—and in addition to more money and freedom than he has ever known, it provides Wrexham with living quarters in Scrivener's luxurious, but otherwise deserted, London flat. In the face of such gratuitous beneficence, Wrexham is passively puzzled but accepting—an attitude he maintains even when various acquaintances of Scrivener's start dropping in, with passkeys as often as not. Wrexham talks to them all about his employer, and is surprised that they know little more than he does. What he learns compounds his ignorance about Scrivener but leads him to a different sort of wis-

50 dom. "To know the facts is one thing: to know the truth is another. Facts are to truth as dates are to history—they record certain events but they do not reveal the significance of those events."[14] He attains an understanding of the understanding of others that echoes Proust's Marcel: "We talk lightly of 'knowing' someone, when in reality we know nothing of the quality of that person's life. As a rule we know only his or her circumstances. . . . To know where a man has been tells you little. It is what a traveller becomes on his pilgrimage which is important, not where he has lodged on the way. . . . The terms we use to describe others usually reveal little concerning them, but much concerning ourselves."[15] Thus, we are early prepared for the Pirandelloesque ending: the sudden appearance of Scrivener and his pronouncing the book's title. Nothing is solved or settled—except that Scrivener really does exist (one begins to doubt even this while reading the book) and that Wrexham may now join the fraternity of those able to interpret him at first hand.

The novel is far from wholly successful. For one thing, the Proustian theorizing, though expressed with a fairly high degree of sophistication, occurs in something of a vacuum because of the characters' thinness of representation. The "real" quality of Proust's characters may be indeterminate, but they are nonetheless portrayed with a fullness that gives them substantiality and vitality. They have the indeterminacy not of cardboard figures but of people we know. Houghton, however, strives for a four-dimensionality in his characters without having first convinced us that they are three-dimensional. And yet *Jonathan Scrivener* remains an interesting experiment in angular perspective, an attempt to portray a protagonist not through representation but, in a sense, by subtraction, minimalization. And Wrexham's remaining wholly un-

---

14 Claude Houghton [Oldfield], *I Am Jonathan Scrivener* (New York: Simon and Schuster, 1930), 86.

15 *Ibid.*, 86–87.

ironic, wholly unwilling to thrust himself into the void
resulting from the protagonist's remaining offstage until
the book's final line, creates both the flat quality of the
novel and its oddly quiet fascination. *Jonathan Scrivener*
is not a great novel, but sometimes such secondary works
have more to teach us about technique than more complex constructs.

Multivolume novels rarely employ secondary-character
narration. I know of only three attempts to employ the
form: Upton Sinclair's *Sylvia* and *Sylvia's Marriage*,
Christopher Isherwood's Berlin series, and Langston
Hughes's Simple series.[16] Typically, the Sinclair pair of
novels is a *roman à thèse*, its subject, prophetically, sex
education and sexual equality. The narrator, Mary Ab-
bott, who has long suffered her self-assumed responsibilities, quits her unhappy marriage as soon as her children are grown; like them, she goes off to make what she
feels will at last be her own life. She eventually becomes
the confidante of poor southern rich-girl Sylvia Castle-
man, whom she not only educates on such taboo subjects
as venereal disease and abortion but enlists for mission-
ary work among the ignorant downtrodden: southern
white womanhood.

Sinclair's ideas in these books are even more strikingly
contemporary than usual. Were they read today, they
would doubtless advance the causes of women's libera-
tion at least as well as most of the tracts specifically designed for that purpose. Unfortunately, Sinclair is really
no novelist; his stock characters and situations vitiate
much of the book's potential impact, and the preaching
tone and orientation trivialize its unusual mode of narration.

Langston Hughes, on the other hand, *is* an adept fic-
tionalizer, and his Simple series achieves exactly what it

16 Salinger's Glass family saga might well be included here, but I prefer to
see the narrator, Buddy Glass, rather than his brother Seymour, as that work's
emerging protagonist.

52 intends. Each of the books is a novel in the manner of
Winesburg, Ohio: a grouping of vignettes linked by their
relationship to the protagonist and their epiphanous
structure. Instead of *Winesburg's* multifarious narrator,
however, Hughes portrays his title character (Jesse B.
Semple) by having an anonymous but fully dramatized
narrator (whom the protagonist considers his only real
friend) record a series of encounters he has with Simple.
The encounters contain almost no action in themselves
(with the exception of the nearly always broke Simple trying to cadge a beer), and very little narrative description
or commentary. They consist primarily of a disquisition
by Simple in the form of a dramatic monologue on such
subjects as money, work, education, women, and race.
Simple's anecdotal style, punctuated by occasional con-
versation with the narrator, leads rather to epigrammatic
conclusions than to direct linkages with other episodes.
Simple Speaks His Mind, as the title suggests, has an
especially loose construction; Simple expatiates on whatever occurs to him, though, as the equally black narrator
chidingly reiterates, primarily on the subject of race. The
book's section-headings—(1) Summer Time, (2) Winter
Time, (3) Hard Times, (4) Any Time—afford convenient
groupings rather than structural unity. *Simple Takes a
Wife*, though similarly constructed, contains the unity of
plot its title suggests, for, while Simple's interests con-
tinue to range widely, he focuses primarily on the com-
plications and expenses of obtaining a divorce in order to
marry the good woman he loves.

The ironically nick-named Simple is a marvelous
character: uneducated yet wise with a wisdom born of
hardship and instinctive wit; self-deprecating and
unique, yet a proud spokesman for all black people; an
affirmer of the American dream, yet a piercing critic of
the American reality; a practitioner of various common
vices (drinking, fornicating, etc.), yet an ardent advocate
of hard work, monogamy, family loyalty, formal educa-

tion, justice. He is a joy to behold and to hear, and Hughes wisely creates a narrator who allows us to do both at length.

As a character, the narrator interacts continuously with Simple while maintaining his subordinate role. Their conversations reveal his blackness, his equability about such matters as race and injustice, and a few other details. Still, we know little of his life, and doubtless should draw no conclusions about it on the basis of his near-permanent presence in the bar. As far as we are concerned, he is there (like Marlow's after-dinner listeners) as a captive audience, though one who makes his presence very much felt through commenting as well as listening and recording. But—and this is the finest thing about Hughes's portrayal of the narrator, in the narrator himself and in his relationship to Simple—his commentary is never distinct from his narrative. That is, all his criticisms and reservations about Simple's attitudes and values are always voiced to him rather than to us; and Simple's rebuttal not only follows but wittily terminates the episode. Thus, though Simple is often opposed and even derided, he is never the victim of condescension or irony; he invariably takes advantage of his having the last word to make a telling point. The brilliance of Hughes's handling of the indirect voice lies in its constantly putting the garrulous Simple in his place—and then implicitly acknowledging that that place is one of triumph.

Why, then, are multivolume novels narrated by secondary characters so rare? I see no theoretical explanation, although immediate difficulties in sustaining the minor perspective with consistency suggest themselves. The indirect, nonironic angle of vision seems to require both a firmness of moral beliefs on the part of the implied author and a desire to personify them in a dramatized narrator who remains, nonetheless, subordinate to the central character or action. Despite Booth, such unquestioned firmness is fundamentally antithetical to the novel's

54 modernist and postmodernist spirit; and earlier novels seek the greater freedom of narrative revelation that results from embodying ethical touchstones in an authorial voice. The only way to afford a secondary character comparable freedom is to allow him scope for ironic commentary—and to do so is to create tension between narrative and commentary, and thereby to promote the speaker's role to major status. The built-in limitations of the form, then, are clearly great; and yet Hughes (and Isherwood to a lesser extent) successfully demonstrates that it can be made to serve his fictional purposes. One can only speculate that even finer and more spectacular writers than Hughes might have attained—and perhaps will attain—even greater successes in their deploying of this rarest of narrative forms.

III
Joyce Cary's Cubistic Morality

Almost all of Joyce Cary's fiction was conceived within a multivolume framework. Of his sixteen published novels, those of Africa (*Aissa Saved, An American Visitor, The African Witch*, and *Mister Johnson*) form a series linked in theme and setting.[17] There are two "Novels of Childhood" (*Charley Is My Darling* and *A House of Children*). *Castle Corner*, the earliest of three "Chronicles" (along with *The Moonlight* and *A Fearful Joy*) was originally conceived as the first of a trilogy.[18] Cary's last novel, *The Captive and the Free*, was to inaugurate a trilogy on the theme of religion. And the work in which conception

17 See Charles G. Hoffmann, "The Genesis and Development of Joyce Cary's First Trilogy," *PMLA*, LXXVIII (September, 1963), 431, Andrew Wright, *Joyce Cary: A Preface to His Novels* (New York: Harper & Brothers, 1958), 57–62, and M. M. Mahood, *Joyce Cary's Africa* (London: Methuen, 1964).

18 See Charles G. Hoffmann, " 'They Want to be Happy': Joyce Cary's Unfinished *Castle Corner* Series," *Modern Fiction Studies*, IX (Autumn, 1963), 217–25. The categories I employ are Wright's, and references for his discussion of them are as follows: "Novels of Africa," pp. 57–62; "Novels of Childhood," pp. 62–65; "Chronicles," pp. 66–71.

crystallized into the major achievement from which
Cary's importance as a modern novelist derives are his
two completed trilogies: *Herself Surprised, To Be a Pilgrim,* and *The Horse's Mouth; Prisoner of Grace, Except
the Lord,* and *Not Honour More.* Each of these contains a
triptych of sustained dramatic monologues as three protagonist / narrators take turns depicting themselves and
their worlds at length. Each of the six novels is a virtuoso
performance by a uniquely individualized narrator whose
subject is himself. As Andrew Wright has said, Cary "can
suit the words to the characters so justly that in the novels
of the two trilogies there are six styles: six metaphorical
structures, six schemes of syntax, six kinds of interior
monologue—indeed six worlds." [19] Events and other
characters—though they assert independent existence of
their own—assume significance only to the extent that
they impinge upon and affect the interpreting consciousness. In effect, Cary's trilogies are *The Ring and the Book*
without the Pope's objective judgment, *The Sound and
the Fury* without Dilsey's transcendence: a multifaceted,
cubistic depiction of reality as a series of personal and
therefore contrasting viewpoints, each of which is doubly
contradicted but not negated.

The two trilogies are structurally identical, and therefore may be read vertically (*Herself Surprised,* then *Prisoner of Grace,* etc.) as well as horizontally (or chronologically). The first books of the trilogies are narrated by
women often bewildered by the world of men, but who
are nonetheless both vital to it and largely defined by it.
Both Sara, in *Herself Surprised,* and Nina, in *Prisoner of
Grace,* seek to explain how they became trapped by in-
stitutions (the judiciary, politics) that are fundamentally
alien to them, while defining themselves in relationship
to marriage, the one institution that makes sense to them
and seems central to societal (and therefore human) continuity. Yet their narrations focus primarily on marital

19 Wright, *Joyce Cary,* 109.

56 failure—for both are betrayed by the men whose lives have largely shaped their own. Both Sara and Nina, having tried to mediate and unite, become trapped between two opposing masculine viewpoints; that they are consequently doomed becomes clear to them and to us later on in the trilogies. Wright expresses it this way: "Sara and Nina are both torn between the free and the unfree man, which is simply to say that their complicated female natures demand a complexity, in fact a contradiction, in response. Sara and Nina succeed as characters by virtue of their relationships. They succeed also—and this is perhaps putting the same matter in other words—because they can tell their own stories, which can be corrected in their turn by the stories of their men."[20]

Like *To Be a Pilgrim*, *Except the Lord* is narrated by "an old man, aware that he is regarded by the young as a fogey.... He is pedantic and fussy, personally a little ridiculous, and he knows it.... he is a little cracked, an old man on the verge of senility."[21] Both accounts tend to be long-winded and round-about, tonally self-indulgent,

20 *Ibid.*, 105–106.
21 Walter Allen, *The Modern Novel in Britain and the United States* (New York: Dutton, 1965), 246. Allen is speaking just of Thomas Wilcher. Wright similarly refers to Chester as "an old man now regarded as hopelessly out of date ... a man who is himself lost" (pp. 144–45). These two narrators do, however, differ in one crucial way: Wilcher honestly confronts and accepts his inadequacies; Nimmo's narration, like his life, attempts to evade his.
　　Other parallels have also been suggested: for example between Wilcher and Nina (Jack Wolkenfeld, *Joyce Cary: The Developing Style* [New York and London: New York University Press and University of London Press, 1968], 92), and between Gulley and Chester (Wright, p. 73). Cary agrees with Wright that a primary analogy exists between Gulley ("a politician in art") and Chester ("an artist in politics"). He says, in the Preface to *Prisoner of Grace* (London: Michael Joseph, 1960), 6, "This is true and penetrating in so far that both are creative minds in the world of a perpetual creation. They are inventing unique answers to problems that are of necessity always new." But none of the analogies necessarily excludes any of the others.
　　Except for *Except the Lord*, Cary's trilogies appear in the uniform Carfax Edition; all six are published in London by Michael Joseph. Following are the dates of initial publication, of first publication in the Carfax Edition, and the reprint consulted, respectively: *Herself Surprised*: 1941, 1951, 1951; *To Be a Pilgrim*: 1942, 1951, 1961; *The Horse's Mouth*: 1944, 1951, 1961; *Prisoner of Grace*: 1952, 1954, 1960; *Except the Lord*: 1953, ——, 1953; *Not Honour More*: 1955, 1966, 1966. Cary's Americàn publishers are Harper & Row and Grosset & Dunlap.

and certainly far different from what seems likely to follow the tensions and questions raised by Sara's and Nina's narrations. Finally, both *The Horse's Mouth* and *Not
Honour More* are self-portraits (and defenses) by younger
protagonists under sentence of death: Gulley Jimson has
just suffered a presumably fatal stroke; Jim Latter awaits
hanging for the murder of his wife. Both are done in a
choppily impressionistic style that accurately reflects the
fact that Gulley and Jim are not writing their accounts but
dictating them while in a state of high excitement.[22]

The second trilogy is the more somber and less exuber-
ant of the two, as if youthful lyricism had been tempered
by the mundane and deadening experience of the world,
the night before yielding to the morning after. The critical
consensus has focused on the first trilogy as the greater
and more interesting achievement—with its enormous
vitality and originality, its "restless experimentation,
what seemed [Cary's] endless fertility of scene and situation."[23] Yet despite many similarities the second trilogy
is not simply a reworking; it is a considerable achievement in its own right—an arguably more successful unity, in fact, than the first.

Cary himself has spoken of the basic structural problem
with regard to the first trilogy. In his Preface to *Herself
Surprised* he reveals that, when confronted with the
choice, he trusted his characters rather than his scheme
whose "object was to get a three-dimensional depth and
force of character. One character was to speak in each
book and describe the other two as seen by that person."[24] Charles Hoffmann explains:

22 For a brief discussion of the parallels between Gulley and Jim, see Wolkenfeld, *Joyce Cary*, 92.

23 Allen, *Modern Novel*, 247. Wolkenfeld (pp. 93–94) and, implicitly,
Wright (p. 142) do, however, see the second trilogy as more complex than the
first. Malcolm Foster, *Joyce Cary: A Biography* (London: Michael Joseph, 1969),
478, 492, and Wolkenfeld (p. 90) see the second trilogy as less unified, but this
may be because, as Cary says, "the contrasts between the different worlds [of
the second trilogy] are much sharper" (*PR*, 59).

24 Joyce Cary, Preface to *Herself Surprised* (London: Michael Joseph, 1951), 7.

58   The different worlds of the three characters became more distinct than Cary had originally planned. It is in this sense that he believed he had failed: "My failure was in the contrast or overlap of these worlds. They were not sufficiently interlocked to give the richness and depth of actuality that I had hoped for." Aware of this technical limitation of the first trilogy, Cary sought to avoid it in planning the second trilogy: "That's why, in planning the second trilogy, I limited it to a single subject, politics, and tied the three chief characters closely together in the same complex development. This did achieve the contrast and conflict I wanted."[25]

In the first trilogy, however, each of the three protagonists in turn usurps center stage to such an extent that the other two, though present at times, recede into the distant background. Consequently, the interplay of multiple perspectives in the first trilogy occurs largely through contrasting tones and outlooks rather than through contradictory interpretations of the same or closely related events and characters. Cary's decision, as far as the individual novels are concerned, was surely a wise one, for all three novels of the first trilogy are virtually flawless; there is scarcely a false or irrelevant note in any of them. But the result is a less than fully unified trilogy, for all three of the protagonist / narrators are such intense individuals that they tend to go blithely (though magnificently) off on their own with relatively little regard for each other or the trilogy's overall unity. Consequently, the books of the *Herself Surprised* / *To be a Pilgrim* / *Horse's Mouth* trilogy (unlike those of more closely integrated multivolume novels like Ford's tetralogy, Durrell's quartet, Tolkien's *Lord of the Rings*) are more commonly read separately than as parts of a greater whole.

The reverse is true of Cary's second trilogy, whose sum is certainly greater than the individual parts.[26] In commenting on their structure, Jack Wolkenfeld says,

---

25 Hoffmann, "First Trilogy," 439.
26 Malcolm Foster begins his discussion of the second trilogy with the assertion that it "does not succeed as well as his first as a unified work. The parts

Both trilogies are unusual in that they are neither strictly circular nor strictly sequential. That is, they do not cover what is essentially the same ground ... from three separate points of view (as does *Rashomon*, perhaps the best known example of the type), nor do they simply follow each other in time. ... Instead, they present a situation which is only very loosely similar in the separate books, told from the conflicting viewpoints of three separate narrators. ... Each individual volume is essentially an apologia—a conscious attempt by each character to explain his general attitude toward life. The trilogies as a whole, however, gain their effect from the juxtaposition of the separate works. Each character's view is different, sometimes radically different, but each view combines with the others—unwilling though the combination may be—to produce the total situation.[27]

But despite the apparent digressiveness of *Except the Lord*, the three novels of the second trilogy are intimately, and inextricably, interlocked; they function as a structural and moral unit. Nina narrates *Prisoner of Grace* in order to define "all these different I's" that she is and was in her relationships with "that great man who was once my husband" and with "my cousin Jim Latter" (*PG*, 9). In *Not Honour More*, Jim Latter details the breakdown of coherence in his relationships with Nina and Chester—and then ultimately their deaths. Chester Nimmo, who completes the triangle and determines the trilogy's domestic and political interactions, narrates the most self-centered account (it virtually ignores Nina and Jim), but *Except the Lord* defines the context (historical, political, and per-

---

do not mesh entirely, the overall theme comes across less clearly, the chronology is too vast ... but most important is the problem of making Jim Latter and Chester Nimmo sympathetic characters." Interestingly, Foster's discussion is largely concerned with demonstrating that, in fact, this trilogy has far greater complexity and unity than readers have often realized—and he never does get around to substantiating his initial negative pronouncement. His conclusion is far more circumspect and judicious: "*Unless* Jim Latter is understood and seen as Cary intended, Nimmo and Nina cannot be seen clearly, and the whole trilogy collapses into contradiction. *If* it fails as a unified work, it is not on this ground" (pp. 478–92; my italics). Foster never demonstrates that it *does* fail.

27 Wolkenfeld, *Joyce Cary*, 21.

60 sonal) within which the other two books—and the trilogy
as a whole—evolve their meaning.[28]

The Nina who narrates *Prisoner of Grace* is Cary's most
complicated woman.[29] She represents herself as a weak
but sympathetic character bent on depicting and confronting her own contradictions and inadequacies honestly. This is not to say that either Nina or her narrative is
straightforward or reliably objective, though Cary refers
to her as "credible . . . trustworthy." He adds, "of course
she had to have her own point of view, she could not
know all Chester. . . . "[30] Rather, as both character and
narrator, Nina is an impressionist who has little respect
for facts as such, or for abstract moral concerns, what
Chester and Jim call principles. And yet, echoing Cary's
defense of deception as sometimes necessary for doing
good,[31] Nina defends the role she played as Chester's

28 Wolkenfeld (p. 182) similarly sees Chester as the focus of the second trilogy and as a force for unity that the first trilogy lacks. Hazard Adams, on the
other hand, makes a case for Sara's centrality in the first trilogy. He notes that
"Cary has spoken of Sara as the central figure by which the three novels are
linked," and he adds: "Sara is a marvelous character in her own story, but in
the other two alone she vindicates Cary's method; she *reflects* Jimson and
Wilcher better in their stories than she describes them to us in her own."
Hazard Adams, "Joyce Cary's Three Speakers," *Modern Fiction Studies*, V
(Summer, 1959), 114, 119. But this should be juxtaposed with Hoffmann's discussion of the triptych concept in the first trilogy, a notion implying that *Herself Surprised* and *The Horse's Mouth* are relatively peripheral. He says: "The
triptych concept is implicit in the idea that Wilcher understands the whole situation [as Cary intended], for *To Be a Pilgrim* as the middle 'panel' of the triptych is the central focus of the whole" ("First Trilogy," p. 436). That Cary did
not succeed in this intention reflects on the trilogy's overall structure. As Fred
Stockholder says, "none of the characters really knows very much about the
others' visions or activities. The formal unity of the novels is not completed on
the realistic plane, for the structure of the novel is a parable on man's isolation.
All of the three characters are in the same position as Gulley Jimson when he
says, 'I can't speak for any one else, I don't know the language.'" "The Triple
Vision in Joyce Cary's First Trilogy," *Modern Fiction Studies*, IX (Autumn,
1963), 233.

29 Wright, *Joyce Cary*, 76.

30 Cary, Preface to *PG*, 7–8. Nina is seen as unreliable by Mahood (p. 88)
and Wright (p. 106), and morally deficient by Giles Mitchell, "Joyce Cary's
Prisoner of Grace," *Modern Fiction Studies*, IX (Autumn, 1963), 268–75,
though Wright (p. 106), Mitchell (p. 273), and Wolkenfeld (p. 178) also stress
her fundamental consistency.

31 Cary, Preface to *PG*, 5.

wife: "The reason why I worked so hard at the letters and
speeches was that I was afraid of being a very bad wife; or,
to speak more truly, I was afraid of what would happen to
me, if I came to hate Chester. My devotion, in fact, was
like those embraces and kisses I had used to give Jim as a
child.... They were a kind of incantation to make me
love." And without irony, she can immediately add that
"I am one of those people (I expect because I am rather
timid by nature) who naturally hate tramplers, and am
especially frightened of lies, of anything cunning and malicious" (*PG*, 61). Though in *Not Honour More* Jim ac-
cuses her of being so, Nina clearly does not think of herself as "cunning and malicious"—nor I think should we.
By the end even Jim has come to view her as, rather, a
victim of corruption.

Nina is certainly an inveterate liar—"Unless I took
great care, I lied to Chester about the smallest trifles" (*PG*,
131)—but her mendacity is usually transparent, and
either well-intentioned or merely a convenience. Her
most elaborate lies result from an instinctive and honora-
ble desire to retain her son's confidence (*PG*, 207–208)—
even if it means sacrificing Chester's. But as she adds, "I
found, to my cost, it was very dangerous to keep secrets
from Chester" (*PG*, 208), and the consequences emphasize the untenability of her moral expedience: Tom's
self-righteous attack on Chester after being lectured about
lying ("'everything in the house is lies'" [*PG*, 193]);
Chester's denunciation of Nina when he learns of her
"deceit" (*PG*, 236–38); and then, just after his shocking
political defeat, his sweeping rant against public and private falseness: "'The country is rotted all through.... We
are afraid of the truth—we are not honest with one
another.... For a long time now we have been lying to
each other—there is no truth anywhere.' And he accused
me of hiding things from him, 'as usual'.... 'Our life is
eaten hollow with falseness'" (*PG*, 330–33). As always,
Nina's understanding of Chester is insightful; to "we are

62 not honest with one another," she responds: "What have I
done? (for when Chester said 'we' he always meant me)"
(*PG*, 330). And yet, though she knows that, as elsewhere,
he is at least partly playing for an effect on her, she generally not only acts to placate him but defends even his
grossest duplicities. When, for instance, Chester lies to
Parliament about some business dealing, Nina insists that
"it would have been *quite misleading* for Chester to have
told the whole story. . . . Chester was quite right . . . to ar-
range his statement so that people were persuaded to believe that he was really innocent, because he *was innocent*" (*PG*, 214–15). But here, at least as Nina sees it, the
end is truth even if the means are not. Yet regardless of
truth, Nina finds virtue in Chester's lying so long as it is
pragmatic and sincere. In the context of Chester's principled abandonment of his pacifist principles, she recalls
a childhood incident when she and Jim, sailing in a storm,
were probably saved only by Jim's "pretending he had
made an enterprise out of the trip . . . he was making a real
difference by suggestion that we could *make* the whole
affair rather glorious instead of a stupid escapade and a
miserable struggle not to be drowned." Her point is that
"No one would dream of calling Jim a hypocrite for pretending to himself and me, in the middle of a violent
storm, that we were doing something reasonable and possible. And no one has any right to call Chester, who had
ten times more imagination than Jim, a hypocrite for pretending in the middle of a political storm . . . that he had
always meant this or that" (*PG*, 229–30). And Nina actually finds Chester's action praiseworthy: "No one on earth
can prove that Chester was not doing a rather noble act
(risking his very honour) when he 'ratted' on his pledges"
(*PG*, 268). And for all that her choice of verb and the quotation marks suggest, her statement of purpose and her
summation of Chester's career are without ironic qualification: "What I am trying to do in this book is not to make
out that Chester was a saint . . . but to show that he was

...a 'good man'—I mean (and it is saying more than could be said of most people) as good as he could be in his special circumstances, and better than many were in much easier ones" (*PG*, 215–16).

This is a remarkably kind and yet astute judgment of Chester—especially coming from a wife who divorces him after thirty years not only of never having loved him but of fearing him as an enemy. But then, for all her passivity and indolence, Nina repeatedly demonstrates that she is not what she appears content to pass for: a simple-minded innocent or the infinitely malleable instrument of others. Her equanimity when confronted by the most outrageous lies (her often passionate defense of them, in fact) is only one manifestation of her rare though odd breadth of outlook. Another is her self-analysis that, for all she endures, never indulges in self-pity because she remains unfailingly aware both of her limited perspective and of alternative ways of viewing and judging. For example, on being married to Chester, she says, "And already I was able to reflect that, though I did not like the man, I was not suffering any intolerable burden in being married to him" (*PG*, 25). After a while she adds, "Of course, each time life became more 'possible' again it was also more complicated" (*PG*, 47). And her attitude towards Chester remains consistently dual: "Even when he was in my arms I would look down on his thick crinkly hair and detest it" (*PG*, 62); "the more I devoted myself to Chester, the more I would criticise" (*PG*, 63). She is capable of praising and mocking him simultaneously: "Chester always rose to occasions ... but also he somehow managed to profit by them. There was perhaps some truth in the old joke that if Chester Nimmo, stark naked, were attacked by two desperadoes, armed to the teeth, there would be a short sharp struggle, and an immense cloud of dust, and then it would be found that the footpads had murdered each other and that Nimmo was wearing the full evening dress of an archbishop with gold watches in

64 every pocket" (*PG*, 138). In virtually the same breath she can assert that "Chester was the best of fathers" and express fear that he will take Tom from her (*PG*, 158–59), or feel intense anguish at Tom's cruel mimicking of Chester and yet find him "so brilliant that I could not take my eyes off him. . . . [And then,] to my horror, I was suddenly seized with laughter" (*PG*, 240–42). Her subsequent analysis of Tom's mimicry reflects an identical ambivalence: "I shall never admit that Tom became an evil person. But I do think that he knew, at least subconsciously, that his mimicry was cruel and false; he simply could not resist the temptations of his 'art', which was, after all, a real art" (*PG*, 348).

Perhaps the oddest manifestation of her dualistic outlook occurs when, having at last given herself "up to hatred" of Chester, she despairingly contemplates suicide. Chester stops her from jumping off the balcony— and "just then Chester's pyjamas . . . began to slip down and he grabbed at them with such an offended look (as if they had tried to 'betray' him) that I had a horrible impulse to laugh." Then she feels submissive but not humiliated ("because it seemed now to me that I was doing the only reasonable thing"), has sex with Chester while detesting him, and then thinks she would have done well as a prostitute (*PG*, 307–309). This extraordinary sequence graphically depicts an emotional agility conforming to no common notion of morality. Nina herself says that "a woman is used to feeling in half a dozen places at once" (*PG*, 271)—and perhaps the relativistic amorality implicit in such a statement defines her as well as anything can.

It is no wonder then that Nina, like the trilogy as a whole, displays an utter contempt for facts, a belief that facts often work to conceal truth rather than express it. Of Chester's political actions, she says, "The more you know of the facts the more uncertain they seem" (*PG*, 48), for "when you are dealing with men like Chester facts simply turn round the other way" (*PG*, 112). Her typical reaction to the common view of anything is "But again the truth is quite different from the facts and much more complicated" (*PG*, 99). But Nina's implication, that her own vision represents the truth beyond facts, is denied by her often convoluted responses to people and events: her detestation of the man she chooses to live with for thirty years; her love-making with Jim as a means of proving love (*PG*, 61, 85); her doing with Chester the bedtricks Jim had brought her from India, and then being surprised that, contrary to what she had intended, "he took this very natural achievement (just as I had done with Jim) as a sign that we were at last 'at one'" (*PG*, 114). Throughout *Prisoner of Grace*, her matter-of-fact tone suggests an obliviousness to the implications of her various startling pronouncements—on money: "Next to living with the man you love and having good health, it is the most delightful thing possible. Even when you can only esteem your husband and are subject to eye headaches, it is a very great consolation" (*PG*, 140); on Chester's acting swaggeringly triumphant after a major breach between them: "My loathing of him passed into a kind of reflective trance; and when, to my astonishment, he had the impudence to make approaches ... I found myself too 'scattered' to oppose him. I said to myself ... 'Very well—do what you like to me', and behaved like a dutiful but rather abstracted slave. But he ... showed no indignation—he behaved like a master who chooses to be a little rough to enjoy his mastery. And I did not hate him, because it was useless" (*PG*, 156–57); on her relationship with Chester after the divorce: "On the very first occasion that we were alone together ... he made an attack on me. . . . You say I should have turned him out of the house. But I was extremely anxious to avoid any kind of contretemps which might upset Jim. . . . and now I did everything possible to

66 give the man what he wanted as quickly as possible, simply to get it over" (PG, 385–88).[32]

Yet despite Nina's exasperating weakness and her endless capitulations to Chester, we remain largely sympathetic. For all her dismissing of facts and employing of lies, she has tried to be honest with Chester about vital matters: Tom's conception, for instance, and her whole relationship with Jim. More important, her portrayal of herself with all her inadequacies intact, her admittedly impressionistic account, her including opposing but equally valid moral perspectives all suggest an honesty with both herself and us. But towards the end Nina pushes us beyond mere annoyance. She finally makes the break with Chester that—since the scene at the train station when she nearly goes off to join Jim after the conception of Sally—we have increasingly desired and decreasingly expected. But it turns out that she has not got free of Chester at all: ultimately, climactically, and despite Chester's diminished public and physical power, he dominates her more fully than ever. And she concludes her account by describing the strange and apparently thrilling tension she feels in living simultaneously with both her husbands.

Thus, where the structure of the novel appeared ready to resolve itself—with the divorce, the remarriage, and the birth of the first child to be openly acknowledged as Jim's—Nina's characteristic qualities (inertia to the point of tragic indecisiveness, indecisiveness to the point of masochism) lead to an ending typical of the impressionistic novel: one that is unresolved, unbalanced, utterly open. We are left to wonder: how long can she fight off Chester? how long can *his* health stand the strain? what

32 This last quotation contains Nina's initial use of the rhetorical "you"—a sign of the defensiveness that dominates the final twenty pages of her *apologia*. Reflecting his career as what Cary calls "the spellbinder, the artist in words, the preacher, the demagogue" (PR, 51)—the performer always consciously manipulating an audience—Chester employs the rhetorical "you" throughout *Except the Lord*.

form will Jim's violence take when he discovers her lies 67
about Chester's behavior, and her own? Thus, though
Prisoner of Grace offers a remarkably complete picture of
Nina's complex perspective, it increasingly demonstrates
the limits of that perspective: she ends the book by an-
nouncing, typically, her complete happiness in the midst
of a precariousness in which imminent disaster is inherent. At this point we can accept Nina in one of two ways:
at face value (she is, after all, charmingly and disarmingly
self-condemning as she gamely struggles with unanswerable moral questions) or its obverse: as hopelessly blind
and masochistic, even morally and mentally unbalanced.
For *Prisoner of Grace* greatly resembles such novels as
The Good Soldier, Felix Krull, and *Lolita,* all of which
remind us that, more often than not, protagonist / narrators present themselves with devastating (if unconscious) irony. The crucial difference, however, is that
Prisoner of Grace exists as part of a larger work; paralleling the Ford of *Parade's End* rather than of *The Good Soldier,* Cary gives equal voice to the other participants in
the common disaster.

Prisoner of Grace is the most important and successful
book of Cary's second trilogy because Nina is its most interesting character and most imaginative narrator. The
trilogy as a whole is essentially spatial rather than temporal; this is what Cary meant when, referring to the first
trilogy, he spoke of desiring "a three-dimensional depth"
in which each narrator describes the other two. The appropriate analogy is a painted triptych or multiple descriptions of a sculpture by several stationary observers,
rather than a process like a film or a concert. Yet *Prisoner
of Grace* has it both ways because Nina, though she is not
obsessed by tradition like Chester and Jim, is the only one
of the three to have an historical consciousness.[33] Thus,
when she has finished her account, with its focus on the

33 In this Nina resembles Tom Wilcher of the first trilogy. See Adams,
"Joyce Cary's Three Speakers," 109–110.

68 present, we have also learned all we need to know about her past—and how the two interact with each other. The narratives of Chester and Jim, on the other hand, are temporally narrow: Chester virtually ignores the present; Jim is locked obsessively into the immediacy of the moment.

Both Nina and Chester see the past as a time of greater happiness, but where she invokes it as commentary upon the present, Chester's narrative aims at shifting our focus of concern from now to then, from a moral ambivalence that cannot help appearing as the hypocrisy it usually is to the innocence of youth—when attending a play represented the outer reaches of sin. *Except the Lord's* quiet, retrospective, and nostalgic narration of a far-from-idyllic and yet not unhappy initiation into the realm of experience goes a long way towards undercutting the antipathy toward Chester built up by Nina's account. As Andrew Wright says, "The second volume of the political trilogy widens the boundary of our sympathy for Chester Nimmo, not least because he cannot explain in his own words the events of his political career."[34] Chester defines his narrative purpose in terms that look beyond family life during growing-up years: "If I draw back now the curtain from my family life, sacred to memory, I do so only to honour the dead, and in the conviction that my story throws light upon the crisis that so fearfully shakes our whole civilisation" (*EL*, 5). Yet despite occasional references to his political and marital life, and even to his biographers (whom he scorns), Chester's account seems not a defensive polemic, but a broad and largely untroubled recollecting of growing up in difficult times: "My memory, despite myself, was full of songs."

What makes *Except the Lord* noteworthy is not its narrative perspective per se, for Chester's reminiscences are straightforward and commonplace and they lack the narrative tension typical of the modern cubistic novel. The

34 Wright, *Joyce Cary,* 148.

book ends as it began, with Chester's contemplation "by
the grave of a noble woman, one of the three noblest I
have ever known, my mother, my sister, my wife" (*EL*, 5).
Yet only at the end does he reveal that the grave is, surprisingly, his sister's—for (after *Prisoner of Grace*) we
expect a book about Nina and his life with her. But she
doesn't appear at all, except as an angelic child of five and
in passing references to her as his dedicated wife of many
years. Even the defensive tone which emerges about two-
thirds of the way through the book is dissipated as Chester returns, towards the end, to the distant past. If Chester's account is ostensible autobiography, then, it is an
odd one, for (like Henry Adams' *Education*) great chunks
of his middle life are passed over. But the novel of course
does not stand by itself, and its significance lies precisely
in its *not* being an ostensible sequel to the tense immediacy of *Prisoner of Grace*. In a temporal sense, the second
trilogy is written out of order;[35] and *Except the Lord*
seems placed in the triptych exactly where it does not belong. Yet the past it portrays serves as context for both the
marriage depicted in *Prisoner of Grace* and the political
and personal machinations of *Not Honour More*. Further,
its virtual ignoring of the *Prisoner of Grace* (and *Not
Honour More*) subject matter suggests the connection—
that Chester seeks to avoid confronting the disturbing reality of his marriage and political career—and thereby
implies a conscious evasiveness on Chester's part corresponding to that depicted by both Nina and Jim. For the
very unself-consciousness of Chester's account, its minimal introspectiveness, leaves everything still hanging
that, after *Prisoner of Grace*, we had expected *Except the
Lord* somehow to resolve—or at least to consider.

Not Honour More thrusts us back immediately into the
Prisoner of Grace subject matter and time scheme. The
much shorter temporal span in Jim's account, which

35 *Ibid.*, 142.

70   picks up from the end of Nina's, suggests a running down
of time, a condensing, as it heads towards some climactic
moment which, for its narrator, will cause it to end. The
tautness builds from the opening sentence: "This is my
statement, so help me God, as I hope to be hung" (*NHM*,
5). In the first few pages Jim recounts his antipathy for
Chester; his discovery of "this old swine, over seventy
years of age, interfering with my wife"; his shooting of
him; his defense of the African Lugas, who "were better
Christians in every way, and better men than any in
Whitehall"; his sense of victimization at having been
"hounded out of the African Service for trying to protect
my people" (*NHM*, 7–8). It is a shock to return, after Chester's self-indulgent and atemporal re-creation of the past
in *Except the Lord*, to the violence and sordid sensuous-
ness of this present. Jim's narrative and moral stance refo-
cuses our attention on the world of personal and political
hypocrisy, of small-minded intrigues, while making us
wonder at Chester's—and Cary's—ability to seduce us
from our sense of disgust, our tendency to make moral
judgments, long enough to read *Except the Lord* with
sympathy for its protagonist / narrator.

   Yet in its own way, Jim's account is as self-indulgent as
Chester's. Jim sees himself as terribly wronged throughout, an embodiment of truth and honor in a world of lies
and trickery, the last principled man left to oppose the
universal moral rot. His self-righteousness wells up
continually—as when he says that others see him as "that
nasty ex-soldier, making a ridiculous fuss. . . . The lowest
form of animal life—an honest freeman" (*NHM*, 205–
206). For all his nominal qualities he is, like Othello, a
moral and emotional infant incapable of enduring complex passions, and he seeks to evade them by action he
calls "duty" and a murder he calls "an execution." Both
Jim and Othello are the egregious fools their trickster-
antagonists call them as they mockingly manipulate

them; both manage to be alternatively tyrannical and insipid in relationships with others. At one point, after unsuccessfully shooting at Nina (Chester had taken the precaution of removing the bullets), Jim gashes her forehead by hurling his pistol at her. The next moment, he blames Nina for failing to respond to his solicitude.

Further, for all his obsession with truth and honesty, Jim, like Chester, is a less than reliable narrator. He claims that Chester "stole this woman, my wife, from me when she was little more than a child and set to work to destroy her body and soul" (*NHM*, 8). But he fails to mention that Nina was pregnant by him at the time, that he had deserted her as soon as he knew, and that Chester was delighted to marry her even knowing of her condition. Jim's highly subjective account, like Chester's, offers glimpses of uncomfortable truths bursting through despite its narrator. When Chester suggests that it is natural for the woman who was his wife for nearly thirty years to retain some feeling for him, Jim says, "She hated you." Jim is right in part, but Chester's response—"She is incapable of hatred."—conforms more significantly to the Nina we have come to know in *Prisoner of Grace*. This is one of those moments when the self-conscious narrator reveals perhaps better than he knows, a type of revelation whose extent is a measure of such a narrator's reliability.

Jim reveals a good deal more elsewhere: when, for example, he offers multiple versions of his initial seduction of Nina [36] and, especially, during the novel's bizarre

36 Foster notes that Jim "tells the story of his seduction of Nina three times, in Chapters 2, 12, and 13," and concludes: "It seems obvious from this that Cary wants it clearly understood that Jim is a liar" (p. 488). Foster is not wrong, but I think he makes too much of the hints of contradictions in these very fragmentary accounts. Granted, Jim cannot tell the same story twice, but then who can? Besides, Jim is just as obviously dependable at times—as in his general depiction of Chester, in his relating the disastrous failure of the general strike, in his noting Chester's contradictory reasons for being in the house with Nina the penultimate time. For the most part Jim strikes me as about as reliable as most of us are.

72 final scene and Jim's defense of it. "They think me a fool who murdered the wife he loved for nothing. But it wasn't murder I did. It was an execution. And I didn't do it for nothing. . . . There was no other choice for a man who wasn't prepared to live like a rat" (*NHM*, 223). We share Jim's moral perspective at the end *only* to the extent that we too can conceive of "no other choice."

Jim's blindness and absurdity are evident; he may even be mad. But it is as superficial to dismiss him as a hopeless lunatic as to consider him Cary's moral spokesman. His devotion to duty, for instance, may be destructive, but it has its nobility as well; like his obsessive hatred for Chester, it is as morally ambivalent as such loyalties generally are. Further, it is not simply ironic that Chester is sterile while Jim produces a child seemingly every time. To note Jim's inadequacies, then, is not to reduce him to a moral cipher, but to emphasize the human quality behind the voice we hear, to acknowledge the validity and the limitations as inherent in his viewpoint as in the others.

Cary has said that the contrasts of the different worlds in the second trilogy are much sharper than in the first (*PR*, 59). But the second deals more centrally (though more narrowly) with sharply divergent moral perspectives. The utterly different outlooks in the first trilogy all evoke empathy and tolerance—even when read together. The reader partaking of Sara's enduring female vitality, Wilcher's honest self-analysis, Gulley's buoyant opting for freedom over justice, could affirm each in turn without having to make ultimate moral distinctions—and thus without being tested himself. The first trilogy's viewpoints are not mutually exclusive; they do not demand each other's destruction or that we side definitively with one of them against the others. Each remains viable and vital; we are free to wish them all well.

The reverse is true of the second trilogy, where the perspectives of none of the protagonist / narrators are ultimately appealing. All of its protagonists are less sympa-

thetic than their counterparts in the first trilogy.[37] It has
by now been convincingly demonstrated that despite the
early critics (who repeated the initial wrong-headed reaction to the Stephen of Joyce's *Portrait of the Artist*), Jim
Latter's perverted values and doubtful sanity disqualify
him as Cary's spokesman.[38] But it is equally untenable to
see Chester as essentially admirable or to defend Nina's
adultery.[39] After *Prisoner of Grace* and *Except the Lord*, it
is clear that Nina and Chester are *not* morally reliable,
and the anticipation of a spokesman-like voice in the
forthcoming third book of the trilogy is natural. But the
fact that Cary did not write *Not Honour More* that way
should not deceive us into going back and viewing Nina
and Chester as better than they are. For all his talent and
devotion, Chester remains a political opportunist of the
worst kind, one indifferent to the destructive effects his
machinations have on others, and a man with no qualms
about employing his wife as tool or slave—and who, after
his divorce, spends his last years in seemingly endless as-
saults on her.

Nina, the most attractive of the three, is perhaps the
most blameworthy. When she says of Chester, "He never

37 See Foster (p. 478) and Wolkenfeld (pp. 94, 153). Wolkenfeld, in fact,
sees all of them as blind, insane, and unreliable, as well as failures (pp. 94. 115,
153–54, 178)—a judgment that strikes me as no more than a half-truth.

38 Mahood (p. 103) and Robert Bloom, *The Indeterminate World: A Study
of the Novels of Joyce Cary* (Philadelphia: University of Pennsylvania Press,
1962), still find grounds for defending the murder. But Foster (p. 490) and Wolkenfeld (pp. 115, 180–81) are convincing in finding it utterly indefensible.
Wolkenfeld quotes Cary as mocking "'Jim's honour.... Afraid of public
opinion—of what people will say. This "honour" is artificial, trivial, it is *really*
cowardice'" (p. 180).

39 Foster, who rightly sees Nina's motivation as highly complex, chides Jim
who "with his narrow, childish mind, can see it only in the narrow terms of
adultery, a breach of faith" (p. 490). But it is easy to be philosophical and
understanding about adultery when someone else's wife is involved. Jim's
moral perspective is blameworthy not because he fails to condone Nina's continuing relationship with Chester (as Foster implies), but because it leads him
to reprehensible action. For Jim's being right about the adultery is surely to his
credit, just as the murder as surely is not. I assume that, though still condemn-
ing the murder, we would feel more unambivalently positive towards Othello if
Desdemona had actually been as she seemed to him.

74 stopped his manoeuvres for a moment; there was trickery in his kindest deed" (PG, 127), we can applaud her fine insight. But as often as not, her actions demonstrate her apparent ignorance of what she knows, for, knowing better, she nonetheless willingly spends her life in bondage to those two moral incompetents, Chester and Jim, and it thus becomes impossible to accept Nina as any more of a reliable moral spokesman than they. She appears *most* responsible for the common disaster because her vision and values are not only closest to our own, but they have sought to mediate, and thus transcend, the two warring extremes, to interpose a viable truth between conflicting abstractions. Actually, she has no more to tell us about objective truth than those she derides for their faith in facts. All she can reveal with authority is her own confused understanding of herself in flux. Of course, this is a great deal—and it is why the book, and the trilogy, matter as they do.

Such cubistic novels as Cary's trilogies, then, novels of multiple participant narration, portray a series of relatively unambiguous moral assertions, each made by a compelling though not necessarily persuasive spokesman for his own uniqueness. Like Sara, Wilcher, and Gulley (though to a lesser extent), Nina, Chester, and Jim create perspectives which, in isolation, would command a fair degree of sympathetic involvement. But each is juxtaposed against the other two, which, because of the intense emotional interconnectedness of the second trilogy, thereby serve as a negating context, a pejorative moral comment. It would seem that none of them can maintain viability in such a context, such an alien environment; and yet all the perspectives Cary creates in the trilogies do so to a surprising extent—because the coupled pair in the implicit two-against-one relationship is a temporary thing, constantly shifting, so that each is not only isolated and under attack, but simultaneously reinforced and, as it were, on the offensive. Walter Allen says of Cary that "more than any writer of our time, English or American, he is the novelist of the creative imagination, for the creative imagination is the quality he most values in human beings. And the creative action of the imagination is unceasing and continuous, each man trying, in Cary's words, 'to create a universe which suits his feelings'. Since each man is unique and his shaping fantasy unique, it clashes inevitably with those of his fellows and, often, with the established order of society." [40] And yet Cary adds, "I am influenced by the solitude of men's minds, but equally by the unity of their fundamental character and feelings, their sympathies which bring them together" (*PR*, 52). The implication for our reading of such novels as Cary's trilogies is that, while a reality beyond the myopic perspectives exists, it is knowable only through the functioning creative imagination, the self-generating and expansive outlook, which remains, nonetheless, mortal, finite. [41]

<hr />

40 Allen, *Modern Novel*, 242.

41 John Teeling attacks Bloom's finding in Cary " 'a relinquishment of authority,' 'the vice of objectivity,' and 'submission to the variety and multiplicity of experience.' The two trilogies, says Bloom, merely give six different views of life, and the result is that 'the kind of ordering which a novelist's particular and precise belief can supply is largely absent in each trilogy as a whole' (p. 39)." John Teeling, "Joyce Cary's Moral World," *Modern Fiction Studies*, IX (Autumn, 1963), 276–83). Teeling shows that, for example, Chester's degradation is "abundantly demonstrated" in the trilogy, but his essentially negative argument takes him not to "Joyce Cary's Moral World," as his title heralds, but only through some of Cary's "Immoral Worlds."

Other critics also try to have it both ways. Wolkenfeld insists on an unequivocally definable reality behind the multiple standards of the two trilogies: "This is given by the implied narrator who controls the viewpoints, the one who actually does the shifting, the consciousness which in the trilogies points to the many connections between the various books. This last level suggests very strongly that there is a single, external, objective reality within which the individual groups find their relative place, and that there is a single pattern of human behavior which subsumes all individual and social differences" (p. 56). But does such a conclusion really follow from the inescapable fact of a writer's creating and manipulating structure beyond the level of his characters? If so, then Browning's Pope and Faulkner's Dilsey are glaringly redundant and the very notion of a nonabsolutist novel would be a contradiction in terms.

Wright similarly maintains that Cary's "worlds constitute different aspects of a single world, and that this world has a 'final' shape is most clearly to be drawn from a consideration of each of the trilogies as a whole. . . .The reader is

76   Consequently, it is not the unique viewpoint (no matter how aberrant) that is doomed and damned; rather, the abstract universe of moral certitude proves its own irrelevance when confronted by unresolvable conflicts defined not by ambiguity but by multiple self-sustaining perspectives. The reader then is thrown back on his own resources. Being triply involved and yet rejecting in turn each of the outlooks depicted in the second trilogy, he finds himself forced to extract and determine values with little but his own predilections and responses to aid him. Thus, though the first trilogy may be the greater aesthetic achievement, the second raises more unanswerable questions and perhaps leaves us more disturbingly touched and tested: surely, in comparable situations, we would not have failed so disastrously as Nina or Chester or Jim—or would we? The equivocality and unresolvability of such a question suggest the extent to which multiple-perspective art like Cary's second trilogy assumes that we too express a moral stance within a world no longer merely round but cubistic as well. In modern literature, the process of squaring the circle has come, simultaneously, to encompass and impel us all.

----

constantly required to compare and assess the versions of the same world presented by competent but interested witnesses. The reader is forced to draw a final conclusion, by himself" (pp. 109–110). But if the world of the novel *is* "final," as in *The Ring and the Book*, then it is absurd to say that the reader is "forced to draw a 'final' conclusion, by himself."

Cervantes, *Don Quixote* All this means very little so far as our story is concerned, providing that in the telling of it we do not depart one iota from the truth.

"And I will say right now," declared Don Quixote, "That the author of this book was not a sage but some ignorant prattler who at haphazard and without any method set about the writing of it, being content to let things turn out as they might."

3
Partially Dramatized and Undramatized Narrators

Regardless of his relationship to the main action he narrates, the participant commentator (as we have seen in Chapter Two) is necessarily dramatized: named (or virtually so[1]) and per-

---

1 In *Beyond Life*, the first of his *Biography of the Life of Manuel* sequence, James Branch Cabell calls his secondary-character narrator "I." But "I," who was originally intended to bear the author's name, still speaks for him in the complex (though anonymous) manner of Henry Fielding's Henry Fielding. Langston Hughes's narrator in the Simple series is also unnamed but still expresses his own individuality.

78 sonalized, limited and subjective, invariably self-conscious to a large extent. Each of the other two main modes of narration shares some of these qualities but differs in basic ways. The multifarious narrator is depersonalized and therefore free to transcend the action when he chooses, essentially a nonparticipant, yet one who is often partially dramatized and therefore limited (though sometimes only by the inherent time-bound, space-bound quality of narration). Third-person-subjective is undramatized and unself-conscious, yet wholly personal because bound up with and locked into the character or characters whose thoughts and values are thus articulated. In this chapter I will be considering, first, the dramatized impersonality of multifarious narration, then the undramatized personality of third-person-subjective, and, finally, the hybrid form created by the combination of the two.

I

Multifarious Narration

From traditional use of the term *omniscience*, it would seem that multifarious narration, at least in theory, would be objective, impersonal, undramatized, and unself-conscious. Scholes and Kellogg maintain that such a narrator is *not* all-knowing, that he is in fact as limited by time and space as the rest of us, but his existence on an essentially human plane would still seem to be impossible. The narrative voice in Wyndham Lewis' *The Human Age* fulfills such negative expectations. The voice is reportorial, effaced, like the framing narrator of a radio play. "The city lies in a plain, ornamented with mountains."[2] Thus he begins and thus he continues—the tone is matter-of-fact, neutral, even when narrating the fantastic, like the characters' rapid alterations in sex, age, form, time, and place. This is simply the way it is, the

2 Wyndham Lewis, *The Human Age, Book One: Childermass* (London: Methuen, 1956), 5.

narrative voice seems to say, in this given that must be dealt with, in this "Scene: Outside Heaven." There are characters, situations, actions—but nothing to suggest that any of it connects with the voice that speaks. And the same is generally true of historical novels set in the past rather than the future—Ford's *Fifth Queen* trilogy, for example.

But Lewis' multifarious narrator is atypical, not unique but very much in the minority. More commonly, multifarious narrators intrude themselves from time to time— sometimes as a nearly effaced editorial "we," but quite often as an anonymous but vitalized "I." Mann's *Magic Mountain* may be taken as exemplifying those works occupying, on the spectrum of dramatization, the place next to *The Human Age*. Mann's narrator intrudes, but infrequently and always as "we." Very little suggests any concerns apart from the tale being told or any discrete moral and aesthetic interests on the part of the narrator. There are perhaps two main hints: an awareness of the gulf between story time and narrative time which mildly recalls *Tristam Shandy,* and an occasional expression of limitation: "How far Madame Chauchat was affected we can only guess."

The next place on the spectrum is occupied by narrators like Robbe-Grillet's in *In the Labyrinth*. He begins and ends as "I" and even becomes sufficiently a participant to take up the burden of carrying a mysterious box which the main character, an unnamed soldier, has gotten himself killed trying to deliver. But in between, the narration is multifarious—objective, external, and undramatized—in the manner of *The Human Age*. Robbe-Grillet's two voices are, in fact, wholly separable; the "I" seems more an accident of composition than an essential or true participant.[3]

Perhaps most characteristic of multifarious narration

---

3 See pp. 97–98 herein for further discussion of this point.

80 are anonymity, occasional self-consciousness, partial dramatization, and extensive but still limited knowledge. One thinks, for instance, of the occasional self-consciousness of Doris Lessing's narrator in *Children of Violence*; of the narrator's submerged identity bobbing to the surface at odd moments in John Cheever's Wapshot series ("I" addresses Moses and Coverly familiarly as "you," knew Moses at school, lives in St. Botolph's[4]); of the narrator in Mann's *Joseph and His Brothers*. This last writes an essayistic Prelude concerning Joseph's ancestry and his place in history, and yet expresses his own vital personality by asserting that, "of this statement probably every word is false" (p. 12), that his story's beginning is necessarily arbitrary, that he shares Joseph's wandering spirit (p. 32), and by often reflecting the world (and thereby himself as well) through Joseph's eyes. Cheever's narrator represents what might be called classical multifarious narration: he maintains a consistently external relationship to those he reveals, and we never do get inside of them (in absolute terms, such externality is what sets multifarious narration apart from the personal modes); yet their actions are detailed so fully and explicitly that we are made to attain a sense of internal revelation and identification. We know Moses and Coverly and Leander fully, we feel; therefore we know them, in effect, from the inside out.

In contrast, Lewis' wholly transcendent and removed voice in *The Human Age* will not only occasionally venture inside his characters (like a puppetmaster inside his performing creatures), but will even, at odd moments, display a vicariously involved emotional response. His comment on Pullman's knocking down of Satterthwaite goes like this: "The fierce little victor steams away and

4 John Cheever, *The Wapshot Chronicle* (New York: Harper & Brothers, 1957), 103–109; *The Wapshot Scandal* (New York: Harper & Row, 1964), 18 ff, 307–309.

leaves the battered monster prone where he lies as he 81
richly has deserved and may all such bullies come to a
similar end amen!" (*Chi*, 142–43). The narrator's identification with Pulley—in third-person-subjective fashion—
seems complete; however, a shift in perspective follows
immediately:

> But with what rapidity his passion deserts him! giving him
> scarce time to relish the swiftly moving event for it has
> quickly come and quickly it has almost gone.
> His calm pulse announces his restoration to the normal
> personal mean of circumspect donnish Pullman, with the
> fading of his aggressive youthful fire the more stable young-
> gish don, studious and alert, with somewhat scanty hair that
> blows in wisps of uncertain colour, returns, in seventy yards
> it has absolutely all evaporated, he is cooler than a hotbed of
> cucumbers. (*Chi*, 143)

Thus Pulley is deflated as surely and completely as Satters.

Lewis' narrator has no compunctions about taking us
briefly inside his characters, creating a degree of sympathetic involvement, and then mocking by shifting quickly
elsewhere—say to some far-fetched literary analogy for
Satters' having stated his liking for Pulley: "The delicious
confession because of the exciting crudity of words thrills
him, it has the sanctity of a pact that a kiss alone could
properly seal and he pauses in confusion; then big burn-
ing Gretchen he yodels on putting into clumsy brazen
words all the sentimental secrecies coveted by the Fausts
with jammy and milky appetites in the dark ages of
simplicity" (*Chi*, 97). Lewis' narrator is extremely clever,
as clever as Conrad's equally abstract and ironic voice in
The Secret Agent. The danger with all such narration is
that it becomes heavy-handed and falls flat to the extent
that the characters fail to come alive, and characters in
such works have a difficult task in asserting themselves
against continual disparagement. Conrad's characters

82 largely succeed because they are sufficiently individualized for their pathos to strike a balance with the narrator's irony. Lewis' ever-changing characters—lacking the uniqueness possessed by such other protean figures as Melville's Confidence Man, Woolf's Orlando, Mann's Felix Krull, or Durrell's Justine—remain stick figures dressed in borrowed clothing, unprepossessing as characters, feeble and insignificant because dead metaphorically as well as literally. As a consequence, the narrative voice appears self-indulgent and arrogant, contemptuous not only of his characters but of us as well—for the Olympian pose masks a moral stance which cannot be simply swallowed whole, which must be weighed to be granted validity, but which is presented so as to preclude our doing so.

As the term implies, the multifarious narrator is capable of the most complex and various role playing, both from one novel to the next and within a single work. At times he may approach omniscience, at others provide only occasional explication of the internal realities of those within his province, at still others become little more than a roving reporter—in Dos Passos' term, a "camera eye." Yet he remains various and nimble, capable of the most intricate shiftings of perspective almost from moment to moment.

Still, despite their apparent refusal to acknowledge rules or masters, multifarious narrators are not nearly so uncircumscribable as this might suggest. Their range does not, on the one hand, encompass narration by someone bearing his creator's name, whether he systematically defines himself as transcending the events he recounts (like Fielding in *Tom Jones*) or inhabits their very center (like Henry Miller or Jan Cremer). Such characters, I suggest, are a special type of participant / narrator, for what they narrate reaches us through a specific, defined voice and viewpoint, a dramatized, named speaker whose values, like those of any other participant / narrator, are there for us to know and weigh. (This type of narration is discussed in Chapter Two, pp. 30–46 above.)

At the other end, the spectrum of multifarious narration stops short of narrators who speak, still in third-person form, mainly from within—the anonymous and undramatized narrative focusing that restricts itself, with relative consistency, to the perspective of named individuals within the action. (Third-person-subjective narration is discussed on pp. 87–96 of this chapter.)

What multifarious narration does best—and perhaps better than any other mode—is to dramatize the evolving fortunes of one or several major characters against the larger backdrop of historical or social affairs. Thus, Mann re-creates a vast Old Testament edifice to contain *Joseph and His Brothers*; Mikhail Sholokhov writes a veritable history of Russia in his Don chronicles; Ford invokes the spirit of Tudor England for his *Fifth Queen* trilogy; Tolkien creates and populates with creatures of every sort a whole new realm, Middle Earth, to retell the age-old fable of good and evil; Harry Kemelman does the same, but in the guise of a seemingly impossible marriage of Talmudic scholarship and popular detective fiction; and a host of writers (Arnold Bennett and John Galsworthy, Henry Williamson and Upton Sinclair, Roger Martin du Gard, John Cheever, and Doris Lessing) employ multifarious narration to recount the novelist's version of contemporary history—sometimes, as in Lessing's *Children of Violence*, taking it into a projected future, or even, as with Lewis' *The Human Age*, creating an utterly new realm (though of course out of the materials of the old) beyond conventional time and space.

But though subsuming aspects of exegesis, philosophy, history, and prophecy, these works remain novels— which means, as much as anything, that individuals emerge, not cast in huge or shadowy relief against their backdrops, but in human scale, with all their hopes and sufferings, fears and needs, and asserting themselves de-

84 spite the larger sweep of events, which never wholly defines or subordinates them.[5] The novelist fundamentally
treats people as individuals, on a domestic scale; the his-
torian is concerned with something greater and less, a
mythical, hydra-headed beast called "the people." Adam
Appleby, David Lodge's harassed protagonist in his
parody of *Ulysses, The British Museum Is Falling Down,*
says, "Literature is mostly about having sex and not much
about having children; life is the other way round." In
this sense, historians write literature and novelists write
life. And the multifarious narrator recounts it multifariously, in all its forms, with sureness, agility, and scope.

Thus, the multifarious narrator is often partially dramatized (unlike the participant / narrator, who always is, and
the third-person-subjective, who never is); he is always
anonymous—though often "we" or "I"—yet even the
most objective of multifarious narrators defines stances
for himself, perspective, and therefore a structured
scheme of values which we, in turn, need to weigh. Yet
again, the difficulties in such considering are often compounded not only by the narrator's refusal to actualize the
values in terms of a dramatized character, but also by the
multifarious narrator's protean nature, his common refusal to become univocal, locked into a single vision,
even in narrating a *Bildungsroman.*

The uses made of documentation further suggest the in-
termediate quality of multifarious narration. Protagonist /
narrators generally feel constrained to reveal both the circumstances of their narrating (Pamela's and Clarissa's
endless letters, Gulley Jimson's "honorary secretary,"
Humbert Humbert's imagined jury, Darley's manuscript

5 It is interesting to note that, in defining the novel, one is often forced to
rely on content rather than structure, for the novel per se has no structure. As
Robert Scholes and Robert Kellogg indicate, the novel is a synthetic literary
construct (combining mimesis and history with romance and fable), "an un-
stable compound, inclining always to break down into its constituent elements." *The Nature of Narrative* (New York: Oxford University Press, 1966),
15.

of the past) and their sources for whatever they know at
second-hand (diaries, letters, hearsay, and the like).
Third-person-subjective is largely devoid of documentation (Stephen's few diary pages at the end of Joyce's *Portrait* are the exception rather than the rule). Multifarious
narration dispenses with them or not as suits the individual work. *The Human Age* and *The Fifth Queen* have
none. Others create a fictional equivalent to the factual
appendices included in such protagonist-narrated historical novels as Mary Renault's *The King Must Die* and *The
Bull From the Sea*, and Robert Graves's Claudius duo:
Lessing's appendix of "Various Documents, Private and
Official, dated between 1995 and 2000," Leander's jour-
nal in Cheever's *Wapshot Chronicle*, Tolkien's elaborate
study of the language and culture of Middle Earth in *The
Lord of the Rings*.

Multifarious narration is an excellent technique for the
unobtrusive recounting of multiple perspectives—and in
this it often becomes multivalent. But even here its emphasis lies not on introspectiveness, a plumbing of internal depths or temporal subtleties, but on the dramatic
immediacy of human interrelationships—plus, sometimes, their theoretical ramifications. Such a technique
deals best not with profundities of thought but with com-
plexities of plot, the richness of human and societal inter-
course; not with Proustian intricacies of time and memory, but with the fullness of their evolving and being.

Occasional multifarious narrators are prevailingly
self-conscious, even ironic—as, for instance, in *Joseph
and His Brothers*, *The Secret Agent*, *A Passage to
India*—and these narrators create special difficulties for
the unwary who would determine the values of their
novels. To the extent that they draw attention to themselves they distract us from simply considering what they
point toward in their narration, and instead we are made
to view the narrative voices themselves—not directly but
in some fascinatingly perverse way—as the locus of

86 meaning. One thinks, in this regard, of the gentle but overt mockery of Mann's partially dramatized narrator, of the passive but heavy-handed irony of Conrad's wholly undramatized one, of the essayistic intrusiveness of Forster's removed voice—all of them offering not value judgments but problems apparently defying solution. Forster's famous last paragraph offers a definitive denial of friendship between Aziz and Fielding, between East and West: "But the horses didn't want it—they swerved apart; the earth didn't want it, sending up rocks through which riders must pass single file; the temples, the tank, the jail, the palace, the birds, the carrion, the Guest House, that came into view as they issued from the gap and saw Mau beneath: they didn't want it, they said in their hundred voices, 'No, not yet,' and the sky said, 'No, not there.'"[6] The implied author, on the other hand, is presumably saying yes, that he *does* want it—but exactly what he wants, and how it will come about, and why it would be a good thing remain, at most, implicit in the novel (in such things as the dialectic of its tripartite structure: "Mosque," "Caves," "Temple"), something he doesn't care to treat overtly, or else cannot. They therefore remain lingering critical questions for those who would ascertain the moral quality of form in such novels.

But multifarious narration, at least in its relatively impersonal manifestations, generally represents authorial presence more straightforwardly. The narrator tends to be reliable and unironical, to embody the values of the novel as they are actually presented, to minimize distance between narrative voice and implicit author. Consequently, one criterion for failure in works like Galsworthy's Forsyte chronicle or Ford's *Fifth Queen* trilogy. Williamson's *Chronicle of Ancient Sunlight* or Sinclair's Lanny Budd series is the extent to which we reject—or even question—both the multifarious narrator's scheme of

6 E. M. Forster, *A Passage to India* (New York: Harcourt, Brace, 1952), 322.

values and his untroubled adherence to them.[7] In an age of anxiety (and which age is not?) the sight of such complacency can be deeply disturbing. The modern novel—which is disturbing in other ways—is characterized by moral confrontation, juxtaposition, multivalence, an open and often self-deprecating admission of its inability to envisage a world predicated upon verities. Multifarious narration, at least to the extent that it pretends omniscience, often assumes that such a world, whether or not it lies within our grasp, does indeed exist—or at least that we should behave as if it does. Consequently, as a technique, multifarious narration—for all the varied forms it has taken in twentieth-century novels—represents the least modern of narrative modes.

II
Third-Person-Subjective

Third-person-subjective is less of a catchall category than multifarious narration. Still, it ranges from the intense immediacy of Joyce's *Portrait*, Richardson's *Pilgrimage*, and Woolf's *To the Lighthouse*, to the more relaxed and comparatively externalized narration of Rolland's *John Christopher*, Farrell's *Studs Lonigan*, Hartley's *Eustace and Hilda*. In the latter type we are very nearly in the realm of multifarious narration that focuses on a single protagonist. The line between multifarious narration and third-person-subjective is difficult to discern, for the two merge like adjacent colors in a prismatic spectrum, and yet they remain just as distinctive.

7 Booth defines a bad novel as one in which the reader is not induced to accept the norms of the implied author (*The Rhetoric of Fiction* [Chicago and London: University of Chicago Press, 1961], 157). But Booth is speaking only of an implied author whose values we reject out of hand. There are also implied authors whose values are theoretically acceptable but who, because of dogmatism rather than ambiguity, present them in a way that makes us tend to deny them nonetheless (*Pilgrim's Progress*, read as a novel, is such a work for many readers). To the extent that such a rejection occurs, regardless of the norms being rejected, we would seem to have a bad novel.

88   Where the two abut they are separated by a difference
of degree. Multifarious narration is wider ranging because free to move away from the individual perspective,
and free to indulge in self-dramatization or generalizing
speculation. Even the loosest and least intensely internal
third-person-subjective narrator moves—whether physically, intellectually, or morally—only rarely and briefly
from the fully dramatized perspective from which and for
which "he" is speaking. Such a narrator, then, can never
be "I," can never attain an independent, dramatized reality, because (though occasionally moving from it) he remains defined by the univocal perspective being portrayed. Arthur Sherbo notes that narrators generally have
two functions: to narrate and to comment.[8] But third-
person-subjective narrators do not comment, at least not
directly. Their only means are selection and ordering,
juxtaposing, stylistic variation—the devices of neither a
participant engaged in the narrated action nor of an indifferent God off somewhere paring his fingernails, but of an
artist actively concerned—professionally if not personally—with the evolving product of his handicraft.

The writer of modern third-person-subjective novels
has a most difficult task: he must create distance without
at first seeming to do so. Deep and unbridgeable chasms
between narrator and protagonist can be created with
such a technique, but morally reprehensible protagonists
function best when they are their own narrators. Browning's dramatic monologists, Ford's Dowell, Nabokov's
Humbert all engage our sympathies while betraying
themselves. On the other hand, a morally straightforward
protagonist may trigger a rejecting mechanism, for we no
longer readily suffer the glib equation of character and
implied author values found in such early multivolume
novels as *Pilgrim's Progress*, *Robinson Crusoe*, Cooper's
Leatherstocking tales, Thomas Hughes's *Tom Brown*. Yet

8 Arthur Sherbo, *Studies in the Eighteenth Century English Novel* (East
Lansing: Michigan State University Press, 1969), 5.

the *appearance* of just such an equation remains basic to third-person-subjective: how else can we accept the convention of implicit identity between, say, Stephen's stream-of-consciousness in *Portrait* or Miriam's interior monologues in *Pilgrimage* and their rendering? Distance between protagonist and third-person-subjective narrator, then, is hinted rather than proclaimed or denied, for such a speaker cannot remove himself physically to a place from which announcements of any sort can be made, or even where irony can be overtly displayed. Since judgmental instincts are strong, the dangers inherent in such a technique are great for both the unwary (who tend to accept immediate representation as ultimate reality) and the overly sophisticated (who tend to view all character portrayal as ironic).⁹ But third-person-subjective opposes both tendencies; for its vision is structurally monolithic—narrator and protagonist seem to be at one with each other—and yet its ends are dual.

One obvious and immediate consequence is that such an anonymous and disembodied voice can never offer the kind of overt irony in his treatment of subject matter displayed by such multifarious narrators as those in *The Pic-*

---

9 For a fine statement of the whole problem, see Booth's discussion of Joyce's *Portrait* and the critical response (pp. 325–36), especially his quite proper sympathy for readers who unquestioningly accepted Stephen at face value. Despite his acknowledging that the irony in the portrait is now plain, Booth still chides Joyce for an ambivalence that permits us to view Stephen as "the artistic soul battling through successfully to his necessary freedom, or [as] the child of God, choosing, like Lucifer, his own damnation" (pp. 327–28). Booth insists on a pigeonholing that Joyce was at great pains to escape; yet the problem remains real, unresolved by Booth's plea for homiletic lucidity or by those who reject the whole judgmental question. In this context, one might, on the one hand, consider the problem of distance between Henry Miller and his identically named protagonist / narrator (see Chapter Two, pp. 30–46 above); on the other, the warning in Saul Bellow's "Deep Readers of the World, Beware!" (New York *Times Book Review*, February 15, 1959, pp. 1, 34) and Booth's similarly titled section (pp. 364–74). A recent essay by Charles Rossman, "Stephen Dedalus and the Spiritual-Heroic Refrigerating Apparatus: Art and Life in Joyce's *Portrait*," in *Forms of Modern British Fiction*, ed. Alan Warren Friedman (Austin: University of Texas Press, 1975, pp. 101–131), goes a long way towards resolving the problem by convincingly documenting the ironic treatment Stephen receives within the *Portrait*.

90   ture *of Dorian Gray, The Secret Agent, A Passage to India,
The French Lieutenant's Woman.* But irony does remain
possible (as the early critics of Joyce's *Portrait* learned to
their dismay) for an author seeking new levels of narrative subtlety within this form. Taking his cue from *both*
the stream-of-consciousness technique employed by
Edouard Dujardin and self-conscious protagonist / narrators like Sterne's Tristram Shandy, Joyce creates an utterly depersonalized implied author against whose values
those of the protagonist are contrasted and thereby
undercut to an extent. The irony lies in our own painfully
gradual awareness that something is fundamentally awry
with the values ostensibly being propounded (Stephen's
aestheticism, elitism, and arrogant nay-saying)—and that
the process by which we come to acquire this awareness
is, for the work we are experiencing, both intentional and
central.

Outermost narrative frames used to matter less in fiction. In *Pilgrim's Progress*, for example, little is lost if we
forget that the entire journey occurs within the
framework of a dream. Traditionally, as in the *Arabian
Nights*, Boccaccio's *Decameron*, and Giovanni Sercambi's
Novelle, frames are conveniences, storytellers' conventions, rather than functionally central. The air of
modernity about *The Canterbury Tales* results from its
frame's penetrating the tales and interacting with them,
rendering them part of the pilgrimage's action and not
merely set-pieces; further, teller and tale have been coor-
dinated.[10] But since the taut and highly conceptualized
structures of James, we are often confronted by a fiction
whose frames, while mattering greatly, are largely
hidden—and whose purposes and values are, therefore,
not immediately evident or accessible; they become dis-
cernible only through some process of indirection. We
know that in the modern and postmodern novel we in-

10 See H. B. Hinckley, "The Framing-Tale," *Modern Language Notes*, XLIX
(February, 1934), 72.

habit a realm presided over (though not necessarily ruled) 91
by that most compelling and articulate of philosopher-
kings, the unreliable narrator. But in third-person-
subjective novels like James's *The Ambassadors,* Joyce's
Portrait, and Ford's *Parade's End,* the unreliable narrator
achieves perhaps his most complex treatment, for wholly
effaced and unself-conscious, he is at odds with the
dramatized central consciousness in the subtlest of ways.
The protagonists of such works are not authorial embodiments, yet they are rendered with the sort of sympathy
and shared values that would, at first, strongly suggest
that they are. With such works as these, we have as many
demands made upon us as by the most deceiving (and
self-deceived) protagonist / narrators, narrators like Ford's
Dowell, Cary's Chester Nimmo and Jim Latter, Nabokov's
Humbert Humbert—but far fewer and less prominent
clues for distinguishing the moral distance between implied author and central consciousness.

Pilgrimage, Dorothy Richardson's highly wrought and
largely neglected masterwork, will serve as case in
point.[11] It is a novel which, sharing the grammatical form
of multifarious narration, attains the level of personal intimacy with its protagonist that we associate with participant narration. "Reading *Pilgrimage,*" Walter Allen
comments, "we are within Miriam as in life we are within
ourselves; we share in her extraordinary capacity for continuous and never-blunted response to current existence,
the ultimate astonisher."[12] From *Pilgrimage's* first
sentence—"Miriam left the gaslit hall and went slowly
upstairs" (P, 15)—both the narrator and the reader partake of Miriam's emotions and angle of vision with a consistency bordering on identification. There seems to me

11 The neglect of *Pilgrimage* has been somewhat reduced by the publication
of the first uniform edition by J. M. Dent & Sons (London, 1967); it includes
March Moonlight, the thirteenth and final novel of the series, which is published for the first time. References in the text are to Volume I of this edition.
Richardson's American publisher is Alfred A. Knopf.
12 Introduction to *Pilgrimage,* 5.

92 no distance between Miriam's response and ours to her experience preparatory to becoming a governess in Germany. "She thought of her lonely pilgrimage to the West End agency, of her humiliating interview, of her heart-sinking acceptance of the post, the excitements and misgivings she had had, of her sudden challenge of them all that evening after dinner, and their dismay and remonstrance and reproaches—of her fear and determination in insisting and carrying her point and making them begin to be interested in her plan" (P, 27). Here, Richardson's periodic prose successfully attains a rhetorical equivalent of Miriam's movements and mounting excitement that carries us—as well as her family—along with them. Such common victories are presented with complete sympathy throughout, with never a trace of irony or qualification. The narrator reflects Miriam directly, with total self-effacement and reliability: "When Miriam woke the next morning she lay still with closed eyes. She had dreamed that . . ." (P, 21).

Yet Miriam and her narrator are not one. To the extent that we may personalize the narrator, the character is clearly younger, less experienced, more insecure and even self-pitying—certainly at the beginning of her 2500-page odyssey and perhaps still at the end, by which time Miriam has largely usurped the narrative function. Many wonderfully lyric passages give free reign to her emotions, expressing them unequivocally, at face value. Listening to music, for example, "Miriam, her fatigue forgotten, slid to a featureless freedom. It seemed to her that the light with which the room was filled grew brighter and clearer. She felt that she was looking at nothing and yet was aware of the whole room like a picture in a dream. Fear left her. The human forms all round her lost their power. They grew suffused and dim. . . . The pensive swing of the music changed to urgency and emphasis. . . . It came from everywhere. It carried her out of the house, out of the world" (P, 43). At other times, however, Miriam is apprehended on a more objective plane. A touch of ridicule colors the portrayal of her horror and shame at having her hair washed in public (P, 59–61), her defensiveness over smoking her first cigarette (P, 208–210), her unthinking repulsion of affection she desires (P, 217–25), her sense of revelation over reading a newspaper for the first time (P, 243–44), and so on. The narrator will sometimes begin a scene with full identification, and then gradually distance himself somewhat from his protagonist. With Miriam we perceive that "Clara's pallid worried face had grown more placid during the hot inactive days, and today her hard mouth looked patient and determined and responsible. She seemed quite independent of her surroundings. Miriam found herself again and again consulting her calm face. Her presence haunted Miriam throughout tea-time" (P, 139). By the end of this passage, a real if indeterminate distance has opened between character and narrator, the haunted and the recounter of the haunting.

But even more ambivalently expressive is the near-juxtapositioning of conflicting responses. At her most self-pitying Miriam indulges in a contrasting glorification of past happiness (e.g., p. 132) which, at other times, she suspects. "Woven through her retrospective appreciations came a doubt. She wondered whether, after all, her school had been right" (P, 81). At times she feels capable, confident, content. "She felt the movement of her own breathing and the cool streaming of the air through her nostrils. She felt comely and strong" (P, 97). "She loved the day that had gone; and the one that was coming" (P, 111). But more often she feels lost, alone, inadequate. "She had longed to feel at home with them and to teach them things worth teaching; they seemed pitiful in some way, like children in her hands. She did not know how to begin. All her efforts and their efforts left them just as pitiful" (P, 93). "She could do nothing. Her fine ideas were no good" (P, 95). Her emotions are powerful and volatile,

94 attaining elation after some momentary human contact, plunging to despairing homesickness after a letter from her sister—and accepting each momentary extreme as ultimate reality. Further, her emotions seem a tap to be switched on or off at the whim of others. When feeling "very near the end of endurance [as her] sense of her duties closed in on her," Miriam is suddenly buoyed up because "evidently Fraulein [the head of the school where she is governess] approved of her after all" (P, 133, 135). Later, excited by his "mannishness," she "looked again and again at Pastor Lahmann.... She felt that only he could feel the beauty of the evening exactly as she did. Several times she met and quietly contemplated his dark eyes. She felt that there was someone in those eyes who was neither tiresome nor tame.... At first he had met her eyes formally, then with obvious embarrassment, and at last simply and gravely. She felt easy and happy in this communion. Dimly she was conscious that it sustained her, it gave her dignity and poise. She thought that its meaning must, if she observed it at all, be quite obvious to Fraulein and must reveal her to her. Presently her eyes were drawn to meet Fraulein's and she read there a disgust and loathing such as she had never seen. The woods receded, the beauty dropped out of them" (P, 156–57). Over and over again, the impression made upon Miriam is so sudden and intense that, if it were not for the depth and solidity of her rendering, she would seem not so much a *tabula rasa* as a vacuum, absorbing all yet containing nothing.

Like all of us, Miriam plays at roles and tries to mask her role playing. "She knew her pince-nez disguised her and none of these girls knew she was only seventeen and a half" (P, 55). What saves Miriam in such passages as this are, first, her self-awareness of the role playing (and therefore her potential for meaningful self-understanding) and, as the narrator subtly emphasizes, her youth. Her

sins are not mortal but only *en passant,* stages in her
journey from conceptual infancy to a plane emotionally,
intellectually, and morally analogous to that of the third-
person-subjective voice. The trap for the unwary in such
a novel as *Pilgrimage,* then, lies not in thinking of the
distance between Miriam and narrator as unbridgeable,
but in considering it bridged from the first. Clearly the
narrator and Miriam are not trying to pull us in different
directions; in a sense, rather, the one marks out the trail
for the other to follow. For, neither at odds nor at one
with the implied author's voice, Miriam is the narrator in
embryo, or at least in potential—and the narrator is unreliable only to the extent that we are led to accept the
evolving Miriam as wholly formed at inception.

To make my point, I have doubtless exaggerated the
sense of distance between *Pilgrimage*'s implied author
and protagonist. In reading the novel (and even rereading) our experience is that the two are, if not one, still in-
extricable. Yet distance remains real and unmistakable—
and at least partly a consequence of Richardson's choice
of narrative technique. For Miriam caught up in a moment of intense feeling may become inarticulate, but the
narrator recounts the experience with unfailing fluency—
and thereby at a remove. This is the essence of the book's
dualism and a prime factor in its evoking complex responses. Our natural tendency to identify completely with
Miriam's emotional variegations is partially checked by
the presence of the narrator as artistic shaper—evolving,
without covert intrusiveness, aesthetic and moral patterns
from the discrete atoms of Miriam's experiences.

Such works as *Pilgrimage,* Joyce's *Portrait,* and Ford's
Parade's End (at least now that we are attuned to them)
provide us with sufficient clues for perceiving distance
between the implied author and his alter-ego protagonist.
In such novels, third-person-subjective narrators become
the most covertly unreliable of all—because not only do

96 they represent themselves as unquestionably reliable but, effaced completely, they display neither motivation nor even the appearance of a personality with potential for motivation. What creates much of the tension in such works, then, is not only the subtlety by which narrative distance emerges, but the fact that the reader himself must do much of the work: spot the clues, define the distance as best he can, and then—what is hardest of all—locate himself and his own values viably within it.

III
The Hybrid Form

Multifarious narration and third-person-subjective are often employed interdependently. In Dreiser and Wolfe, Dos Passos, Sartre, and Waugh, the multifarious narrator has, as it were, come down to earth. He still maintains his right to roam and soar—to offer impersonal essayistic tales of cities (like Dreiser's Chicago, Wolfe's New York) or rapid, "objective" scene shifting (as in Dos Passos, Waugh, and Sartre). But the focus is basically the evolving protagonist or (in the case of Lawrence, Dos Passos, Sartre) protagonists, whose experiences we share in third-person-subjective form. To a large extent we come to know, identify with, and judge characters like Dreiser's Frank Cowperwood, Wolfe's Eugene Gant / George Webber, Waugh's Guy Crouchback in much the same way as we do Richardson's Miriam, Joyce's Stephen in *Portrait*, Ford's Tietjens and Henry Martin Aluin Smith (in *The Rash Act* and *Henry for Hugh*). Thus, through more complex means this hybrid form attains effects similar to those of simple third-person-subjective.

As a point of departure, other compound types—first the hybrid of multifarious plus participant narration, then the multiple third-person-subjective of Ford's *Parade's End*—may serve as context for our considering this most common of hybrid narratives. One of the most interesting

examples of the former is Camus' *The Plague*.[13] Much like
Henry Adams in the *Education*, Camus' speaker takes
great pains to establish his objectivity (see especially pp.
198–211)—but as narrator rather than phenomenon, as
one transcending events rather than as subject of an autobiography cast in the guise of biography.[14] Yet Camus'
narrator also wants it both ways: he expresses multifariousness (that is, objectivity, superior knowledge), but
simultaneously claims to be a participant. He cites
sources for his knowledge (personal experience, accounts
of others, public documents), is occasionally self-
conscious and dramatized, and moves from apparently
total removedness to "we," to "I," and then finally reveals
himself as Rieux, *The Plague*'s protagonist, who "ex-
pressly made a point of adopting the tone of an impartial
observer" (p. 271) in order to recount without emotional
embellishment the supercharged experience of the
plague. Even at the end, Rieux continues to refer to himself as "he," thus framing the personal revelation with the
multifarious.

Camus' structure is the converse of Alain Robbe-
Grillet's *In the Labyrinth* (in which multifariousness is
framed by the personal voice, an "I" narrator)—yet both
achieve an objectivity of narration which simultaneously
sustains the personal level of involvement. But Camus' is
the greater achievement at least partly because manner
and matter are organically interrelated: Rieux, a doctor
whose life is disrupted both personally and professionally, needs a degree of objectivity if he is to function effectively, survive the plague, and recount its horror without
breaking down. Robbe-Grillet successfully creates a tone
of existential hopelessness within which his protagonist,
anonymous and doomed, struggles gamely and fatalisti-

---

13 Albert Camus, *The Plague*, trans. Stuart Gilbert (New York: Alfred A.
Knopf, 1960).
14 Contrast Gertrude Stein's *The Autobiography of Alice B. Toklas*, a biography in the guise of autobiography.

98 cally against ruthlessly indifferent forces. But why then the "I" frame? The most plausible suggestion—that it reveals the ultimate efficacy of human control—seems impossibly at odds with the rest of the book. Here we have not multivalence achieved through the narrator's plausibly assuming multiple moral stances (as in *The Plague*), but the sort of confused ambiguity Booth rightly decries in *The Rhetoric of Fiction*.

In other kinds of novels, the framing personal voice may of course be used precisely in order to exercise overt control. In *Tom Jones* and the *Brave New World* sequence (as in Cabell's *Biography of the Life of Manuel*, Miller's trilogies, Jan Cremer's sequence) the author creates himself—literally or in effect—as a participant in the action. Yet both the Henry Fielding who narrates the essayistic chapters of *Tom Jones* and the Aldous Huxley who writes *Brave New World Revisited* and the 1948 Preface to *Brave New World* inhabit realms transcending those occupied by other personae created by the writers named Henry Fielding and Aldous Huxley. Such narrators who bear their authors' names determine structure and direction, explicitly shape, define, and control all they narrate, and seek to establish absolute moral norms beyond which there can be no appeal. The intentions and effects are far different from those who, like Cabell, Miller, and Cremer (and Henry Adams and Gertrude Stein in *The Autobiography of Alice B. Toklas*, for that matter), create themselves as central characters rather than as framing ones, and then risk themselves and their values in the common fray. Thus there are two distinct forms of self-representation: multivalent (author as creator) and integrated (author as creature).[15]

---

15 Of course the integrated form is really multivalent as well, but more subtly so, for we are always aware of the author's inability, regardless of intention, to surrender his framing power to remove himself from the action should he so choose. One of the many nice touches in John Fowles's *The French Lieutenant's Woman* is the author's casting himself in *both* roles simultaneously: superior to his story's participants and yet three times appearing as character (once in narrative present, and twice in story present).

Hybrids of multifarious and third-person-subjective also employ frame narration, but apparently only in single-volume novels. The outermost voice in such novels as *Nostromo, Three Soldiers, Under the Volcano,* and *Lord of the Flies* contracts into third-person-subjective at key moments (in the first three) or for almost the whole book (*Lord of the Flies*), but we always return to it for implicit moral commentary at the end. The variations on this form are numerous; but perhaps two novels may serve to illustrate the possibilities. William Golding's *The Inheritors* omits the first part of the frame (unless one counts the title and the epigraph from H. G. Wells's *Outline of History*), and the perspective of the first nine-tenths of the book locks into the anachronistic simple goodness of the neanderthals. The radical and sudden shift away from their moribund perspective, from subjective to objective, recalls us to our own; we can never really share theirs, for we, the morally ambivalent inheritors of the title, invariably brush our predecessors aside with the abruptness and dismissive indifference of Golding's structural transition.

To the Lighthouse reverses this frame structure. The two large sections, "The Window" and "The Lighthouse," are wholly multiple third-person-subjective; the brief but temporally extensive middle section, "Time Passes," is multifariously factual. Felt reality is thus played off against linear reality—much to the detriment of the latter.

Most commonly, perhaps, hybrids of multifarious and third-person-subjective employ not a frame structure but a continuous interweaving of the two. In Woolf's *Between the Acts* and Nathalie Sarraute's *Between Life and Death,* for instance, the two narrative modes are inseparable and virtually indistinguishable, united in an untransitioned compounding that reflects its two elements no more than salt reflects sodium and chlorine. Usually, however, and especially in multivolume novels, such hybrids assume the form of the *Bildungsroman,* with the two strands in-

100 terwoven but separable. The protagonist matures (in third-person-subjective revelation) against the backdrop of multifariously related larger events and within a chronological context. Thus, in Dreiser's Cowperwood trilogy, Wolfe's novels, Waugh's *Sword of Honour*, multivalence results from the structural antagonism between the protagonist's perspective and that of the world at large.

The narrative patterning in all three of these works, like Ford's multiple-subjective *Parade's End*, creates an immediate and relatively superficial duality of response— for we naturally tend to identify with the inadequately equipped protagonist struggling to make a go of his world and his life; and yet we are made to view him from Olympian heights as well as, therefore, an inferior creature whose aspirations are at best hollow and at worst doomed. It thus takes a major talent to employ such a technique with proper balance, without sinking to sentimentality or rising to condescension. The extent of failure in Dreiser and Wolfe has long been rehearsed—as has, by now, their extraordinary achievements in the face of their own failings. A comparison of Ford's *Parade's End* and Waugh's *Sword of Honour*, two unique yet remarkably similar multivolume successes, would seem to offer greater opportunity for considering the moral and aesthetic consequences of structure in this type of hybrid novel.

Evelyn Waugh's *Sword of Honour* trilogy does for World War II what Ford's *Parade's End* tetralogy does for World War I. The two are virtually identical in tone and style as they recount the deaths of the old ideals, the old civilization, the old easy assumption that history equals continuity. In a world that mocks them for attempting to translate moral goodness into action, both Ford's Christopher Tietjens and Waugh's Guy Crouchback, saddled with faithless bitches for wives, remain—for good or ill—Tory gentlemen to the last. They inevitably appear ridiculous in the process, for their tender virtues seem

trivially anachronistic when confronted by the arbitrary
grotesqueness of modern warfare and the gross corruption and inefficiency, masquerading as corporate wisdom, of its attendant machinery. The human gesture
would seem to have no validity in a world spinning
violently out of control. In both works, the structure emphasizes just this point, for each begins by portraying its
emerging protagonist through third-person-subjective
narration, and then shifts away from him to create radically contrasting perspectives. In both cases, the initial effect of the contrast is to reduce the protagonist's stature,
to undercut his uniqueness, to make us view him as object rather than subject—and yet the end result is far different from this.

The basic plot is identical in the two novels. Both
Christopher and Guy, products of a dying traditionalism
personified by their fathers and expressed by their own
unwillingness to divorce openly faithless wives, are set
upon by the forces of mass warfare and bureaucracy
seemingly bent not only on destroying them (rather than
the proclaimed enemy), but denigrating them in the process. Fathers die and wives deny them; the old touchstones
by which they had defined and sustained themselves are
mocked and dismissed; they confront condescension
from all sides (including the multifarious narrator)—yet
both refuse to break or to compromise. In best British
fashion, they "muddle through" and earn not only second wives of sympathetic natures, but the grudging respect of those who had patronized them. At the end of
The Last Post, Christopher's brother Mark, paralyzed and
dying throughout that novel, speaks at last to urge Valentine to blunt her sharp tongue against Christopher, a good
man. And Valentine, in the tetralogy's last words, acknowledges the significance of what Mark has said. She
tells the doctor, "Perhaps it would be best not to tell Lady
Tietjens [Mark's wife] that he spoke.... She would have
liked to have his last words.... But she did not need them

102 as much as I" (*LP*, 836). Similarly, the final words of *Sword of Honour*, spoken by Guy's resentful brother-in-law, are: "things have turned out very conveniently for Guy" (*US*, 240). In both works, then, the shift from monolithic focusing on the protagonist to a broader and more distant perspective ultimately strengthens rather than undermines his human and moral centrality.[16] For all its efforts, the world neither destroys nor dismisses him, nor succeeds in reducing him—as seemed likely all along—to the ridiculous or pitiful. Instead, Christopher's and Guy's steady perseverence (acting as if verities were still possible in a hopelessly relativistic realm ruled by the machinery of violence and authority) achieves a kind of triumph that implies the ultimate triviality not of themselves but of the blind, destructive forces arrayed against them.

How does this come about? The protagonists in both works, for all the third-person-subjective energies devoted to them are rather shadowy at first, animated postures of limited individualization, perhaps because so clearly, in Pound's phrase, out of key with their time, and at a loss to understand or cope. The shifts away from them, however, tend, perhaps despite our expectations, to *decrease* our sense of their hollowness, to render them figures of a substantiality sufficient to occupy the time and energy of others. For both Ford and Waugh, narrative hybridization is the proper and necessary means for achieving the desired dualistic outlook.

Robie Macauley has called *The Last Post*, the fourth book of *Parade's End*, "the strangely inconclusive conclusion of the Tietjens story." In form it is the most oblique of any of the books, the most extreme example of what must be called Ford's 'tangential relevance.' Christopher

16 In 1965, Chapman & Hall (London) published a single-volume edition that Waugh labeled "A Final Version of the Novels." The revisions were not intended to be substantive, but they do two important things: they conceal the fact that *Sword of Honour* was originally three separate entities and they keep the focus more narrowly and consistently on Guy's perspective.

Tietjens is present physically for only one moment at the end of the book and yet he is the most central being in it."[17] No more than Guy's is Christopher's point of view maintained with complete consistency from the first, for the narrator moves at times into other characters or to discursive comment. Yet the basic narrative focus remains on Christopher throughout the tetralogy's first three books. When, for example, Christopher and Macmaster are initially presented, it is Christopher who "felt certain" or "was not so certain," who "could not remember," who "disliked" and "knew" various things, who "didn't disapprove." In typical third-person-subjective fashion, descriptions of Christopher are integrated with intimate and unattributed knowledge of what he is: Tietjens "could not remember what coloured tie he had on.... He was a Tory—and as he disliked changing his clothes, there he sat, on the journey, already in large, brown, hugely welted and nailed golf boots, leaning forward on the edge of the cushion, his legs apart, on each knee an immense white hand—and thinking vaguely." His companion Macmaster, on the other hand, receives no autonomy of representation; he exists essentially through Christopher's perception of him. Macmaster wore "a tie confined by a gold ring, steel-blue speckled with black—to match his eyes, as Tietjens knew.... Macmaster ... was leaning back, reading some small, unbound painted sheets, rather stiff, frowning a little. Tietjens knew that this was, for Macmaster, an impressive moment. He was correcting the proofs of his first book" (*SDN*, 3–4). And it is not until *The Last Post*, with its breakdown of form into the apparent anarchy of nine interior monologues, that Ford's implied author departs radically from Christopher's point of view.

Waugh handles his multiple perspectives somewhat differently, yet with the same ultimate effect. The first

17 Robie Macauley, Introduction to *Parade's End*, xvii.

104 book of the trilogy is almost wholly third-person-subjective, though even here there are variations. It begins with a Prologue (Chapter 1 in the one-volume edition) offering background information on Guy's parents and then on war. The point of view is certainly Guy's at times: "He was not loved, Guy knew, either by his household or in the town" (*MA*, 15). At other times attribution is less clear: "Only God and Guy knew the massive and singular quality of Mr Crouchback's family pride. He kept it to himself"; "Mr Crouchback acknowledged no monarch since James II [England's last Catholic king]"; "He had a further natural advantage over Guy; he was fortified by a memory which kept only the good things and rejected the ill" (*MA*, 34–35). Yet his respect and deference to his father suggest that none of this is alien to Guy, that in fact the point of view might be obliquely his.

The first major shift in perspective, then, does not occur until the conclusion of *Men at Arms*, for the funeral of Apthorpe (Guy's *bête noir* and the character whose name supplies the titles for the first volume's three sections) occurs while Guy is flying back from England—and it leads directly to the book's multifariously related valedictory: "Already the Second Battalion of the Halberdiers spoke of Guy in the past tense. He had momentarily been of them; now he was an alien; someone in their long and varied past, but forgotten" (*MA*, 245–46).

Officers and Gentlemen, the second book of the trilogy, begins inside Guy: "As he passed the guard-room he had a brief, vague impression that there was something odd about the sentry" (*OG*, 16). But from here on, Guy's unique perspective, though never entirely lost, is decreasingly dominant. The shifts take us into a dozen different characters, into Ludovic's aphoristic and cynical diary, into the "Catch-22" world of mindless bureaucracy,[18] to

18 There is only one instance of this in the first book of the trilogy (pp. 159–60), but at least four in each of the other two: *OG*, 30–33, 115–18, 141, 154–55; *US*, 26–31, 126–27, 141–43, 185–87.

glimpses of world figures like Churchill and Roosevelt
acting for all the world as if in control of things, to
virtually abstract commentary: "Of the nine weeks which
had passed since X Command sailed from Mugg, five only
had been spent on the high seas. In the war of attrition
which raged ceaselessly against the human spirit, anti-
climax was a heavy weapon" (*OG*, 110–11). The third-
person-subjective glimpses into others, the panoramic
overviews, and perhaps especially the many choppily
presented vignettes (paralleling the "camera eye" sections of Dos Passos' *USA*), suggest as with Ford a breakdown of narrative control (though not the author's) corresponding to the chaos of thought, planning, and action
that represents Waugh's view of war. Then, too, Guy's
unexpected and apparently arbitrary happy ending conforms with honesty and irony to the world of moral anarchy in which good intentions generally destroy, evil
and stupidity are favored as often as not, and the individual viewpoint seems constrained to yield to a pseudo-
omniscience lacking all purpose, order, and moral validity.

Yet Guy, like Ford's Christopher before him, is not
simply the chance survivor of society's equivalent of the
principle of indeterminacy. Both have not only clung to
their old values before the holocaust, but have managed,
in their very manner of survival, to revivify them and, in
the process, make the world take notice. Guy's climactic
moral decision—to take back his wife not despite but because she is pregnant by another man—does more than
what he intends: save at least the one soul offered him.
His superficially gratuitous creative act (the act of a fool,
as others see it) fulfills the sense of destiny that invades
him after the death of his father, "the best man, the only
entirely good man, he had ever known" (*US*, 65). "In the
recesses of Guy's conscience there lay the belief that
somewhere, somehow, something would be required of
him; that he must be attentive to the summons when it
came. They also served who only stood and waited. . . .

106 One day he would get the chance to do some small service which only he could perform, for which he had been
created. Even he must have his function in the divine
plan" (*US*, 66).[19] Certainly in Waugh's plan, Guy's life-
affirming action weighs in the scales against the far more
gratuitous destruction he has witnessed, experienced,
and now surely earned the right to survive.

In both these complex novels, then, form beautifully
follows function. Waugh's multifarious narration, like
Ford's multiple third-person-subjective, prevents our
maintaining the simple dualistic response the initial narrative form establishes: identification with the sympathetically portrayed protagonist and yet condescension
because of his obviously anachronistic outlook and values. Instead, moving from them, we experience first-hand
the forces arrayed against them—and from close up they
seem much smaller, ultimately impotent because merely
destructive—and, moving full circle, we come to bear
witness to a world's yielding, making room for what it
cannot destroy. It is in this way, this shifting from a univocal focus, that Christopher and Guy can be seen to earn
not only the world's reluctant approval but ours as well.

Through the initial monolithic third-person-subjective,
we come to know Christopher and Guy well but narrowly,
to feel that theirs is, though far from the ideal outlook on
the world, the only one possible for us to experience. But
the shifts away from them to all we have been missing
serve not to denigrate but to enlarge, not to undercut their
uniqueness but to validate it—as well as all the labor ex-
pended to portray them fully in the first place. The structure of both works, then, may be represented by a double
funnel with the large bases congruent. In terms of
perspective, we move out and away from the initial fixed

19 Appropriately, Tietjens also quotes the Miltonic line as he and Valentine
agree that she will not now become his mistress: " 'As for us,' he had concluded, 'they also serve who only stand and wait' " (*MA*, 284).

point; but at the end we arrive, somewhat surprisingly, at
a place corresponding morally to our point of departure.

We have traveled far away from the superficial and outdated world view that Christopher and Guy have seemed to represent, and then found it too precious to deny. We come back in the end to where they have undeviatingly been because all the alternatives have negated themselves. But this is something we could never have appreciated without the trial of form. We experience—with a relief turning to suspicion and then revulsion—the visions of others that Ford's and Waugh's implied authors involve us in toward the latter part of their works, so that we may, in Eliot's words, "arrive where we started / And know the place for the first time."

Joseph Conrad, "Author's Note" to *Chance*: Every subject in the region of intellect and emotion must have a morality of its own if it is treated at all sincerely; and even the most artful of writers will give himself (and his morality) away in about every third sentence.

W. B. Yeats, "Among School Children": How can we tell the dancer from the dance?

4
Conrad's Picaresque Narrator: Marlow's Journey from *Youth* to *Chance*

Read as a unit, Conrad's Marlovian fictions—*Youth, Heart of Darkness, Lord Jim,* and *Chance*—differ markedly from what they are in isolation. In the four works taken together, Conrad's primary narrator, Marlow, himself becomes the moving center of an episodic, larger fiction in which characters and incidents spin off and revolve about him, as in one of the

inner circles Lord Jim seems to emit characters like
Brierly and the German captain, Brown and the French
lieutenant—all aspects of the whirling, prismatic protagonist of one experiential focus. Conrad's seemingly
depersonalized narrator emerges over the course of several works first as character and then as protagonist. In
the beginning of *Heart of Darkness*, Marlow says, "'I
don't want to bother you much with what happened to
me personally,'" which provokes the narrator to comment that Marlow showed "in this remark the weakness
of many tellers of tales who seem so often unaware of
what their audience would best like to hear" (*HD*, 179).
Yet Marlow immediately indicates that his purpose in recounting his Congo experience is to have his listeners
"understand the effect of it on me." Marlow's tales are
self-revelatory above all.

Conrad constructs the Marlovian tales on two main series of relationships and two dynamic sequences. First,
Marlow interacts both with the protagonists of his narratives and with the narrators who frame him; second, temporal revelations portray not only the young Marlow,
Kurtz, Jim, and Flora, but also Marlow's own picaresque
journeying from one narrative stage to the next. The
stories within the stories express an independent reality
and validity like that which Chaucer creates in *The Canterbury Tales*—and as great a symbiotic interdependence
with the framing context. The narrated tales are beguiling
in their own terms, for each dramatizes an extraordinary
sequence of adventures and misadventures in which an
energetic questor reaches, with varying degrees of success, toward identity and control. The four narrated sequences lose in chronological ordering but gain in significance by being filtered through what James calls the
"interpreting consciousness"—Marlow's plus at least
one other. Yet the four also exist—and perhaps most fundamentally, certainly most organically—as temporal
stages in the development of Marlow himself. For

110 through Marlow, Conrad achieves at once the intimacy
and distance he sought in the shifting perspectives of *The
Nigger of the "Narcissus."* It is our task, then, to consider
how this oddly constructed tetralogy—growing much
longer and more cumbersome each step of the way—
negotiates the personal, moral, and aesthetic evolution of
its central spokesman.

Youth and *Heart of Darkness* are both narrated by an
anonymous former seaman, one of the five characters
(along with the director of companies, the lawyer, the ac-
countant, and Marlow) who recall and verbalize a similar
past. "Between us there was, as I have already said
somewhere [in *Youth*], the bond of the sea. Besides holding our hearts together through long periods of separa-
tion, it had the effect of making us tolerant of each other's
yarns—and even convictions" (*HD*, 175). But *Youth*, the
earliest of the four, is straightforward and its dualism assumes a traditional order; like Pip in *Great Expectations*,
an older and more reflective Marlow both narrates and
comments upon the active, uncontemplative innocence
of his own younger self. Yet the structure of *Youth* is far
simpler than that Dickens employs, for the younger and
older Marlows are virtually identical. No lesson has been
learned, no initiatory trauma separates the two; it is only
that one is older, more experienced, and consequently
sadder. For all its vitality and vibrance, its humor and
bravura, its briefly but fully realized characters, *Youth* is
slight because in it Marlow experiences no crisis beyond
the physical; consequently, he has no moral lesson to
teach or learn.

Tonal, structural, and narrative differences between
Youth and the three later works parallel the deepening
passage from *Tom Sawyer* to *Huckleberry Finn*. Kurtz in
Heart of Darkness, Jim in *Lord Jim*, and Flora and Powell
in *Chance* take us away from Marlow to a large extent;
they appear to us with the force and validity of protagonists in their own right. We may even be annoyed at

times by the incessant verbalizing of that infuriating word
spinner who seems congenitally incapable of telling his
tale (each a rehearsing of yet another of "Marlow's inconclusive experiences" [HD, 179]), and who keep intruding himself between us and it. Wayne Booth, however,
suggests that teller and tale, like Yeats's dancer and
dance, are indistinguishable. "Is 'Heart of Darkness' the
story of Kurtz or the story of Marlow's experience of
Kurtz? Was Marlow invented as a rhetorical device for
heightening the meaning of Kurtz's moral collapse, or
was Kurtz invented in order to provide Marlow with the
core of his experience of the Congo? Again a seamless
web, and we tell ourselves that the old-fashioned question, 'Who is the protagonist?' is a meaningless one. The
convincing texture of the whole, the impression of life as
experienced by an observer, is in itself surely what the
true artist seeks."[1] And yet the question has meaning if
we treat the four Marlow narratives as a whole, as Conrad,
by his intertwining of them, encourages us to do.

Lord Jim, the greatest of the four Marlovian tales, is
unique in including an extra narrative layer, a multifarious commentator who begins with ostensible objectivity
to portray the title character—"He was an inch, perhaps
two, under six feet, powerfully built, and he advanced
straight at you with a slight stoop of the shoulders, head
forward, and a fixed from-under stare which made you
think of a charging bull" (LJ, 1; my italics)—parlays that
"perhaps" into a full-scale attack on the validity of just
such narration—"They wanted facts. Facts! They deman-
ded facts from him, as if facts could explain anything!"
(LJ, 23)—and then merges into an auditor-narrator analogous to the one in Youth, Heart of Darkness, and Chance:
"And later on, many times, in distant parts of the world,
Marlow showed himself willing to remember Jim, to remember him at length, in detail and audibly. Perhaps it

1 Wayne C. Booth, The Rhetoric of Fiction (Chicago and London: University
of Chicago Press, 1961), 346.

112 would be after dinner, on a verandah draped in motionless foliage" (*LJ*, 27). The main difference between the multifarious and personal voices lies in the breadth of "many times" and the vagueness of that last "perhaps"; but from this point until the return to multifarious narration at the end of Chapter 35, the narrative perspective of *Lord Jim* is identical in form and effect to that of the other three tales: a companion of Marlow's narrates Marlow's narrative.

Why does Conrad employ a multifarious frame narrator for *Lord Jim*? The question may best be approached by considering why Conrad abandons the strategy for the bulk of the novel. In a manner likely derived from the depiction of Henry Fleming early in *The Red Badge of Courage* (a novel Conrad knew, admired, and consciously sought to surpass[2]), Conrad's multifarious narrator takes us inside Jim's youthfully foolish ego. "At such times his thoughts would be full of valorous deeds; he loved these dreams and the success of his imaginary achievements. They were the best parts of life, its secret truth, its hidden reality. They had a gorgeous virility, the charm of vagueness, they passed before him with a heroic tread; they carried his soul away with them and made it drunk with the divine philtre of an unbounded confidence in itself. There was nothing he could not face. He was so pleased with the idea that he smiled, keeping perfunctorily his eyes ahead" (*LJ*, 16). The narrator's mocking attitude speaks through the hollow rhetoric of "valorous deeds," "the success of his imaginary achievements," "gorgeous virility, the charm of vagueness," "heroic tread," as well as the climactic self-deception of "There was nothing he could not face," and the devastating betrayal of trust implicit (and retrospectively explicit) in "keeping *perfunctorily* his eyes ahead." As elsewhere, the narrator here verges on turning into the sarcastic presiding genius

2 See Jocelyn Baines, *Joseph Conrad: A Critical Biography* (New York: McGraw-Hill, 1967), 205.

of *The Secret Agent*. The intense derision directed at
Jim—increasingly obvious with each rereading—requires
counterbalancing if Jim is to be afforded any sort of sympathetic response. Thus, Conrad conceals from his reader
what everyone else knows—that the *Patna* failed to sink—
and abandons the frame narrator by offering Marlow as
intercessor between Jim and us.

One further important distinction between the narrators of *The Secret Agent* and *Lord Jim* is that the latter
never really engages in dry, ironically detached, and
near-solipsistic narration and manipulation. Rather,
when Marlow passionately declares to Jewel that Jim is
not good enough (because no one is good enough), it
seems clear that he speaks also for the novel's uncertain
multifarious narrator who, in the novel's first line, an-
nounces Jim's height as *perhaps* five feet ten inches and
then rails out against facts just before the anonymous lis-
tener and Marlow take over the narration. Such a narrator
is far removed from that of *The Secret Agent*, who accepts
as valid the irony of facts and the triviality of all human
endeavor.

Lord Jim's frame narrator, however, after denouncing
facts in a manner wholly sympathetic with Jim's perspective, then depicts Jim's attitude toward the Inquiry as follows. "After his first feeling of revolt he had come round
to the view that only a meticulous precision of statement
would bring out the true horror behind the appalling face
of things. . . . He wanted to go on talking for truth's sake,
perhaps for his own sake also; and while his utterance
was deliberate, his mind positively flew round and round
the serried circle of facts that had surged up all about him
to cut him off from the rest of his kind. . . . He was made to
answer another question so much to the point and useless, then waited again" (*LJ*, 24–26). Such an approach to
facts precisely parallels the attitude and technique of the
book as a whole and Marlow in particular—and has as a
central purpose our continuing deception.

114   Here is the technique at its most blatant—although we do not realize this on first reading. Marlow is speaking about the Inquiry: "There was no incertitude as to facts—as to the one material fact, I mean.... Its object was not the fundamental why, but the superficial how, of his affair.... the questions put to him necessarily led him away from what to me, for instance, would have been the only truth worth knowing. You can't expect the constituted authorities to inquire into the state of a man's soul—or is it only of his liver?" (*LJ*, 47–48). The problem here for us is that we who are ignorant of factual reality are also made to believe that "there was no incertitude as to facts," and so we are unprejudiced by their actuality—or, rather, we are prejudiced by what we are deceived into assuming they are. We share Marlow's outrage at official insensitivity because we think we share his superior moral insight. Only later do we discover that we have done so because we have been duped. Yet such is the nature of moral commitment that it becomes a near impossibility for us to betray our initial identification, to distance ourselves from the moral trap that Marlow (perhaps unintentionally) and certainly Conrad have laid for us. Perhaps the only way out is to recognize, as R. W. B. Lewis has said of Faulkner, that the difficulty of such narratives "lies in the order of their telling.... What *happens* in a Faulkner story is the most important thing in it, except perhaps the moral excitement that produces the happening. But we are let in on the event secretively, gradually, almost grudgingly, from different viewpoints and at different times." [3] Despite the narrator, one of the things we ultimately learn, as Marlow himself must, is that a knowledge of the facts is as fundamental for a proper response to *Lord Jim* as for *Oedipus Rex*. Marlow begins to see this halfway through: "The truth seems to be that it is impossible to lay the ghost of a fact . . ." (*LJ*, 169).

3 R. W. B. Lewis, *The Picaresque Saint* (Philadelphia and New York: Lippincott, 1959), 197.

And more complexly, as he later comes to contradict himself when he begins detailing Jim's death, Marlow acknowledges that what he calls "the language of facts" is "so often more enigmatic than the craftiest arrangement of words" (*LJ*, 295).

But *Lord Jim's* frame narrator—with his uncertainty and his attack on facts from a perspective we first accept as "omniscient"—creates an aura of excessive reliability around Marlow's tale. It is the frame narrator preceding the introduction of Marlow who empathizes with Jim's Platonic equation of aesthetics and morality in responding to the German captain on board the *Patna*: "The odious and fleshy figure . . . fixed itself in his [Jim's] memory for ever as the incarnation of everything vile and base that lurks in the world we love" (*LJ*, 17). Without this context, this subtle and seductive use of the plural personal pronoun by the multifarious narrator, Marlow's similar perspective would be immediately suspect—the defensiveness of a partisan—and would thereby fail to elicit our sympathetic involvement with Jim, an involvement basic to the vertiginous ambivalence at which the novel aims. The multifarious narrator both gives license to Marlow's unreliability and, at least on first reading, lulls our suspicions concerning what Conrad is having him foist on us. In this sense, *Lord Jim* is simply an elaboration of *Heart of Darkness*, for Marlow's concealing from us what fact Jim flees (thus causing us to assume a less damning one) reworks in daringly expanded form the trick of keeping Kurtz from us until we, like Marlow, make the mistake of choosing him.

As character and narrator, Marlow typically experiences and expresses what seem at first commonplace approach / avoidance attitudes—toward lies (smacking of mortality though sometimes necessary), toward work (dislikes it, but likes "what is in the work, the chance to find yourself. Your own reality" [*HD*, 203]), toward exoticism ("the fascination of the abomination" [*HD*, 177], to-

116 ward youth and the sea (the time and place of fleeting glory), toward women (human beings "very much like myself," yet devoid of "masculine decency" [*C*, 53, 63]). The accreted effect of such dualism, however, is ambivalence carried to the point of confusion, and Marlow, his masks of sarcasm and human sympathy simultaneously in place, becomes a curious Janus-faced guide whom we trust at our peril.

Thus, much of the tension in *Heart of Darkness* and *Lord Jim* arises from Marlow's failure to resolve, often even define, major contradictions. The "one of us" theme in *Lord Jim*, for example, is as central to *Heart of Darkness*, though in the earlier work it goes by the name of "idea." Marlow complacently begins his Congo tale by dubiously asserting the moral superiority of English colonists to Roman conquerors. He adds: " 'The conquest of the earth, which mostly means the taking it away from those who have a different complexion or slightly flatter noses than ourselves, is not a pretty thing when you look into it too much. What redeems it is the idea only. An idea at the back of it: not a sentimental pretence but an idea; and an unselfish belief in the idea—something you can set up, and bow down before, and offer a sacrifice to' " (*HD*, 179). Marlow reiterates this notion halfway through *Lord Jim* when he speaks of being deeply impressed by earlier adventurers and traders: " 'It seems impossible to believe that mere greed could hold men to such a steadfastness of purpose, to such blind persistence in endeavor and sacrifice. . . . To us, their less tried successors, they appear magnified, not as agents of trade but as instruments of a recorded destiny, pushing out in the unknown in obedience to an inward voice, to an impulse beating in the blood, to a dream of the future. They were wonderful' " (*LJ*, 195–96). Certainly this is historically a popular view—witness "manifest destiny"—and were it not that Marlow also repudiates this position in *Lord Jim* it might be anachronistic to claim hindsight's advantage on Mar-

low and Conrad: that we know too much by now to doubt
that more outrageous inhumanity is committed in the
name of ideas than for purposes of sheer criminality. If, as
the *Heart of Darkness* narrator anticipates, this tale portrays yet another of "Marlow's inconclusive experiences," it may well be in part because, despite Marlow's
pronouncements, it depicts not only "the utter savagery"
of the uncivilized, but the far more frightening darkness
at the heart of men of ideas. Thus Marlow, heading for the
crisis, begins to think of the howling natives as other than
human—and then worse, *as* human: "one of us."

Similarly, Gentleman Brown, who in *Lord Jim* may be
seen as playing Kurtz to Jim's parallel role as *Heart of
Darkness's* Marlow, is also treated as "one of us" (e.g., pp.
337, 344). Marlow takes pains to distinguish him from his
accomplices. The "'others were merely vulgar and
greedy brutes, but he seemed moved by some complex intention'" (*LJ*, 306). In Brown's murder of Dain Waris and
his men, Marlow adds, "'There is a superiority as of a
man who carries right—the abstract thing—within the
envelope of his common desires. It was not a vulgar and
treacherous massacre; it was a lesson, a retribution—a
demonstration of some obscure and awful attribute of our
nature which, I am afraid, is not so very far under the surface as we like to think'" (*LJ*, 352). Further, Marlow insists that "while Jim was one of us," Dain Waris was "one
of them" (*LJ*, 314). And when Marlow comes to choose a
soul mate to receive word of Jim's death, that "privileged
man," like Gentleman Brown, embodies Marlow's racial
biases carried to their logical extreme. "You said," Marlow writes, "that 'giving up your life to them' (*them* meaning all of mankind with skins brown, yellow, or black in
colour) 'was like selling your soul to a brute.' You con-
tended that 'that kind of thing' was only endurable and
enduring when based on a firm conviction in the truth of
ideas racially our own, in whose name are established the
order, the morality of an ethical progress.... In other

118 words, you maintained that we must fight in the ranks or our lives don't count" (*LJ,* 294). Marlow's response is an ambiguous "Possibly!" because a clear-cut response would deny the validity of either his racial views or else of what he sees as Jim's magnificent triumph of fate. Marlow characteristically wants it both ways.

The same concern for "us" and "them" surfaces as early as *Youth,* where Marlow identifies with humanity (rejecting Carlyle who was not a man but "either more— or less" [*Y,* 146]), with Caucasians (fearing the fascination of the abomination, "the lands of brown nations, where a stealthy Nemesis lies in wait, pursues, overtakes so many of the conquering race, who are proud of their wisdom, of their knowledge, of their strength" [*Y,* 170]), with Englishmen (exalting the *Judea's* ragged crew: " 'It was something in them, something inborn and subtle and everlasting. I don't say positively that the crew of a French or German merchantman wouldn't have done it, but I doubt whether it would have been done in the same way. There was a completeness in it, something solid like a principle, and masterful like an instinct—a disclosure of something secret—of that hidden something, that gift of good or evil that makes racial differences, that shapes the fate of nations' " [*Y,* 161]).

But the concept of otherness is most central to *Heart of Darkness.* On first encountering the Congo, Marlow discovers an absurd world antithetical to the natural or grotesquely mocking it: a boat "shelling the bush" causing nothing to happen; a "dead" railway truck "lying there on its back . . . [like] the carcass of some animal"; "objectless blasting"; emaciated slaves wearing masks of "deathlike indifference [who] were called criminals" (*HD,* 186–88). And since the "civilizing" outsiders are the unnatural element, Marlow must carve out a stance for himself apart from them. With typical sarcasm, Marlow speaks of being greeted by the despicable manager as "a part of the great cause of these high and just proceed-ings" (*HD*, 189). In a similar tone he later alludes to the human heads on Kurtz's posts: " 'I am not disclosing any trade secrets. In fact, the manager said afterwards that Mr. Kurtz's methods had ruined the district. I have no opinion on that point, but I want you clearly to understand that there was nothing exactly profitable in these heads being there. They only showed that Mr. Kurtz lacked restraint in the gratification of his various lusts, that there was something wanting in him—some small matter which, when the pressing need arose, could not be found under his magnificent eloquence' " (*HD*, 234). Curiously and characteristically, Marlow suggests that Kurtz's actions are somehow less reprehensible because motivated not by greed but by undefinable desires.

Immediately there follows Marlow's climactic summary of Kurtz—"he was hollow at the core"—a chilling conclusion to his quest: "I was curious to see whether this man who had come out equipped with moral ideas of some sort, would climb to the top after all and how he would set about his work when there" (*HD*, 205). Thus Marlow's thesis concerning the redemptive nature of ideas (above all, "the white man's burden") and his implication that the Congo represents unfortunately uncongenial soil for their implantation are wholly misleading: Kurtz's "moral ideas" are hollow and he brings with him the evil he encounters. Like *Lord Jim, Heart of Darkness* becomes a very different work in second and subsequent readings because we become sensitive to the hollowness of Marlow's own position—the subtle horror of his thesis, perspective, choice, action, and justification—all of which he offers in the narrative with little or no examination. Similarly, he takes no note of his own telling imagery—for example Kurtz's "ivory face" (*HD*, 247) and the Intended's "forehead, smooth and white" (*HD*, 254), which echo the reference to Brussels as a "whited sepulchre," suggest that we become what we seek and that what we seek is death. The imagery is wonderfully sar-

120 donic in mocking our self-delusion, but Marlow merely tosses it out without comment; its impact is great almost despite him. Thus, Marlow's pose of Buddha-like inscrutability seems in the end to deceive no one so much as himself.

Marlow's first use of the term "one of us" occurs early in *Lord Jim*. He is fascinated by the dichotomy in Jim of what, with reference to Brierly, he later calls his "sham and reality." Jim's appearance is compelling—"clean-limbed, clean-faced, firm on his feet, as promising a boy as the sun ever shone on." And Marlow is furious: "I was as angry as though I had detected him trying to get something out of me by false pretences. He had no business to look so sound." Not for the last time, Marlow finds Jim's casualness odious. "I waited to see him overwhelmed, confounded, pierced through and through, squirming like an impaled beetle—and I was half afraid to see it too." And then comes Marlow's identification and generalization, the basis for fear greater than that encountered in the heart of savage darkness: "From weakness that may lie hidden, watched or unwatched, prayed against or manfully scorned, repressed or maybe ignored more than half a lifetime, not one of us is safe. . . . he was one of us. He stood there for all the parentage of his kind, for men and women by no means amusing, but whose very existence is based upon honest faith, and upon the instinct of courage. . . . backed by a faith invulnerable to the strength of facts, to the contagion of example, to the solicitation of ideas. Hang ideas! They are tramps, vagabonds, knocking at the back-door of your mind, each taking a little of your substance, each carrying away some crumb of that belief in a few simple notions you must cling to if you want to live decently and would like to die easy!" (*LJ*, 33–36). Having experienced the indecency of Kurtz's life and the difficulty of his death, Marlow now condemns the moral supremacy of ideas, the thesis of *Heart of Darkness*. Now older and tireder, he rejects them here as he had exalted them there. In *Lord Jim* he espouses something more substantial, the reality and validity of appearance and imagination—and they betray him as well.[4] Maybe this partially explains why, in *Chance*, Conrad has Marlow return to the simpler stance of *Youth*—though (as discussed below) by then it's too late to carry it off.

The theme of "one of us," of "idea," intertwines as well with that of imagination and duty. Conrad's simple "good" men—Singleton in *Nigger of the "Narcissus,"* Captain MacWhirr in *Typhoon*, *Lord Jim's* French lieutenant—function well because their intellectual and moral makeup precludes their seriously entertaining alternative courses of action; in *Chance*, Captain Anthony is essentially and ultimately of this same order. The practical successes of such characters are wholly admirable (and precisely what Jim is circuitously seeking), yet they themselves are inadequate because they seem mechanical, lacking in divergent impulses, not "one of us"—though these are the very characteristics that ensure their successes. The extreme of this type are the presumably nonintrospective helmsmen in *Heart of Darkness* and *Lord Jim*. Marlow says of Kurtz, "'I can't forget him, though I am not prepared to affirm the fellow was exactly worth the life we lost in getting to him. I missed my late helmsman awfully. . . . Perhaps you will think it passing strange this regret for a savage who was no more account than a grain of sand in a black Sahara. Well, don't you see, he had done something, he had steered; for months I had him at my back—a help—an instrument'" (*HD*, 226–27). Marlow opts for the nightmare Kurtz represents over that of the rapaciously bourgeois manager—"'Ah! but it was something to have at least a choice of nightmares'" (*HD*,

4 Marlow never seems to learn the lesson of appearances. His initial reaction to the French lieutenant is that "he looked a reliable officer . . . he was seamanlike" (*LJ*, 120). Marlow happens to be right in this case—as Jim happened to be right about the *Patna's* captain—but such judgments reduce values to a dangerously myopic conflating of morality and aesthetics.

239)—without ever noting the possible unnightmarish choice that the helmsman's example offers. He compares Kurtz unfavorably to his helmsman (as he later does Jim to those of the *Patna*), but his racial scorn is strongly evidenced. The helmsman's surprising devotion to duty and his failure to act like a bestial savage—like the cannibal crew's extraordinary restraint, their failure to "have a good tuck in for once" (*HD*, 216) as white men in their position would presumably have done—merits the respect due a faithful pet or a useful tool. Kurtz, a true savage in word and deed—"hollow at the core"—receives from Marlow, like Jim and Gentleman Brown, the homage due to "one of us."

Throughout his narratives but especially in *Lord Jim*, Marlow's unreliability undercuts the values on which he and we presume to stand, while seeming at first to reinforce them. Intentionally or not, Marlow works to arouse our sympathy for Jim while denouncing him. He speaks of being pitiless and says, "I was not in a merciful mood. He provoked one by his contradictory indiscretions" (*LJ*, 68, 72). But then, indulging in one of his own "contradictory indiscretions," he immediately adds, "You must remember he believed, *as any other man would have done in his place*, that the ship would go down at any moment" (*LJ*, 73; my italics). Marlow exploits the advantage he has of us: at this point, near the start of his narrative, *we* still believe that the *Patna* did sink, and that Marlow is therefore holding Jim up to extraordinary moral criteria. Yet he then reverses himself and damns with faint praise where he had praised with faint damnation. "'He was not afraid of death perhaps, but I'll tell you what, he was afraid of the emergency. His confounded imagination had evoked for him all the horrors ... of a disaster at sea he had ever heard of. He might have been resigned to die but I suspect he wanted to die without the added terrors, quietly, in a sort of peaceful trance'" (*LJ*, 75). As usual, Marlow's prophetic impulse is correct in a sense, in a way we would not have anticipated: Jim does "die . . . quietly, in a sort of peaceful trance," but orchestrating it fully himself, on centerstage, with all eyes fixed upon him as on the noblest of tragic heroes or oddest of mortal phenomena.

Halfway through *Lord Jim*, Marlow gives us what he calls "the last word" on Jim's Patusan success while characteristically denying the possibility of anyone's doing so:

> "The last word is not said,—probably shall never be said. . . . I have given up expecting those last words, whose ring, if they could only be pronounced, would shake both heaven and earth. There is never time to say our last word. . . . The heaven and the earth must not be shaken. I suppose—at least, not by us who know so many truths about either. My last words about Jim shall be few. I affirm he had achieved greatness; but the thing would be dwarfed in the telling, or rather in the hearing. Frankly, it is not my words that I mistrust but your minds. I could be eloquent were I not afraid you fellows had starved your imaginations to feed your bodies. I do not mean to be offensive; it is respectable to have no illusions—and safe—and profitable—and dull. Yet you, too, in your time must have known the intensity of life, that light of glamour created in the shock of trifles, as amazing as the glow of sparks struck from a cold stone—and as shortlived, alas!" (*LJ*, 194–95)

As elsewhere, Marlow gives himself away in every line: in forgetting the lesson of *Heart of Darkness* (that "those last words" may indeed be pronounced, and that they change nothing), in forgetting the lesson of *Youth* (that for him too "the romance of illusions" has long since yielded to "Pass the bottle!"), and especially in his typical thrusting of conclusions at us before the evidence. We are surely meant to question the ultimate authority of such a grand pronouncement occurring, as it does, halfway through the novel and then being repeated later on, but still before his narrative proper concerning Patusan: Jim attained a "greatness as genuine as any man ever achieved" (*LJ*, 212). Had we been allowed to experience

124 Patusan uncontaminated by Marlow's prejudicial contextualizing, we would be in a position to distance ourselves from his conclusion and would likely do so. In addition, Marlow's attack on his listeners' lack of imagination has the force and validity of a non sequitur since only two pages before he had asserted that, unlike Jim, "I have no imagination."

Marlow's own *final* conclusion about Jim's achievement is very different from this early one. He first speaks with bemused wonderment of Jim's being " 'satisfied . . . nearly. This is going further than most of us dare. I—who have the right to think myself good enough—dare not. Neither does any of you here, I suppose? . . . But he is one of us, and he could say he was satisfied . . . nearly. Just fancy this! Nearly satisfied. One could almost envy him his catastrophe. Nearly satisfied' " (*LJ*, 281). But then after detailing Jim's death in richly lyrical terms, he says, " 'Is he satisfied—quite, now, I wonder? we ought to know. He is one of us—and have I not stood up once, like an evoked ghost, to answer for his eternal constancy? Was I so very wrong after all? . . . Who knows?' " (*LJ*, 362–63). Further, as Marlow reminds us, our experience of Jim is very different from his: " 'He existed for me, and after all it is only through me that he exists for you. I've led him out by the hand; I have paraded him before you' " (*LJ*, 194).[5] For us, Jim is a work of art and Marlow the artist with words— and as the narrator of *Under Western Eyes* tells us, "Words, as is well known, are the greatest foes of reality."[6] No wonder, then, that we perceive Jim initially as Marlow would have us, and yet that Jim defies the static definition the artist would impose upon him. It thereby

5 At the end, as Marlow writes to the "privileged man," Jim is even further removed from us, even more an artifice of others' constructing. Marlow says, "It is impossible to see him clearly—especially as it is through the eyes of others that we take our last look at him" (*LJ*, 294). Oddly, as Marlow would have it, the more Jim becomes shaped and final for some, the more he becomes inconclusive process for others.

6 Joseph Conrad, *Under Western Eyes* (New York: Anchor Books, 1963), 1.

becomes incumbent upon us not only to perceive the product as process, but also to call into profoundest questioning the voice of the artist—not *qua* artist, but as purveyor of reductive pronouncements concerning what his art has wrought.

As he almost invariably does, Marlow again anticipates us, for he strikes exactly this note when, on taking leave of Jim for the last time, he speaks of reentering the world of moral complexity and uncertainty. " 'I had turned away from the picture and was going back to the world where events move, men change, light flickers, life flows in a clear stream, no matter whether over mud or over stones. . . . But as to what I was leaving behind, I cannot imagine any alteration. . . . They exist as if under an enchanter's wand. But the figure round which all these are grouped—that one lives, and I am not certain of him. No magician's wand can immobilise him under my eyes. He is one of us' " (*LJ*, 286–87). This may be the clearest indication yet of what "one of us" means: those born to inhabit the world of moral challenge and inadequacy, those doomed to imagination, freedom, flux—as if this were not, as Marlow himself indicates elsewhere, the common fate of all mankind.

Marlow's response to Jim alternates from one extreme to the other throughout his narrative. He maintains that Jim had no business looking so sound (pp. 33–34) since there was a "subtle unsoundness" about him (p. 77), that there could be no "convincing shadow of an excuse" for his action (p. 43), for its "real significance [lay] in its being a breach of faith with the community of mankind" (*LJ*, 135). Jim had, Marlow tells us, "jumped into an everlasting deep hole. He had tumbled from a height he could never scale again" (*LJ*, 96). No wonder that Marlow's attitude is pitiless (p. 68), not merciful (p. 72), that he directs a "deep-rooted irony" at Jim. At a climactic moment, he declares himself "unexpectedly to be thoroughly sick of him" (*LJ*, 204). And yet, to counterbalance, he

126 immediately adds, "Youth is insolent; it is its right—its necessity; it has got to assert itself, and all assertion in this world of doubts is a defiance, is an insolence." Further, Marlow simultaneously asserts a wholly opposed analysis, one that defines Jim as the victim of "a fiendish and appalling joke" (*LJ*, 104–105), and who, on the *Patna*, "believed, as any other man would have done in his place, that the ship would go down at any moment" (*LJ*, 73, 84). He had helplessly faced and "had survived the assault of the dark powers" (*LJ*, 213), and then at the end "was overwhelmed by the inexplicable; he was overwhelmed by his own personality—the gift of that destiny which he had done his best to master" (*LJ*, 296). Marlow agrees with Jim that "You've been tried" (*LJ*, 107), that he is a gentleman (p. 112); he is pleased that the French lieutenant takes "the lenient view" (*LJ*, 127); he asserts Jim's greatness and devotion in the face of Jewel's bitter love and sense of betrayal.[7]

Ultimately and typically, Marlow seeks to resolve polar contradictions, to synthesize antitheses. Jim, he says, "appealed to all sides at once" (*LJ*, 80); at times Jim seems not univocal but unclear to Marlow and perhaps "not clear to himself either" (*LJ*, 152); it was hard to know "whether his line of conduct amounted to shirking his ghost or to facing him out" (*LJ*, 169); and finally Marlow sees Jim as great and pitiful "in the loneliness of his soul" (*LJ*, 343)—as, that is, a tragic hero who necessarily embodies *all* the contrarieties with which Marlow attempts, without success, to fix Jim in place like one of Stein's butterflies.

Perhaps the strangest and most glaring inconsistency in Marlow's entire narrative concerns Brierly's offer of money if Jim will flee. Marlow first tells us, " 'Of course I declined to meddle. . . . I became positive in my mind that the inquiry was a severe punishment to that Jim, and that

---

7 This encounter, like Marlow's earlier one with Kurtz's Intended, also emphasizes that "one of us" is a sexual as well as a racial distinction.

his facing it ... was a redeeming feature in his abomina-
ble case.... Brierly went off in a huff'" (*LJ*, 58). Later,
Marlow recasts the events in a wholly different light.
"'He was guilty—as I had told myself repeatedly, guilty
and done for; nevertheless, I wished to spare him the
mere detail of a formal execution.... I don't defend my
morality. There was no morality in the impulse which induced me to lay before him Brierly's plan of evasion.'"
And Marlow's bitter anger at Jim's failure to run—
"'Better men than you have found it expedient to run, at
times'" (*LJ*, 131–33)—comes to sound very much like
Brierly. As elsewhere, Marlow successfully manipulates
us both ways: his "Of course I declined to meddle"
arouses our "braving it out" instinct; his laying before Jim
"Brierly's plan of evasion" appeals to our sense of arrogant defiance—and only the most alert reader catches the
blatant contradiction. Marlow plays upon the sen-
sibilities of his listeners and readers with the sure touch
of a skilled surgeon and the gall of a buccaneer.

Marlow's own untrustworthiness may be seen as finally
focusing on Stein, whom he calls "one of the most
trustworthy men I had ever known" (*LJ*, 174). Stein begins his self-revelation by suggesting that man is the
product of an "artist [who] was a little mad" (*LJ*, 179), and
then unconsciously offers himself as exemplum. He tells
of calmly killing three men and finding "the clean earth
smiling at me,"[8] and then of rapturously capturing a
unique butterfly. "'When I got up I shook like a leaf
with excitement, and when I opened these beautiful
wings and made sure what a rare and so extraordinary
perfect specimen I had, my head went round and my legs

8 It is no mere coincidence that Jim, become a killer, replays with uncanny
exactitude the Stein role, as Marlow describes it. "He held his shot, he says,
deliberately. He held it for the tenth part of a second, for three strides of the
man—an unconscionable time. He held it for the pleasure of saying to himself,
That's a dead man!... He found himself calm, appeased, without rancour,
without uneasiness, as if the death of that man had atoned for everything" (*LJ*,
261).

128 became so weak with emotion that I had to sit on the ground.... On that day I had nothing to desire; I had greatly annoyed my principal enemy; I was young, strong; I had friendship; I had the love ... of woman, a child I had to make my heart very full—and even what I had once dreamed in my sleep had come into my hand, too'" (*LJ*, 181–82). The clue to Stein—and to Marlow who finds him trustworthy—lies in the disproportion not only of emotion but also of language: "annoyed" as a euphemism for three killings. In the tradition of life-denying artists, Stein now lacks all that his values implicitly negated: youth, friend, wife, child, and soon strength. Stein himself is what he tags his butterfly—"a remarkable specimen"—but hardly what Marlow proclaims him: a reliable, Virgil-like guide through *Lord Jim's* moral Inferno. His deflation at the end, the revelation of hollowness we have previously associated with Kurtz, is in fact implicit in this moment of our first encounter with him.

Before depicting that deflation, Marlow offers us a description of Jim's death that is as lyrically ambiguous as anything Conrad ever wrote. He speaks of Jim's "last flicker of superb egoism," of his final "proud and unflinching glance," of " 'the alluring shape of such an extraordinary success! For it may very well be that in the short moment of his last proud and unflinching glance, he had beheld the face of that opportunity which, like an Eastern bride, had come veiled to his side.' " And he concludes: " 'But we can see him, an obscure conqueror of fame, tearing himself out of the arms of a jealous love at the sign, at the call of his exalted egoism. He goes away from a living woman to celebrate his pitiless wedding with a shadowy ideal of conduct'" (*LJ*, 362). Marlow's romanticizing of Jim's death offers rich, metaphoric counterpointing to his early assertion of Jim's greatness. What seems to happen is that Jim's ritual suicide—unlike his youthful dreams and Patusan successes—offers no moral guidance for Westerners ("us"), no exemplum for

Marlow to puff and pass on. So he finds both Jim and the significance of his actions obscured by impenetrable shadows at the last.

Marlow then concludes *Lord Jim* with a series of unsettling questions concerning Jim and his death, and an even more unsettling picture of those who remain behind. " 'Is he satisfied—quite, now, I wonder? We ought to know. He is one of us—and have I not stood up once, like an evoked ghost, to answer for his eternal constancy? Was I so very wrong after all? . . . Who knows? He is gone, inscrutable at heart, and the poor girl is leading a sort of soundless, inert life in Stein's house. Stein has aged greatly of late. He feels it himself, and says often that he is "preparing to leave all this; preparing to leave . . . " while he waves his hand sadly at his butterflies' " (*LJ*, 363). Marlow seeks a final note of mystery, poetry, and sadness; yet what really is inscrutable here is not Jim—who is clearly defined by his own sense of worth and a repeatedly amazed awareness of his failure to realize it, a common enough form of schizophrenia—but Marlow's pervasive despair over Jim's lack of single-facetedness. Marlow's refrain, "one of us," *should* suffice to define Jim as white and English, duty-bound, a successful embodiment of Western notions of fidelity and progress. As Marlow revealingly says: " 'He was like a figure set up on a pedestal, to represent in his persistent youth the power, and perhaps the virtues, of races that never grow old, that have emerged from the gloom. I don't know why he should always have appeared to me symbolic. Perhaps this is the real cause of my interest in his fate' " (*LJ*, 229). But despite appearances Jim fails to play the part he and Marlow assign him: " 'He was the kind of fellow you would, on the strength of his looks, leave in charge of the deck—figuratively and professionally speaking. I say I would, and I ought to know. . . . I would have trusted the deck to that youngster on the strength of a single glance, and gone to sleep with both eyes—and, by Jove! it

130   wouldn't have been safe. There are depths of horror in that thought' " (*LJ*, 36–38). Such a truth (and Marlow's need to learn it) invalidates his central assumption concerning racial superiority and the equation of appearance and reality—just as both *Heart of Darkness* and *Lord Jim* repudiate his faith in the nobility of evil done in the service of professed ideals.

Marlow's depictions, therefore, are *necessarily* of "inconclusive experiences," for they neither support his initial theses nor indicate that he confronts and revises them after their refutation by events. Marlow's virtues as man and narrator are also his vices: charming self-deprecation, humane and open questioning, refusal to make definitive pronouncements where warranted (or else an asserting of contradictory ones), sensitive if fruitless intruding of himself into the lives of others—and they represent a compelling self-depiction of one who is surely "one of us." Yet Marlow's hesitations and irreconcilabilities reflect an unreliability seriously at odds with the surface dependability of his narrative stance. A moral and intellectual Hyperion to Dowell's satyr, he nonetheless suggests the repeated "I don't know. It is all a mystery" of Ford's protagonist / narrator in *The Good Soldier*—as well as portraying Jewel at the end in a way that strikingly foreshadows Dowell's depiction of Nancy Rufford—when he proclaims hopeless ambivalence to avoid the responsibility of balanced judgment. After he has tried and failed to effect events, he writes to the "privileged man"—and to us—"I affirm nothing. Perhaps you may pronounce—after you've read ... " (*LJ*, 294).

The one work of Conrad's that Wayne Booth cites in his "Gallery of Unreliable Narrators" at the end of *The Rhetoric of Fiction* is *Heart of Darkness* (presumably for Marlow's narration rather than that of the anonymous frame commentator); yet *Lord Jim* warrants inclusion equally as much. In both of these, Marlow becomes profoundly, dynamically, and grotesquely unreliable—

"grotesque" in the sense that Sherwood Anderson's writer uses that term at the beginning of *Winesburg, Ohio*: "It was his notion that the moment one of the people took one of the truths to himself, called it his truth, and tried to live his life by it, he became a grotesque and the truth he embraced became a falsehood."[9] As we have seen, Marlow seizes grotesquely on the morality of ideas (any ideas) in *Heart of Darkness*, and on the congruence of appearance and substance in *Lord Jim*—and yet his dartingly vital imagination causes them to remain problematical, a matter demanding continual struggle, always in motion. *Chance*, however, is radically different, for such dynamics offer sharp contrast to the bland superiority of tone Marlow assumes toward Flora, Anthony, Powell, and the others in his last narrative. T. S. Eliot has noted that we are alive to the extent that we do good or evil; Marlow's intellectual and moral detachment in *Chance* has about it a stench of death and decay, what he calls mediocrity. He says, in *Chance*, "'It's certainly unwise to admit any sort of responsibility for our actions, whose consequences we are never able to foresee. . . . the incapacity to achieve anything distinctly good or evil is inherent in our earthly condition. Mediocrity is our mark'" (*C*, 23). There was a time, he notes, when he saw the world with different eyes: "'When one's young human nature shocks one'" (*C*, 15). Nothing shocks, or even interests, Marlow very much in *Chance*—certainly not human nature, which he ceases to encounter on any but a mocking or trifling level. Conrad's mistake, like Shakespeare's in *Merry Wives of Windsor*, consists of reducing to domestication the natural scope and conflict of a profoundly mistaken moral spokesman; a mellow Marlow speaks to our deepest needs and joys no more than does a Falstaff playing at love.

Marlow seeks not only depth but scope as he journeys

9 Sherwood Anderson, "The Book of the Grotesque," *Winesburg, Ohio* (New York: Viking Press, 1967), 25.

132 from *Youth* to *Chance* (each subsequent work is much longer than its predecessor), yet Marlow has come full circle by *Chance*. *Chance* is fifteen times longer than *Youth* but, as Conrad's defensive Preface implies, its amplitude depends largely on verbiage. The problem with *Chance* (Conrad's first popular success) may be emblematized by the fact that *Chance* begins, with trivialized nostalgia, at the end not of *Lord Jim* but of *Youth*. Marlow concludes *Youth* by asking rhetorically, "'Wasn't that the best time, that time when we were young at sea; young and had nothing, on the sea that gives nothing, except hard knocks—and sometimes a chance to feel your strength—that only—that you all regret?'" (*Y*, 170); and many years later he begins *Chance* by agreeing with Powell "that the happiest time in their lives was as youngsters in good ships, with no care in the world" (*C*, 4).

Marlow's attitude toward the sea represents a singular failure to evolve. Upon failing his first test, the youthful Jim scorns "the spurious menace of wind and seas. He knew what to think of it. . . . he exulted with fresh certitude in his avidity for adventure, and in a sense of many-sided courage" (*LJ*, 6–7). We expect *Chance*'s Marlow to sound a good deal different, but halfway through his final narrative Marlow himself echoes Jim's naïve assertion that the sea is "unchangeable, safe . . . sheltering man from all passions, except its own anger" (*C*, 292).

Surely one of Jim's functions is to complete the process that Kurtz began: Marlow's initiation into disillusionment, his alienation from earlier visions of youth and sea. He speaks of Jim's being "'the sort whose appearance claims the fellowship of those illusions you had thought gone out, extinct, cold,'" and then of the destruction of that fellowship.

> "Surely in no other craft as in that of the sea do the hearts of those already launched to sink or swim go out so much to the youth on the brink. . . . In no other kind of life is the illusion

more wide of reality—in no other is the beginning *all*
illusion—the disenchantment more swift—the subjugation
more complete. Hadn't we all commenced with the same desire, ended with the same knowledge, carried the memory of
the same cherished glamour through the sordid days of im-
precation? . . . He was there before me, believing that age and
wisdom can find a remedy against the pain of truth. . . . I was
aggrieved against him, as though he had cheated me—
me!—of a splendid opportunity to keep up the illusion of my
beginnings, as though he had robbed our common life of the
last spark of its glamour." (*LJ*, 111–13)

After such an anguished outcry, it is no wonder that the
opening note of *Chance*—harking back as it does to the
end of *Youth*—rings false.

In both *Youth* and *Chance* Marlow wryly but enviously
shakes his head over the bravura successes of youth, but
such nostalgia, while valid once, becomes brittle and artificial after the confrontation with youth's flagrant excesses of ideas and imagination, and its consequent heart-
rending doom, in *Heart of Darkness* and *Lord Jim*. James
Baldwin has noted that "people who shut their eyes to reality simply invite their own destruction, and anyone
who insists on remaining in a state of innocence long
after that innocence is dead turns himself into a monster." [10] An analogous perversity reduces Marlow in
Chance to anachronism, a banal commentator on the subject he admittedly knows least—women. For *Chance*'s
title is misleading: the novel's small philosophical energy
expends itself primarily on the subject of women rather
than accidents of fortune. Like *Youth* and unlike *Heart of
Darkness* and *Lord Jim*, *Chance* lacks a moral core and
Marlow a moral stance. The problems of its plot are situa-
tional; they bear no relationship to the crisis of nightmare
and conscience Marlow, along with Kurtz and Jim, experiences in *Heart of Darkness* and *Lord Jim*. Though
used in various ways, "chance" primarily means coinci-

10 James Baldwin, "Stranger in the Village," *Notes of a Native Son* (Boston:
Beacon Press, 1955), 175.

134   dence rather than providence, happenstance rather than
      moral and symbolic aptness.[11] Thus Powell tells us that
      he got his first chance by chance—a casual display of
      verbal irony indicative of the novel's lack of profundity
      and wit. The story is the vehicle not for symbolic,
      philosophical, or moral exploration, but for what Marlow
      calls "the commonest sort of curiosity" (C, 40), for he
      finds what he narrates only mildly interesting, and his
      lack of temperamental involvement utterly denies any
      tension at the novel's core.

   The tone of *Chance* is one of casual and bland superiority. The anonymous narrator tells us that Marlow "had
the habit of pursuing general ideas in a peculiar manner,
between jest and earnest" (C, 23), which we might expect
of someone motivated by "the commonest sort of curiosity." Marlow exhibits intense emotion rarely and incon-
gruously, as when he rails out against confessions after
presumably having sought to elicit Flora's. He says,
"'Never confess! Never, never! ... a confession of whatever sort is always untimely. The one thing which makes
it supportable for a while is curiosity.... And all of them
[confessors] in their hearts brand you for either mad or
impudent.'" The narrator says, "I had seldom seen Marlow so vehement, so pessimistic, so earnestly cynical before" (C, 212). Marlow may be correct about his motivation, but curiosity is an oddly feeble basis on which to
construct the vast edifice of *Chance*.

   In the analogous passage in *Lord Jim*, Marlow also contemplates himself as confidant, wondering what loosens
men's "'tongues at the sight of me for the infernal confidences; as though, forsooth, I had no confidences to make
to myself, as though—God help me!—I didn't have
enough confidential information about myself to harrow
my own soul till the end of my appointed time.... I am
not particularly fit to be a receptacle of confessions'" (LJ,

11 See, for example, *Chance*, pp. 16, 126, 272, 311, 328, 446.

28). Marlow's conclusion here is presumably wrong, and in fact he later qualifies it: " 'I would have been little fitted for the reception of his confidences had I not been able at times to understand the pauses between the words' " (LJ, 90). Marlow asserts, " 'My weakness consists in not having a discriminating eye for the incidental' " (LJ, 80), but he implies the opposite when he proclaims his admiration for the French lieutenant's discrimination. " 'He had made out the point at once: he did get hold of the only thing I cared about' " (LJ, 125). Yet with all their contrarieties, such pronouncements are not simply misleading—they are profoundly, grotesquely, supremely so, and they express something central and significant about Marlow in the same way as does the confession passage in Hamlet that this self-judgment seems to echo. Hamlet defines himself to Ophelia: "I am myself indifferent honest; but yet I could accuse me of such things that it were better my mother had not borne me: I am very proud, revengeful, ambitious, with more offences at my beck than I have thought to put them in, imagination to give them shape, or time to act them in. What should such fellows as I do crawling between earth and heaven: We are arrant knaves, all; believe none of us" (III, i, 123–32). The uses of literary sources are subtle and powerful in Lord Jim; in Chance they are cheap and patronizing, as when Marlow refers to Flora and de Barral as " 'Figures from Dickens—pregnant with pathos' " (C, 162).

Marlow's attitudes toward Chance's central concerns—the sea and women—are also disturbing, for his complacent categorization of each confronts endless contradictions while remaining unchanged. As with Typhoon's Captain MacWhirr, the sea in Chance is defined as free from all moral challenge, "free from the earth's petty suggestions" (C, 310), offering professional satisfaction plus adventure with its simple, direct claims (C, 31–32). Thus, life on the Ferndale (as on the Narcissus, the Patna, and the Sephora—in fact, most of Conrad's ships) must be

136 seen as aberrant, its unrestfulness atypical of the sea but very like that associated with the land. In *Chance*, this aberrance is compounded by the marriage of Flora and Anthony, for another of Marlow's ex cathedra pronouncements blithely generalizes about marriage and then marriage at sea. "'With what we know of Roderick Anthony and Flora de Barral I could not deduct an ordinary marital quarrel beautifully matured in less than a year—could I? If you ask me what is an ordinary marital quarrel I will tell you, that it is a difference about nothing.... There are on earth no actors too humble and obscure not to have a gallery, that gallery which envenoms the play by stealthy jeers, counsels of anger, amused comments or words of perfidious compassion. However, the Anthonys were free from all demoralizing influences. At sea, you know, there is no gallery. You hear no tormenting echoes of your own littleness there'" (*C*, 326). Once again, Marlow remains unperturbed by the failure of his definition and picture to square with each other.

Marlow maintains that he is out of his element on land (*HD*, 179; *C*, 33–34), and he is certainly out of his depth with women, although early in *Chance* he asserts the opposite: "There is enough of the woman in my nature to free my judgment of women from glamorous reticency.... A woman is not necessarily either a doll or an angel to me. She is a human being, very much like myself" (*C*, 53). Actually, this asserted affinity, this willful misuse of his "one of us" thesis, serves merely as license for Marlow's endless pronouncements in the face of ignorance and gross inconsistency. Occasionally he sees women as beyond men—in desiring all virtues, power, sensations (*C*, 63), in criminality (*C*, 93–94, 100–101), in cleverness, diabolism, passion, pedantry, courage (*C*, 157–59), in holiness (*C*, 311)—but his basic attitude toward them in *Chance*, in fact through all his narratives, is one of condescension: women are acute but irrational (*C*, 145, 206), inexperienced and ignorant of reality (*C*, 193,

330), usually to blame for problems between the sexes (*C*, 327), inwardly unsettled (*C*, 330); they "can stand anything. The dear creatures have no imagination when it comes to the solid facts of life. . . . Man, we know, can live by bread alone, but hang me if I don't believe that some women could live by love alone" (*C*, 352). Marlow speaks here for all of the Conrad canon, for with the possible exception of Mrs. Gould in *Nostromo*, there are no female narrators or even listeners, not a single woman who is "one of us," none who is not irredeemably "other."

Marlow then offers us a telling abstraction that gives the show away: "You say I don't know women. May be. . . . But I have a clear notion of *woman*" (*C*, 352). Of course Marlow has nothing of the kind; he not only knows far less than he asserts (having had virtually no experience of women), but he cannot keep his assertions straight. Thus, he defends his lie to Kurtz's Intended at the end of *Heart of Darkness* by insisting that he had a duty to keep from her a truth that, as a woman, she would have found "too dark—too dark altogether" (*HD*, 256). But in *Chance* he reverses the formula while managing to remain equally patronizing. " 'I call a woman sincere when she volunteers a statement resembling remotely in form what she really would like to say, what she really thinks ought to be said if it were not for the necessity to spare the stupid sensitiveness of men. . . . We could not stand women speaking the truth. . . . It would cause infinite misery and bring about most awful disturbances in this rather mediocre, but still idealistic fool's paradise in which each of us lives his own little life—the unit in the great sum of existence. And they know it. They are merciful' " (*C*, 144). Trying to determine his complexly ambivalent attitude toward Jim, Marlow reveals something of his own depths. "It is when we try to grapple with another man's intimate need that we perceive how incomplete, wavering, and misty are the beings that share with us the sight of the stars and the warmth of the sun. It is as if

138 loneliness were a hard and absolute condition of existence" (*LJ*, 155). This sort of intensely personal confrontation with human relationships lies at the polar extreme
from the "common curiosity" that motivates Marlow in
Chance.

In his "Author's Note" to *Youth*—which appeared five
years after *Chance*—Conrad identifies Marlow as his alter
ego from first conception to last farewell. Conrad is credible when he denies that Marlow is a charlatan, "a clever
screen, a mere device, a 'personator,' a familiar spirit, a
whispering 'daemon.'" Their relationship, he continues,
grew "very intimate in the course of years.... The man
Marlow and I came together in the casual manner of those
health-resort acquaintances which sometimes ripen into
friendships. This one has ripened. For all his assertive-
ness in matters of opinion he is not an intrusive person.
He haunts my hours of solitude, when, in silence, we lay
our heads together in great comfort and harmony; but as
we part at the end of a tale I am never sure that it may not
be for the last time. Yet I don't think either of us would
care much to survive the other."[12] Conrad's statement has
a poignant validity whose outline has become clear in ret-
rospect, for though Conrad lives and writes until 1924,
both Marlow and his important writings are behind him
by *Chance* in 1913. And this fact seems more than coincidence, no more mere chance than Jim's arrival in Patusan
or the marriage of Flora and Powell through Marlow's
intercession. Jim's death seems to necessitate that of Marlow as artist; Marlow's demise heralds that of Conrad as
artist. Art imitates life and life returns the compliment.

Conrad had reached a dead end from which, apparently, there could be no returning. Marlow's rites of passage from *Youth* to *Lord Jim* expand parameters and
deepen vision, but *Chance* depicts a narrowing, a domes-

12 "Author's Note," to *Youth*, quoted in *"Heart of Darkness": An Au-
thoritative Text, Backgrounds and Sources, Essays in Criticism*, ed. Robert
Kimbrough (New York: Norton Critical Editions, 1963), 155.

tication, as Marlow shifts from morally involved participant to fussily detached busybody making banal pronouncements: "'Pairing off is the fate of mankind'" (*C*,
426). Marlow's concern in *Chance*, motivated by "the
commonest sort of curiosity," lacks empathy, the deep
solace and despair of his earlier narratives—Flora, after
all, is much younger, alien in temperament as well as inferior in sex. Unlike Powell, Marlow doesn't take her seriously until the very end—and even then he manipulates
her with condescending superiority and against his own
initial condemnation of such interference (*C*, 23–24).
Marlow intrudes at the end to change the shape and direction of Powell's and Flora's lives, but apparently without the conviction that his is a significant action. And that
the consequences may be presumed unequivocally
fortuitous—like Marlow's banality throughout—suggests
that Conrad himself respects and shares Marlow's cheery
and dull complacency. No wonder Conrad abandons him
here—no beyond is possible once he ceases to take him
seriously.

One central question remains concerning the Marlovian narratives. Is Marlow himself aware of and controlling the attitude implicit in his perspective—and thus as
cynical as *The Secret Agent*'s narrator from first to last?
Or is he as unconscious of many of his words' implications as is the professor of languages who narrates *Under
Western Eyes*? By and large, *Chance* does not raise such
questions because in it Marlow's sarcasm and sympathy
are both distinct and superficial. But *Heart of Darkness*
and *Lord Jim*, which are, in Booth's word, "seamless,"
remain two of Conrad's inscrutable fictions because they
both raise such questions and seem to deny all the possible answers. Yet whether or not Marlow is fully a party to
the plot, Conrad is surely at great pains to frustrate the
part of us craving certitude. In one sense, Conrad (an
ironist in all his major fiction) is simply having fun at our
expense and Marlow's; yet he is also recognizing that our

140   deepest experiences never sort themselves out neatly: they berate and confound us with their multiple moral claims; they perversely demand contradictory responses of us—and in the process truth and validity must sort themselves out as best they can. Our most difficult and important task may well be to dismiss the ambivalent "possibly" Marlow offers *Lord Jim*'s "privileged man" as wholly inadequate, and yet to perceive that it lies at the heart of truth—if, that is, one may even speak of truth as having a heart. Marlow's journey, though it finally loses the momentum that is its raison d'être, derives its validity by becoming what it seeks—the way into the self-confronting realm of modern art and life, where the artist, burdened by tradition like all of us, nonetheless asserts his claim to "making it new," to striking out for unknown territories of the human psyche like the bold, free, but criminal Leggett of *The Secret Sharer*. Marlow agrees with Jim that his clean slate is a magnificent chance and then adds, "But chances are what men make them, and how was I to know?" (*LJ*, 209). The only answer to such a question must be the quest implicit in the question.

Ford Madox Ford, Preface to *Joseph Conrad: A Personal Remembrance*

It is the rendering of an affair intended first of all to make you see the subject in his scenery. It contains no documentation at all; for it no dates have been looked up.... It is the writer's impression of a writer who avowed himself impressionist. Where the writer's memory has proved to be at fault over a detail afterwards out of curiosity looked up, the writer has allowed the fault to remain on the page; but as to the truth of the impression as a whole the writer believes that no man would care—or dare—to impugn it.

Ronald Paulson

An object or even a word [in *Tristam Shandy*] is responded to and misunderstood in as many different ways as there are people trying to understand it.

5
Faulkner's Snopes Trilogy: Omniscience as Impressionism

The fourteen novels of Faulkner's Yoknapatawpha cycle constitute, in its largest sphere of meaning, a single work—a vast multivalent novel as organically alive as the country and society it portrays. From *Sartoris* (1929) to *The Reivers* (1962), Faulkner's central impelling concern has been to flesh out ever more fully the seemingly endless recesses of that world of which he is the self-proclaimed and unchal-

142 lenged "sole owner and proprietor." That he has successfully created an extraordinarily rich and pulsatingly alive
realm can no longer be seriously doubted. It is equally
certain that—in individual works like *The Sound and the
Fury, Light in August,* and *Absalom, Absalom!*—he has,
in the process, created more than his share of enduringly
brilliant American novels. But what has been less than
universally accepted is that other parts of the Yoknapatawpha cycle are all that they could or should be—either
by themselves or within the larger context. Still, as I argue, the most significant of these problematical works—
the Snopes trilogy—is a large and complex multivolume
novel within a much larger and much more complex
multivolume novel. It is a work which has dismayed and
baffled a wide variety of readers, but which, since Warren
Beck's ground-breaking (if poetically idolatrous) *Man in
Motion: Faulkner's Trilogy,* has been gathering about it
an expanding body of sensitive and insightful criticism.[1]

One of the distinctive features of Faulkner's major fiction is its experimentation—not only with language and
syntax, but also with narrative structure and moral
perspective. *The Sound and the Fury* (1929) is a miniature quartet, for it turns roughly the same story through
three intensely subjective and uniquely mad points of
view, and then through Dilsey's transcending but still
impressionistic sense of human continuity. *As I Lay
Dying* (1930) is an atypical picaresque adventure that un-

1 Warren Beck, *Man in Motion: Faulkner's Trilogy* (Madison: University of
Wisconsin Press, 1961). See, for example, Irving Howe, *William Faulkner: A
Critical Study* (New York: Vintage, 1962), 243–52, 282–94; Cleanth Brooks,
William Faulkner: The Yoknapatawpha Country (New Haven and London:
Yale University Press, 1963), 167–243, 369–70, 402–414; Lawrance Thompson,
William Faulkner: An Introduction and Interpretation (New York: Holt, Rine-
hart and Winston, 1963), 133–58; Edmond L. Volpe, *A Reader's Guide to Wil-
liam Faulkner* (New York: Farrar, Straus, 1964), 304–343; Michael Millgate,
The Achievement of William Faulkner (New York: Random House, 1966),
180–200, 235–52; Richard P. Adams, *Faulkner: Myth and Motion* (Princeton:
Princeton University Press, 1968), 115–29, 158–61; Donald A. Petesch, *Theme
and Characterization in Faulkner's Snopes Trilogy* (Ph.D. dissertation, University of Texas, 1969).

folds itself not through a single observer but through
vignettes narrated by fifteen sharply individualized participants. *Absalom, Absalom!* (1936) offers a Chinese-box
structure of narrators within narrators—the anonymous
voice, Rosa Coldfield, Mr. Compson, Quentin, Shreve—
each unreliable in his own way, and each interlocked
with the others on a spectrum ranging from near immediacy to a yet equally intense temporal and spatial distance.
One commentator has noted that, in consequence, "The
Sutpen tragedy is the novel's center of dramatic interest,
but the narrators are the center of the novel.... The narrators frame the legend as well as relate it."[2] Not only
Henry and Bon but Quentin and Shreve as well are riding
those horses back to Sutpen's Hundred and the moment
of fratricide; and we are along too, not only serving as the
outermost Chinese box of narration,[3] but also participat-
ing in action that occurs in the present for us as well.
What happens in all these works is typical of the disloca-
tions of time and space in Conrad and Ford as well as
Faulkner. As Robert Scholes puts it, "They involve the
reader in the constructive process, making him help to
create the story."[4] We are no longer free to remain apart
and above; there are no fixed terms, no a priori prem-
ises—only the truth that evolves for us during the action
we call reading.

Taken as a single work within the vast structure of the
Yoknapatawpha cycle, the Snopes trilogy (*The Hamlet*,
1940; *The Town*, 1957; *The Mansion*, 1959) is Faulkner's
most ambitious and complex experiment in narrative
technique, yet one that may be seen as a logical extension

2 Isle Dusoir Lind, "The Design and Meaning of *Absalom, Absalom!*," in
William Faulkner: Three Decades of Criticism, ed. Frederick J. Hoffman and
Olga W. Vickery (East Lansing: Michigan State University Press, 1960), 282,
284.

3 See Harvey Breit, Introduction to William Faulkner, *Absalom, Absalom!*
(New York: Modern Library, 1951).

4 Robert Scholes, *The Fabulators* (New York: Oxford University Press,
1967), 74.

144 of the earlier work. Conceived and written over a period
of three and a half decades, the trilogy nonetheless
functions as a unit.⁵ It is, among other things, a saga of
moral perspective, a rich interaction of narrative stances
as much concerned with the manner of its telling as with

5 Certainly Faulkner intended it as such. See *Faulkner in the University*, ed.
Frederick L. Gwynn and Joseph L. Blotner (Charlottesville: University of
Virginia Press, 1959), 96 and 193, and the author's note to *The Mansion*. Beck
also argues effectively for its unity. And yet that there are discrepancies as well
as purpose behind the form and conception of the trilogy, Faulkner himself is
the first to acknowledge: for he came, as he puts it, to know "more about the
human heart and its dilemma" during the thirty-odd years of its composition.
(See also *Faulkner in the University*, pp. 107–108). For a sampling of those
who see the trilogy as ununified, see Howe, pp. 282–92; Volpe, pp. 317–43;
Adams, pp. 158–61. Various minor discrepancies have been noted by Brooks.
p. 412; Volpe, pp. 402–403; Steven Marcus, "Snopes Revisited," in *Three Decades*, ed. Hoffman and Vickery, pp. 387–88; Robert W. Kirk and Marvin Klotz,
Faulkner's People (Berkeley and Los Angeles: University of California Press,
1963), 309–313; and others.
    Many of the substantive arguments raised in these works are considered in
the present study. The strongest, and perhaps the strangest, position is that of
Howe, ordinarily the most perceptive and rational of critics. "One can antici-
pate scores of essays which will trace the ways in which each incident or episode in the trilogy contributes to the total scheme and which will thereby create
the false impression that a satisfying congruence exists between the conceptual
design and the novels as they actually are. Yet, as regards both *The Town* and
The Mansion, such a congruence is not to be found, for only fitfully do those
novels realize the needs and possibilities of Faulkner's over-all design" (p.
285). I will be arguing the opposite view, but beyond mere disagreement,
Howe's position here seems to me *fundamentally* unsound and intellectually
suspect. It is one thing to demonstrate and maintain one's own approach and
evaluation; it is quite another to damn in advance all attempts at a different one.
Howe's discussion of *The Town* and *The Mansion* is also undercut by its de-
pendence on such condescending phrases as "Faulkner never seems able to
face up to . . . " (pp. 289, 292, etc.). Brooks offers effective repudiation of many
of Howe's interpretations (on the trilogy, see especially pp. 234–35, 369–70,
412–13). I will attempt additional ones where necessary for the purpose of my
own study.
    The opposite extreme may be represented by Steven Marcus who, asserting
an analogy with "the post-Homeric fragments," subsumes and exalts even trivial discrepancies: "In those almost entirely lost cyclic poems the stories of *The
Iliad* and *The Odyssey* were recreated and amplified with the same character of
variation that one finds in *The Town* and in parts of Faulkner's other works. As
one reads about them one gets a renewed sense of how one of the primal powers
of literature is to raise mythology to the level of history, to treat the material of
the imagination as if it were indistinguishable from the actuality it invades and
transcribes" (p. 388). Beck agrees that the discrepancies are both minor and a
successful part of the scheme (pp. 16 ff). Marcus' statement may be largely
valid, but no more than its opposite does it follow from the fact that the trilogy
contains minor discrepancies.

its ostensible subject matter. "This technique of multiple presentation," as Cleanth Brooks says in discussing an earlier Faulkner novel, "has everything to do with the solidity and power of *As I Lay Dying*. The author does not commit us to the experience and sensibility of one character whom we see only from the inside and whose world we apprehend only from his point of view. Instead, Faulkner has attempted the much more difficult role of putting us in some kind of sympathetic rapport with an individual character and yet constantly forcing this character back into the total perspective of the world—the world of the family and the larger world of the community."[6] On a similar but larger scale, Faulkner has done this in the Snopes trilogy as well.

Yet at first glance, the narrative structures of the three novels of the trilogy seem to have little in common with each other. *The Hamlet*'s four books are all told by a voice traditionally called the omniscient narrator, though Faulkner does offer us V. K. Ratliff as commentator within that frame. The twenty-four chapters of *The Town* are all subjective statements: ten by Charles Mallison, eight by Gavin Stevens, and six by Ratliff. *The Mansion* seems a hodgepodge combination of these two approaches. None of its three main sections is narrated by the title characters: Mink (five chapters), Linda (six), and Flem (seven)—but two of Mink's chapters have personal narrators (one each by Ratliff and Montgomery Ward Snopes) as do all of Linda's (three by Charles Mallison, two by Ratliff, and one by Gavin). What sort of narrative unity lies behind such a structure?

Warren Beck has written of it in this way: "The three books not only complement but blend into each other. The omniscience of *The Hamlet* richly furnishes the stage and gives the narrative its tremendous impetus; the first person reports which make up *The Town* turn illumina-

6 Brooks, *William Faulkner*, 159–60.

146 tive speculation upon emergent facets of character and action; *The Mansion* emphasizes theme and resolution by apposing the two methods. . . . By alternating third person omniscient narrative method, like that of *The Hamlet*, with extended first person accounts like those which make up *The Town*, *The Mansion* achieves a wider range of tone than either of the preceding volumes, while echoing and fulfilling them."[7] Actually, as I hope to demonstrate, it is a remarkably subjective and often dramatized, though still anonymous, multifarious voice with which Faulkner begins and concludes and unites the Snopes trilogy.

The narrator of *The Hamlet* demonstrates his humanness by articulating the shared values and perspective—though not always the language and imagery—of the chorus like gallery inhabitants. He says, for instance, "A few days later they learned that the new smith was living in the house where his cousin (or whatever the relationship was: nobody ever knew for certain) Flem lived" (*H*, 66). Typically, the narrative voice tells us only what "they" see and know and feel. Thus, his portrayal of Eula Varner expresses the presumably common emotional reaction the narrator himself shares; further, such passages are often ascribed, directly or indirectly, to a particular character. Here, for instance, is Eula in the classroom: "By merely walking down the aisle between them she would transform the very wooden desks and benches themselves into a grove of Venus and fetch every male in the room . . . importunate each for precedence in immolation" (*H*, 115). In this section the narrator has taken us inside Labove; appropriately, then, the language, imagery, and sentiments are exactly what we might expect from the pedantic and frustrated schoolmaster.

The narrator performs a second major function in treating Ratliff as both just a character and something more.

7 Beck, *Man in Motion*, 31, 43.

Ratliff remains in the third person throughout *The Hamlet*, but in what might be termed third-person-subjective (in the manner of Joyce's *Portrait of the Artist*). He is the only individual we get significantly inside of in *The Hamlet* and the only one who comments with anything like consistent authority. The narrator himself emphasizes that we should pay close attention to what Ratliff says: "If he had lived in Frenchman's Bend itself . . . he would have known no more" (*H*, 149). The implication is that Ratliff knows all anyone can know, perhaps all there is to know.

The multifarious narrator of *The Mansion* similarly plays both these roles: he voices the communal values of Jefferson and he speaks out of the consciousness of a protagonist figure, in this case Mink Snopes. Thus in both *The Hamlet* and *The Mansion* the multifarious narrator is neither omniscient nor objective: he takes stances, adopts perspectives, enters into the fray. To this extent he is, like all of us, limited, involved, unreliable.

Within the framework of the multifarious perspective lie the single-faceted narrators, most notably Ratliff, Gavin Stevens, and Chick Mallison. Theirs may be called participant voices since they are named characters in the action and also narrators in their own right; to the extent that they dominate the action they narrate, they may be termed protagonist voices. Ratliff is the most important of these for his moral perspective, his relative reliability, and (since he alone appears in all three novels of the trilogy) his serving as a unifying device. Shrewd, bland, cool, and yet deeply concerned, Ratliff is the most sensitive, incisive, and trustworthy narrator in the trilogy, the closest to a touchstone of enduring and what might be called natural human understanding. Only he, we are told, will recognize the returned Mink after thirty-eight years. "Ratliff alone out of Yoknapatawpha County would know Mink on sight. To be unschooled, untravelled, and to an extent unread, Ratliff had a terrifying capacity for

148 knowledge or local information or acquaintanceship to match the need of any local crisis" (*M*, 381). It is Ratliff who both points a moral in Flem's story (he got what he deserved) and then, in the appropriate note of mocking sympathy, sums up Gavin Stevens' position: "I dont know if [Linda's] already got a daughter stashed out somewhere, or if she jest aint got around to one yet. But when she does I jest hope for Old Lang Zyne's sake she dont never bring it back to Jefferson. You done already been through two Eula Varners and I dont think you can stand another one" (*M*, 434).

Ratliff's actions similarly reflect the communal values he shares with Faulkner's implied author and presumably with Faulkner himself: he warns Frenchman's Bend against Flem's ponies; he separates Ike Snopes from his cow;[8] he refuses to go to New York to celebrate Linda's sleeping with Barton Kohl, but goes happily for the wedding; he unfashionably insists that Stalin is as evil and dangerous as Hitler and Mussolini (*M*, 160–61). Yet Ratliff never embodies omniscience, absoluteness; his wisdom and understanding emerge from the context of mortal confines—even domestic ones: he is an unabashedly good cook, seamstress, housekeeper (*M*, 231). In *The Hamlet*, Ratliff's serious illness and his falling for "the oldest trick in the book" in buying the Old Frenchman place from Flem (especially after having warned the others against Flem's ponies) emphasize his finiteness as character.

Ratliff's reconstruction, in *The Mansion*, of Eula's impregnation similarly underscores his impressionistic narration. "I think what I prefer is, that them five timorous local stallions actively brought about the very exact thing they finally nerved their desperation up to try to prevent.... I wont have nothing else for the simple dramatic verities except that ever thing happened right there that

---

8 Brooks seems to me convincing on the virtue of this action (pp. 407–410).

night and all at once . . . that it taken all six of them even
to ravage that citadel, let alone seed them loins with a
child." And Ratliff adds: "My conjecture is jest as good as
yourn, maybe better since I'm a interested party, being as
I got what the feller calls a theorem to prove. . . . I dont
even insist or argue that it happened that way. I jest simply decline to have it any other way except that one because there aint no acceptable degrees between what has
got to be right and what jest can possibly be" (M, 119–24).
Ratliff's position—that having a conjecture to prove (that
is, being involved with events rather than removed from
them) makes him relatively reliable—represents a repudiation of omniscience. There may be paradox in Ratliff's
implied aesthetics, but his view nonetheless is central to
the tradition of the modern novel. It is, further, Ratliff's
way of affirming what Faulkner calls verities. In response
to Bookwright's cynicism about God, Ratliff says, "I dont
know as I would believe that, even if I knowed it was
true" (H, 83). In *The Town*, he says "Between what did
happen and what ought to happened, I dont never have
trouble picking ought" (T, 100). For Ratliff "ought" is
truer than "did" or "is"—truer morally, truer aesthetically, truer humanly.

As might be expected, Ratliff is at times as inadequate
in narration as in the action concerning the Old Frenchman place. He is, for example, at a loss to explain Flem's
failure to free Montgomery Ward from prison (M, 63–64);
he is wrong in speculating on why Linda, in her senior
year of high school, avoided meeting Gavin (it was Gavin,
fearing a growing intimacy, who avoided Linda); and he
offers us boredom as the identical, glib, and, at best,
superficial explanation for Eula's and Flem's deaths.[9]

9 Both Brooks (pp. 209–210) and Faulkner (F *in* U, 195), on the other hand,
offer strong argument for accepting Eula's motivation at face value. (R. P.
Adams, who finds Eula rather unconvincing anyway, offers a third view: he
maintains that the suicide is illogical because useless and ineffective [p. 161].
But surely our retrospective knowledge of the consequences gives us unfair ad-
vantages over Eula, allowing us to be coolly reasonable where the emotionally

150 And yet Ratliff—having been burned once, having learned not to "tangle with Flem" (*M*, 57)—not only completely regains and thereafter maintains his equilibrium, his reputation for sagacity, but he also enters into another business arrangement with another Snopes (Wall, this time) with complete success—and to this extent serves if not as check 'then at least as counterweight to Flem's rise.

What emerges, I think, is a somewhat mixed picture of a superior, even extraordinary, but very real and therefore limited human being. And if Ratliff—"too damned innocent, too damned intelligent" (*T*, 33)—is this far from being the trilogy's definitive spokesman, how much farther are the more obviously flawed participant narrators? The most important of these, Gavin Stevens and Chick Mallison, narrate with much force, convincingness, and reliability. They are rendered largely sympathetic because, from the inside looking out, we are made to see—and mostly share—their attitudes toward Snopesism, Eula and Linda, Ratliff, America's wars, and so on. And yet it is absurd to condemn Faulkner, as some have done, for failing to make them perfect authorial mouthpieces when it is clear from the novels that they were never conceived as such.

Gavin Stevens, for one, commits so many acts of perverse folly and willful self-blinding—the feud with De Spain, his pseudo-chivalric and feeble posturing towards Eula and Linda, his adopting Montgomery Ward as his protégé, his despairing surrender (of not only himself but his whole generation) before the threat of Clarence Snopes, his refusal to acknowledge Linda's motive for freeing Mink—that we tend to lose track of them and to adopt Ratliff's attitude of frustrated and patronizing, if sympathetic, bemusement.

Irving Howe offers us an easier view, that Faulkner's ar-

---

trapped Eula cannot be.) Ratliff's explanation of Flem's "suicide" stands up better—but perhaps because we know so little of Flem's inner workings that there is nothing to contradict it.

tistry failed him. "How else," he asks rhetorically, "can
one explain the frantic verbal outpourings of Gavin Stevens, the District Attorney with a degree from Heidelberg
and a passion for rant, who serves so disastrously as
Faulkner's 'alter ego'?"[10] One could do worse, however,
than note Faulkner's response to this very question, a response that clearly suggests the absurdity of glib author-
character equations: "You don't really have time to identify yourself with a character except at certain moments
when the character is in a position to express truthfully
things which you yourself believe to be true. Then you'll
put your own ideas in his mouth, but... when you do
that they'll become his.... It just happens that this man
agrees with you on this particular point and so he says
it." And Faulkner goes on specifically to suggest Gavin
Stevens' inadequaces in *The Town*. "Well, he had got out
of his depth.... He got into a real world in which people
anguished and suffered, not simply did things which
they shouldn't do. And he wasn't as prepared to cope
with people who were following their own bent, not for a
profit but simply because they had to. That is, he knew a
good deal less about people than he knew about the law
and about ways of evidence and drawing the right conclusions from what he saw with his legal mind. When he
had to deal with people he was an amateur" (*F in U*,
25–26, 140). This seems to me a valid if redundant statement. For the trilogy makes unambiguously clear that
Gavin, for all we like and sympathize with him, was conceived and created as an inadequate spokesman for inadequate views. As Brooks indicates, Faulkner knows
what he is up to: "Gavin again and again in the novel is
made to play the fool. As a Snopes killer, he is not impressive, and in much of [*The Town*] we are invited to
smile at his follies."[11]

So far from being Faulkner's mouthpiece, Gavin is his

10 Howe, *William Faulkner*, 284.
11 Brooks, *William Faulkner*, 194.

152 mirror image for Flem's impotence. On this subject
Brooks notes that "Gavin's conduct seems so strange that
some commentators have concluded that he is impotent;
but his behavior throughout the novel is not that of an
impotent man."[12] Yet Brooks, despite his largely convincing treatment of Gavin as a de Rougemont Tristan, offers little evidence of his potency. The only solid piece is
Gavin's eventual marriage to Melisandre Backus, but as
Brooks himself says, "his marriage involves friendship
and even affection, but presumably not much passion. . . .
there is in the marriage none of the anguished passion
that Gavin associates with his Helens and Iseults. It may
well have been a happy marriage, but the very fact of
happiness would for the gun-shy Gavin have removed the
possibility of a romance in the grand manner."[13] The lack
of passion is obvious; one wonders about even the friendship and affection. The marriage receives little development in the novel; that it has the force and form of a di-
gression suggests its relative insignificance and negative
impact on Gavin's life. He hates his wife's expensive
wedding present and pedigreed horses. "At first his
wife's money was a problem," the narrator (mildly
amused because distanced) tells us. "In fact, if it hadn't
been for the greater hysteria of the war, the lesser hysteria
of that much sudden money could have been a serious
one" (M, 363). Chick Mallison also compares Gavin's
marriage to the war: "By which time I was married too, to
a bombsight" (M, 256). When Gavin himself speaks of his
wife, he tells Linda it is nonsense to think she will be
jealous (jealousy, after all, exists only where there is passion); and when he speaks to her as he goes off to see
Linda, he says, "I love you. . . . Yes. No. I dont know. Dont
wait up" (M, 364). There is something far more ambivalent in this relationship than in Eula's with Flem.

   Faulkner comments that Gavin "was probably afraid to

12 *Ibid.*, 196.
13 *Ibid.*, 200, 203.

be married. He might get too involved with the human race if he married one of them" (*F in U*, 141). Gavin's marriage to Melisandre represents a reversion, an attempted escape into the past, to the girl who preceded Linda as his protégé. Gavin had earlier vicariously identified himself with Hoak MacCarron (*T*, 135, 342–43) and therefore as Linda's father. Given Gavin's convoluted logic, this may well be anticipatory rationalization to preclude his later having to marry Linda. Chick's view is that "his Uncle Gavin might already have been a grandfather before he even became a bride" (*M*, 356). But Gavin never has any children, and he seems incapable of having any. His most intimate female relationships are with prepubescent girls and postmenopausal mothers; his most obsessive emotions focus on hollow chivalry and Flem's impotence. How pathetically revealing of his own masculine feebleness is his comment that Eula, always ready "for anything that just wore pants," was like any woman always ready for "anything in pants just named Gavin Stevens" (*T*, 219). Regardless of the physiological technicalities, Gavin is sexually worse off than the unambiguous Flem because his caring for people causes him little but anguish and frustration; and the reader tends to ask, along with Chick, "Is it virginity or just celibacy?" (*M*, 193)—in the exact non sequitur tone that is used whenever someone (Gavin, *T*, 94; Montgomery Ward, *M*, 70) realizes that Flem is impotent.

For all its romantic trappings, Gavin's relationship with Linda is no more a vital or positive expression of mature heterosexual love than Gavin's marriage. Its symbol is the wall separating their otherwise co-joined beds the night they spend in a hotel (*M*, 250–53). For both Linda and Gavin, the relationship is remarkably static—in fact, sterile. Playing at omniscient narrator, Gavin had pronounced Linda's fate. Ratliff tells him: "Doomed to fidelity and grief, you said. To love once quick and lose him quick and for the rest of her life to be faithful and to

154 grieve" (*M*, 158). As character, Gavin acts on the apparent
assumption that his pronouncement represents a revealed
truth. Ratliff knows better: "It wasn't her that was
doomed, she would likely do fine; it was the one that was
recipient of the fidelity and the monogamy and the love,
and the one that was the proprietor of the responsibility"
(*M*, 163). For all his claims of victimization, Gavin has
willed or allowed his own fate, for Linda is remarkably
consistent in her proffers not merely of her body (her
mother's offer), but of love (with or without marriage).
Even at the end—after her marriage, Barton's death, Gavin's marriage, Flem's death—she can still say: "I love
you. . . . I have never loved anybody but you" (*M*, 425).[14]
But Gavin cannot allow himself to hear this, any more
than he can allow himself to hear her say he can do "the
explicit word" to her (*M*, 238).[15] In fact, Gavin censors the
word out of his narrative just as he has effaced the act
from his life. He registers his shock to Linda's explicit
offer (or plea) by blushing and hastily writing: *"because
we are the 2 in all the world who can love each other
without having to"* (*M*, 239), and by trying to block it out,
as he does again later with the image-destroying knowledge of her motive in freeing Mink.

Linda's deafness, Chick tells us, removes her from the
flux of time and motion, renders her (like the bride on
Keats's Grecian urn) "immobilised by a thunderclap into
silence. . . . herself no mere moment's child but the in-

14 Somehow missing this, Volpe makes much of Linda's "undying love" for
Barton Kohl (p. 337). Beck similarly speaks of "Linda's inconsolable grief for
her lost husband" (p. 108).

15 Howe is understandably upset by Gavin's obsessive puritanism, and he
quite rightly notes the lack of sensuality in this trilogy of passion. Yet though it
is surely critically untenable to blame an author for the sins of his character,
Howe nonetheless condemns Faulkner for Gavin's lack of sexual candor. Beck,
though unquestioningly praising Faulkner for it, also sees Gavin as mouthpiece
(p. 51).

Millgate has a brief discussion of Gavin's impotence (expressed in "his adolescent sexual attitudes and behavior," p. 247) that parallels mine in several
respects; and, along with Marcus (pp. 386–87), Millgate compares him to
Eliot's Prufrock—a character I presume no one takes as his author's spokesman.

violate bride of silence, inviolable in maidenhead, fixed, forever safe from change and alteration" (M, 203). Yet Linda does hear the world's noises and tries to improve it, and she is extraordinarily articulate on the fullness of time continuously evolving the present from the past (M, 248); while Gavin (embodying and reflecting Linda's deafness as much as he does Flem's impotence) censors out the reality Linda embodies and retreats into stasis. Chick says that females "had to be alive for him to notice them, and they had to be in motion to be alive, and the only moment of motion which caught his attention, his eye, was that one at which they entered puberty" (M, 197). Gavin's marriage, then, is an imaginative construct not unlike the relationships with Eula and Linda; for Gavin, as Ratliff tells us, is bound by the self-willed imposition of his own blinkered vision upon reality. "It was his fate. He jest got run over by coincidence. . . . It wasn't that he was born too soon or too late or even in the wrong place. He was born at exactly the right time, only in the wrong envelope" (M, 128). That is, to be Gavin Stevens is to be doomed to be Gavin Stevens. It's as simple, and complex, as that.

For all his intensity and energy, Gavin initiates surprisingly little action. Such actions as do involve him—the feud with De Spain, the beating by Matt Levitt, the "adoption" of Montgomery Ward—not only defeat but also humiliate him. There is one significant exception, one wholly successful act, yet it too winds up tasting like failure. Gavin had looked absurdly foolish during the rise and fall of Clarence Snopes because (playing again at prophetic voice or omniscient narrator) he had made one of his typically sweeping and erroneous pronouncements to Ratliff: "'It's too late for us now. . . . we are just too old. Call it just tired, too tired to be afraid any longer of losing. Just to hate evil is not enough. You—somebody—has got to do something about it. Only now it will have to be somebody else. . . . it wont be us'" (M, 307). Immediately

156 after Ratliff's successful exorcising of Clarence, Gavin
himself, apparently having learned the lesson of the master, acts and defeats the inevitable next Snopes, Orestes.
But the upshot only reinforces his sense of frustration and
impotent bitterness. "'It's hopeless. Even when you get
rid of one Snopes, there's already another one behind you
even before you can turn around.'" And he lapses back
into a lassitude that leaves him floundering and foolish
before the coming of Mink. Ratliff agrees with his thesis—
"'That's right,' Ratliff said serenely. 'As soon as you look,
you see right away it aint nothing but jest another
Snopes'" (M, 349)—but the tone and emphasis are utterly
different: calm, broad in vision, actively satisfied without
being complacent, believing in the meaningfulness (if not
always the efficacy) of human values and action, and
therefore never defeated or despairing over mortality.
"Fate, and destiny, and luck, and hope," Ratliff says,
"and all of us mixed up in it . . . until cant none of us tell
where it stops and we begin. . . . I used to think that hope
was about all folks had, only now I'm beginning to believe that that's about all anybody needs—jest hope" (M,
373–74).

In the end, Gavin is hope*less* (both enfeebled and devoid of hope): a failed humanist and self-convicted cow-
ard (M, 377); absurdly irrelevant first on Mink's cosmic
significance ("By God, God Himself is not so busy that a
homicidal maniac with only ten dollars in the world can
hitchhike a hundred miles and buy a gun for ten dollars
then hitchhike another hundred and shoot another man
with it" [M, 389]), and then on Mink's imagined "death"
(M, 392–93); willfully self-deceiving about Linda's
motivation; feebly denying her pitying: "You haven't had
very much, have you. No, that's wrong. You haven't had
anything. You have had nothing" (M, 424). And finally,
telling Ratliff that Flem was impotent, Gavin sounds like
he is confessing something from the depths of his own being: "When he got in bed with a woman all he could do

was go to sleep. Yes! ... The poor sons of bitches that
have to cause all the grief and anguish they have to cause!
Drive on!" (M, 430). Worn out, used up, Gavin "was too
old now and the real tragedy of age is that no anguish is
any longer grievous enough to demand, justify, any sacrifice" (M, 392).

Yet Gavin was already old, exhausted, and feeble in
The Town. He ages during the course of that novel without maturing; in fact, the mocking of Matt Levitt's car and
the beating Gavin takes from him (a replay in miniature
and parody of the De Spain feud) suggest enfeeblement
rather than maturation. The regressive note had been
sounded earlier, when Gavin, after his abortive attempt to
impeach De Spain, cries out, "What must I do now, Papa?
Papa, what can I do now?" (T, 99). Gavin may learn some
things along the way but he is essentially unaltered by
events. At the beginning he seems younger even than
Chick (who isn't even born yet); after a while, he is suddenly old, older than anyone else, older than anyone has
any right to be; and at the end of *The Town* he seems not
to have grown up, but only to have gone through it all.

In Chapter 20 of *The Town*, his most introspective
chapter, Gavin expresses a sense of being old beyond
time. He offers us his helpless frustration over Eula's
summons (*"Why cant you let me alone? What more can
you want of me than I have already failed to do?"*), a
briefly calm view of sunset from a hill with all of
mortality "supine beneath you," followed by a very un-
transcendent statement that "life itself is always prema-
ture which is why it aches and anguishes"; and then the
final meeting with Eula during which he again refuses to
marry Linda (T, 319–34). In this long and intricately constructed chapter, Gavin presents himself at his most compelling and also most self-pitying. We are meant to sympathize, even identify, yet if we do so completely and
then subsequently resent having yielded to Gavin's self-
indulgent sentimentality, we have only ourselves to

158 blame. Faulkner's multifarious narrator, though he likes
Gavin, knows better than to take him simply at face value:
he frames the entire chapter with the same mockingbird
voice that (along with Ratliff and Mrs. Littlejohn) offered
ironic commentary on those bidding for Flem's ponies (*T*,
310, 334).

Throughout the trilogy, Ratliff is often referred to as a
know-it-all minding everyone else's business. Yet Ratliff
himself calls Gavin a meddler (e.g., *M*, 194, 204). Is there a
difference? For one thing, with rare exception Ratliff can
play his role without imposing or doing harm. His one
major lapse is his being duped by Flem over the salting of
the Old Frenchman place, but as he suggests, if he hadn't
been there to allow Flem his egress to Jefferson there
would have been someone else. Other than that, he gets
involved with Snopes and Snopesism only through purposeful and morally impelled acts of volition: removing
Ike's cow, his partnership with Wall, helping Gavin sanc-
tion Linda's marriage, and the like. In virtually all he says
and does, Ratliff demonstrates his interest in people and
their "active" values ("he always said active for actual,"
Gavin tells us [*T*, 142]). Gavin, however, is concerned
only with those who somehow touch his life: he doesn't
simply hate Snopesism for its evil power, he is obsessed
by it because, like Don Quixote with his windmills, he
feels it as a direct and personal affront to his beautiful and
doomed vision of reality. An impassioned if sterile
romantic, Gavin can be objective about nothing, and thus
often rushes blindly in where Ratliff is too wary to tread.
Thus he winds up playing impossible vicarious roles—
Eula's outraged husband; Linda's high school sweetheart
and protective father; in general, Jefferson's self-
appointed guardian of puritanical virtue—and looking
absurd in the process.

So far from being Faulkner's mouthpiece, Gavin is the
most pathetic of the developed characters in *The Town*,

in fact in the entire trilogy. Yet because of his gallant championing of stasis, his often inept attempt to frame and maintain verities in the unequal battle with continual flux—as well as his intense, if not always wholly honest, introspection—Gavin is also the trilogy's most complex, interesting, and sympathetic human being. Ratliff may be the most incisive and attractive, Flem the most dynamic, Eula the most compelling, Chick the most impressionable and impressionistic—but Gavin is the most tortured, the most besieged, and he alone compels our attention and involvement in a manner suggestive of our reaction to a tragic protagonist.

The third major participant voice in the Snopes trilogy is Chick Mallison. Like Gavin, he has been viewed as an authorial spokesman—with Faulkner praised or condemned according to how well or badly Chick is considered to succeed in this role.[16] Yet as both narrator and

16 Howe, who condemns Faulkner for being only rarely aware "that Stevens is very far from what he has tried to persuade us he is" (p. 287), considers Chick Mallison even more of a failed spokesman: "Nothing in the text, so far as I can see, provides any ground for supposing that Faulkner takes a caustic view of [his] sophomoric wisdom, or that he wishes us to see Mallison in any but a sympathetic light" (p. 288). Marcus is equally patronizing with regard to Stevens: Faulkner is "too involved with him personally to admit that Stevens never was and never could be that fountainhead of moral enlightenment and of a gallant, embattled tradition which in the crisis of his culture and therefore of his art Faulkner needs to portray." Unlike Howe, though, Marcus sees Chick as simply "a decent and perspicacious young man" in *The Town* and, therefore, as a generally successful Faulknerian spokesman (pp. 386–87).

We need the sort of corrective that Brooks offers. He says that anyone making the mistake of taking Gavin as mouthpiece in *The Town* "is very likely to miss the tone and even the basic meaning of the novel. For if any one thing about this novel soon becomes clear, it is that Gavin, and not for the first time in Faulkner's fiction, is treated as a figure of fun—almost as the butt of the author's jokes" (p. 194). And in response to Marcus' view that Chick's comments on the South are Faulkner's, Brooks adds: "The novels of Faulkner can tell us a good deal about the quality of Southern culture, but the way to read them is not to seize upon remarks made by the characters to support our own conceptions or preconceptions. We compound the folly involved in this kind of reading when we decide hastily that this or that remark made by a character bears the stamp of Faulkner's personal approval" (p. 370). The point, surely, is that Faulkner, like any good artist, does not use characters to make authorial statements in the simplistic manner implied.

160 character Chick is no more trustworthy than Gavin—and
perhaps a good deal less.[17] Each of the first three chapters
Chick narrates in *The Town* begins with his emphasizing
that "I wasn't born yet . . ." (*T*, 3, 45, 103), and Ratliff later
underscores the warning when he implies that Chick was
"doomed to be too young."[18] Further, he receives most of
his information from his cousin Gowan, who was himself
first too young and then too peripheral to the events he
speaks of to know or care what they were really about.
Chick himself comments: "But then Gowan was seventeen; he had a few other things to do, whether grown
people believed it or not. . . . he didn't always listen to all
Ratliff would be saying . . . so that afterward he couldn't
even say just how it was or when that Ratliff put it into his
mind and he even got interested in it like a game, a con-
test or even a battle, a war, that Snopeses had to be
watched constantly like an invasion of snakes or
wildcats" (*T*, 106). Chick, then, so far from being an omniscient or multifarious narrator, is triply removed in
both time and space from much of what he narrates. His
role is that of an artist uncertain of his relationship to his
materials. "I was only thirteen," he tells us, "when Mrs
Snopes shot herself that night so I still dont know how
much I saw and remembered and how much was compelled onto or into me from Uncle Gavin, being, as Ratliff
put it, as I had spent the first eleven or twelve years of my

17 Faulkner himself, though at one point he says Chick had more judgment
than Gavin (*F in U*, 140), was fully conscious of the limitations of Chick's narration. "I thought it [*The Town*] would be more amusing as told through the innocence of a child that knew what he was seeing but had no particular judgment about it. That something told by someone that don't know he is telling
something funny is sometimes much more amusing than when it's told by a
professional wit who is hunting around for laughs. Also, to have it told partly
by a child, partly by a grown man. It's to hold the object up and look at it from
both sides, from two points of view" (*F in U*, 116).
18 *Tristram Shandy*, a book ostensibly about its title character, similarly focuses on events largely occurring before its protagonist / narrator's birth. If
Sterne's book is the influence on Faulkner's comic vision that it seems to be,
then the ludicrousness inherent in Chick's removedness from the events he recounts and passes judgment upon may be seen as all the more intentionally
comic.

existence in the middle of Uncle Gavin, thinking what he thought and seeing what he saw" (*M*, 211). He might have said "filtered" as well as "compelled"—because the process includes Gavin's experiencing (sometimes vicariously through Ratliff and others), recreating, and transmitting, followed by Chick's own ingesting, reenvisaging, and now attempting to communicate.

Chick is additionally removed from events by the moral perspective he adopts as his own. On the first page of *The Town* he says, "When I say 'we' and 'we thought' what I mean is Jefferson and what Jefferson thought" (p. 3). And what are the values inherent in that perspective? "We were his [De Spain's] allies, his confederates; our whole town was accessory to that cuckolding. . . . It was not because we were against Mr Snopes. . . . Nor were we really in favor of adultery, sin: we were simply in favor of De Spain and Eula Snopes, for what Uncle Gavin called the divinity of simple unadulterated uninhibited immortal lust which they represented . . . ours the pride that Jefferson would supply their battleground" (*T*, 15). Chick then parallels and displaces the multifarious narrator of *The Hamlet*, for just as his predecessor spoke the communal voice of Frenchman's Bend, Chick speaks that of Jefferson. In this context, many of his prejudices and predilections may be seen as not merely adolescent pseudo-sophistication, but small-town and southern narrowness—like the fear and hatred of the outsider (Linda Kohl, Colonel Devries) whether he be called communist, Jew, or nigger-lover. Our position as reader is therefore a treacherous one, for we tend to think events are as someone we like describes them: but in doing so here, we would be as far removed from a fixed center of reality as if we accepted as literal truth the re-created past Quentin and Shreve offer us in *Absalom, Absalom!*

Chick's narration is in fact as intensely subjective as are those of that earlier vorticular novel; for from his perspective, the trilogy is a *Bildungsroman*, and on his quest for

162 education he generally gains not wisdom but experience, knowledge, temptation. Faulkner suggests the same thing when he says that Chick evolves in *The Town*. "He grew up in that book. And of course, his point of view changed" (*F in U*, 140). Chick's journey, which (like Tristram Shandy's) seems to have begun long before his birth or conception, is an initiation—into the mysteries and dangers of Snopesism, women, money, war, all the traditional attractions and threats of this world—conducted by the ally-seeking efforts of Ratliff and Gavin.

The results for Chick are as ambivalent as they invariably are. A third of the way through *The Mansion*, as Linda is returning to Jefferson from the war in Spain, Ratliff pronounces Chick ready to share fully in the action. "This time he wouldn't be no innocent infantile bystanding victim" (*M*, 112). Yet *The Mansion* is as replete with Chick's sophomorisms as is *The Town*. He is jealous of Gavin's relationship with Linda (*M*, 112–13), yet sees her as a whore (p. 210) and mockingly asks Gavin, "Is it all right with you if I try to lay her?" (p. 353); he insensitively ridicules Linda not only for her communism and Jewish husband (e.g., pp. 110, 210), but also for her deafness and her voice (e.g., p. 209); having mocked Gavin for his "is it virginity or just celibacy?" (p. 193), he then leeringly speculates on his arrangements for sleeping with Linda (pp. 210–12) and sardonically concludes: "So all that remained for her and Gavin was continence. To put it crudely, morality" (*M*, 212). And he offers us a comprehensive view of the human condition that is harsh, bleak, and cheap—"Man stinks" (p. 230)—especially if juxtaposed with the hard-earned final view that Ratliff and Gavin wearily arrive at together. "'There aren't any morals,' Stevens said. 'People just do the best they can.' 'The pore sons of bitches,' Ratliff said. 'The poor sons of bitches,' Stevens said" (*M*, 429).

Yet Chick is also capable of learning, of real growth. At one point, after Chick had just made jokes to himself about Linda's deafness, Gavin tells him, "When you are a little older you will discover that people really are much more gentle and considerate and kind than you want right now to believe" (M, 201)—and he finds himself reluctantly agreeing. In addition, his experience in the war had—perhaps against his own intention and desires—effected knowledge and change: "The tragedy of war was that you brought nothing away from it but only left something valuable there; that you carried into war things which, except for the war, you could have lived out your life in peace with without ever having to know they were inside you" (M, 354–55). And as a consequence, and despite all his speculative coarseness, he recognizes that Linda is not for him, and he gives up the bad attempt before he makes it.

Even more impressively, Chick achieves an ability to compare himself unfavorably to the uncle he has long patronized. He had considered Gavin foolish and hopelessly dense for being at a loss to explain Barton Kohl's sculpture, but standing before it, he thinks "that, if Gavin was still looking for first base, I had already struck out because I didn't even know what it was, let alone what it was doing" (M, 232). Chick's self-revelation here (and elsewhere) momentarily pierces his facade of cynicism and reveals it as the obverse of Gavin's romantic excesses. Just as we came to see through Gavin's posturing and to reject it as silly and hopeless (though still largely retaining our sympathy for him), so *The Mansion* indicates we are meant to do the same with Chick and his adolescent antiromanticizing. I think Faulkner strikes the right note about Gavin when he suggests that, like Quentin Compson, he creates the "sad and funny picture" of a Don Quixote defending nonexistent virtues in a world that believes in none. "It is the knight that goes out to defend somebody who don't want to be defended and don't need it. But it's a very fine quality in human nature. I hope it will always endure. It is comical and a little sad" (F in U,

141). Chick's climactic dual view of Gavin—because earned and apropos and quiet—is not only similarly valid but applies equally well to himself: "He is a good man. Maybe I was wrong sometimes to trust and follow him but I never was wrong to love him" (*M*, 230). Even more important, this statement may be seen as precisely capturing our ambivalence toward Gavin and Chick not only as characters but also as narrators. For all their aberrations, we are instinctively right to want to trust them; but we are intellectually wrong to do so without corroboration.

What we have, then, are three major participant narrators, each (like the sections of the three Compson brothers in *The Sound and the Fury*) limited to representing a view of truth. "Just as," as Faulkner puts it, "when you examine a monument you will walk around it, you are not satisfied to look at it from just one side. Also, it was to look at it from three different mentalities" (*F in U*, 139–40). But the trilogy's structure is more complex than that. The "mentalities" in *The Town* are not only spatially equal perspectives but also concentric circles: Chick speaking for community, Gavin for "the poets," Ratliff for the oracles. On this last point, Gavin says, "After this many years of working to establish and maintain himself as what he uniquely was in Jefferson, Ratliff could not afford, he did not dare, to walk the streets and not have the answer to any and every situation which was not really any of his business. Ratliff knew . . ." (*T*, 141). In addition, each of these characters moves through time not only linearly (his own chronological aging) but also in something of a spiraling relationship to the expanding phenomenon of Snopesism. Snopesism itself moves in complex ways. Paralleling the Snopesian invasion of Frenchman's Bend in *The Hamlet*, *The Town* at first offers a kind of peristaltic movement into Jefferson of one Snopes after another; this is followed by the dual movement of Flem up the social and commercial ladder and, reversing the earlier process, a simultaneously contracting gyre as other Snopeses are removed one by one from Jefferson. The climactic moment for both occurs at the utmost point of contraction, at what we might call "the frozen moment" of Flem's death.[19] The denouement follows as Mink fades into the west and the earth in a final scene that completes what is, among other things, the saga of the place detailed in the trilogy's opening paragraph: "Hill-cradled and remote, definite yet without boundaries, straddling into two counties and owing allegiance to neither... some of the once-fertile fields had long since reverted to the cane-and-cypress jungle from which their first master had hewed them" (*H*, 3). Back in Frenchman's Bend and again experiencing the perspective of the frame narrator, we—like Mink—make our peace with the ambivalent land (dual-countied, waste and fruitful, tamed and wild) that first endures our struggles and then contains them.

The land, then, as in Conrad's similarly framed *Nostromo*, remains as a symbol of abiding certitude, the closest we come to eternal truth within ceaseless flux. The land itself seems to participate in the trilogy's ritual of renewal (Mink's killing of Flem), for Mink—who had felt himself owned by it (*M*, 91) and had come to fear it (*M*, 402–407)—at last finds peace and freedom within it (*M*, 434–35). Mink's essential spatiality suggests that he could never be a narrator in any traditional sense. His dominant characteristic from the first is an indifference, even an obliviousness, to time, an expansive patience that sits in ambush for Houston for "he couldn't remember how many days it had been," and then wishes "there had only been time, space, between the roar of the gun and the impact of the shot" to explain to Houston why he had to die (*M*, 39); and that can endure thirty-eight years in prison as an instant in order to contract all time into the

19 See Robert Penn Warren, "William Faulkner," in *Three Decades*, ed. Hoffman and Vickery, 124.

166 elongated moment of Flem's death. All of this is counterpointed by events, of the largest scope, occurring at the
opposite end of the human scale—events that serve to
measure not only passing but deteriorating time: the
Spanish civil war, Munich, Poland, the fall of Paris, the
battle of Britain, the atomic bomb.

At the end, we see the town indifferent to its war
heroes, and Chick, using his uncle's imagery, asserting
that the war had created social justice and economic
plenty for all: "It was the fall of 1945 now and the knight
had run out of tourneys and dragons, the war itself had
slain them, used them up, made them obsolete" (M, 350).
This is of course wildly untrue. Only Mink, whose journey from murder to murder parallels and parodies the
world's turning from war to war, slays any dragons, and
only his act of destruction makes sense—first, because we
have seen it in a human dimension and, second, because
it is worked out as purposeful rather than chaotic: a halt-
ing but single-minded rediscovery of time and space as
Mink moves with ceremonial inexorability out of the
timeless aridity of Parchman, through the modern urban
wasteland of Memphis, through the gaudy veneer of Jefferson and its decadent mansion, and finally back to
Frenchman's Bend and the land and cessation from time
and motion. Visiting Europe in the summer of 1939,
Chick saw "a kind of composed and collected hysteria"
(M, 208); in contrast, Mink and Jefferson enact a con-
trolled ritual of Greeklike necessity. And it completes the
cycle and renews the world so that, regardless of what
happens elsewhere, Frenchman's Bend and Jefferson are
able to go on. Brooks may have something like this in
mind when he says that "in this last novel of the trilogy,
Mink becomes a hero."[20]

Thus, unity and purpose do exist despite what some
have seen as the trilogy's breakdown of form. Perhaps the

20 Brooks, *William Faulkner*, 220.

central unifying device, Flem Snopes, is often discussed
as personifying this question because of the different
perspectives on him that the trilogy offers. Leslie Fiedler
notes that " in *The Town* . . . Flem, though still a comic
figure, loses the last vestiges of Faustian grandeur and
begins to be proffered as an object of pity; revealed as
impotent, and, if not chastened by the death of his never-
possessed wife, at least on the verge of sensing the empti-
ness of his triumph."[21] Howe, on the other hand, maintains
that "Faulkner has made the mistake of softening Flem,"
and he consequently indulges in some condescending rewriting. "In composing *The Mansion* Faulkner seems to
have been unwilling to face the possibility that Flem,
having reached the top of his world, might snugly remain
there, or more simply, that it would make for a better
novel to let him remain there. . . . By the time Faulkner
came to completing *The Mansion*, he seems to have felt
a strong need to destroy Flem."[22] What Faulkner may or
may not have considered and rejected we will never
know, but to complain that he has not sustained the wry,
comic note of *The Hamlet* throughout all of the trilogy
is to condemn him for not writing the work we anticipated, and to fail to read the one he *has* written. Fiedler's
view of Flem seems to me far more incisive and apropos:
"The most abiding creation of Faulkner is the Snopes
family, especially Flem Snopes, that modern, American,
bourgeois, ridiculous version of Faust."[23]

Faulkner himself makes it clear that he knows what he
is doing, and that in fact he too dislikes the change in
Flem. He has a grudging admiration for Flem "until he
was bitten by the bug to be respectable, and then he let me
down." He can feel pity for Thomas Sutpen but none for
Flem. "I never did feel sorry for him any more than one

21 Leslie Fiedler, *Love and Death in the American Novel* (Cleveland and
New York: Meridian Books, 1962), 447.
22 Howe, *William Faulkner*, 289.
23 Leslie Fiedler, *Waiting for the End* (New York: Delta, 1965), 10.

168 feels sorry for anyone who is ridden with an ambition or demon as base as simple vanity and rapacity and greed. I think that you can be ridden by a demon, but let it be a good demon, let it be a splendid demon, even if it is a demon, and his was a petty demon. So I don't feel sorry for Flem for that reason" (*F in U*, 33, 80, 120). The intentional fallacy, of course, proves nothing either way, but it does suggest the absurdity of a reading grounded in Faulkner's putative psychological phobias.

If we read *The Hamlet* with care, we will see that even there Flem is not the "marvellous monster" Howe discerns and whose lack he deplores in the subsequent books of the trilogy. Even in that early book, little is monstrous about Flem; rather, monstrosity resides largely in the panic-filled responses others make to him. Jody's is typical; his intense fear of Flem, out of all proportion to the implicit threat of a burnt barn, is sufficient to set Flem's career in motion. Similarly, the likelihood of Flem's duping them with the spotted horses seems to impel the townspeople into mass self-sacrifices in the spirit of public confessions at Russian show trials (as graphically depicted, for instance, in Orwell's *Animal Farm*). Henry Armstid, for one, is a pitiful fool before his encounter with Flem reduces him to a pitiable madman. Flem is not so much demonic, then, as he is demonized by timorous and insecure men who cannot deal with anything even vaguely resembling the forcefulness of unscrupulous and ruthless determination.

The clearest example of this reaction is Ratliff's hyperbolic nightmare vision of Flem taking over hell (*H*, 151–55). Occurring as it does early in Flem's rise, it demonstrates that Ratliff, as we might expect, sees the danger before anyone else. Fiedler says, "The voice of reason in the novel belongs to the sewing-machine salesman, Ratliffe [*sic*], who speaks for Faulkner more directly than any other character in *The Hamlet*; but it is Ratliffe who dreams, or perhaps, more properly, has a vision of Flem's

Descent into Hell."[24] "Actively" knowing better, Ratliff
nonetheless succumbs to the temptations Flem embodies—
not, it should be noted, to an overwhelming force but to
something far more treacherous: an uncamouflaged trap,
which Flem's victims, as Ratliff says over and over again,
compete for the privilege of entering: "I reckon there aint
nothing under the sun or in Frenchman's Bend neither
that can keep you folks from giving Flem Snopes and that
Texas man your money" (*H*, 282); "I never made them
Snopeses and I never made the folks that cant wait to bare
their backsides to them" (*H*, 326). Certainly, Flem, taking
advantage of every opportunity, is evil, but his is not a
supernatural imposition that overwhelms the good man's
defenses. It is the perverse and self-willed blindness of all
the others (with rare exception: Mrs. Littlejohn, Uncle
Dick Bolivar) that represents the real villainy even in *The
Hamlet*. Of course, it is Flem who brings the spotted
horses and seeds the Old Frenchman place, yet his function seems to be less the active creation of evil than the
comparatively passive reaping of the inevitable fruits of
human folly. Ratliff himself is the climactic example as
he struggles for three days to suppress what he realizes
from the first about Eustace Grimm's appearance in Frenchman's Bend (*H*, 355–67).

Yet Ratliff succumbs only once in the entire trilogy,
and the experience serves as a valuable moral lesson for
him. Thereafter, Ratliff remains alive to the very real and
grave dangers Flem represents; but he also both tries to
aid Flem's victims as best he can and tends to humanize
Flem. It is thus ironic that Gavin appoints Ratliff to watch
and fight Snopesism as he goes off to war—Ratliff was
there first, equated Flem with evil, and, having been
burned, has moved beyond a purely negative response.
Ratliff subsequently is most consistent in seeing Flem as
merely evil—something smaller but more deadly because

24 Fiedler, *Love and Death*, 477.

170 it is as much internal as external, insidious, unconquera-
ble because human, very much a part of ourselves ("one
of us" Conrad's Marlow would have said), the part Ratliff
calls "nothing but jest another Snopes."

Flem, then, is not simply and unequivocally condemned even in and by *The Hamlet*—despite his being
praised only by those we despise even more (like Lump).
His motion is real and consistent, even though it is defined more by the stages (social, economic, communal) he
occupies in acquiring status and possessions than by
frontal action. But as we are constantly reminded, such
progress is not inevitable—except in the sense that others
persist in perversely creating the moral vacuum into
which nature seems to thrust this apparently ironic but
actually most appropriately named of all Snopeses. For
all the dynamics of motion others read into him, his is the
phlegm of indolence and apathy; he cannot spit it out—
and by *The Mansion* he stops trying. From the moment of
his initial, passive appearance to the "frozen moment" of
his death, he embodies the qualities implicit in his name:
"want of excitability or enthusiasm; coldness, dullness,
sluggishness, apathy; coolness, calmness, self-possession,
evenness of temper" (*New English Dictionary*). He displays a laconic passivity throughout: in Varner's store, at
the corral, selling the Old Frenchman place to Ratliff, in
The Hamlet; paying for the brass fittings, occupying res-
taurant, power plant, and bank, allowing Linda to leave,
in *The Town*; inhabiting De Spain's role, going with Linda
for whiskey, accepting his death, in *The Mansion*. The few
times he does act are memorable because they are rare and
because, while they reveal him as purposeful and evil,
they are too small and trivial to sustain the notion of
subhuman monstrosity: the scornful five cents worth of
candy for Mrs. Armstid (*after* Armstid had insisted on
losing his money), the planting of liquor in "Atelier Monty"
(after Montgomery Ward had already been arrested), the
summoning of Varner over Eula's adultery (after he and

everyone else had tacitly sanctioned it for eighteen years), and so on.

Before he dries up and dies in the shell that is his mansion and himself, Flem interrelates the endings of *The Hamlet* and *The Town* by spitting, in contempt and farewell, at those he has used and superseded. *The Hamlet* ends with Flem spitting as he passes beyond Henry Armstid's frenzied avarice and Frenchman's Bend's narrow confines. Flem takes the earth goddess Eula and, trailing clouds of Snopeses, goes on to richer fields in Jefferson. Near the end of *The Town*, Flem similarly spits in farewell to Eula—whose death has brought him power, status, respectability (symbolized, respectively, by the bank presidency, De Spain's house, and deaconship in the Baptist Church)—and, having dissipated all those clouds of Snopeses, now sends Linda off as well. Flem's characteristic spitting gesture is as expressive of the situation as is, at the other end of the human spectrum, such an act of homage and expiation as Aufidius' royal funeral for *his* victim, Coriolanus. Flem displays utter contempt for the unending, willful folly of men—and women too if we recall the parallel gesture Mrs. Armstid receives as she comes—obsequiously, grayly, impotently—to beg for the return of her money. And who is to deny Flem his scorn when even such as Ratliff and Bookwright are self-seduced to the folly of greed?

Unlike *The Hamlet*, however, *The Town* contains an additional episode beyond the spitting, that of Byron's four wild children. Ratliff tells us that their departure signifies "the end of a erea.... The last and final end of Snopes out-and-out unvarnished behavior in Jefferson, if that's what I'm trying to say" (*T*, 370). But just as Ratliff's folly at the end of *The Hamlet* opens Jefferson up to Flem, his equally deluded comment at the end of *The Town* should forewarn us of Snopesism yet to come in *The Mansion*: the "unvarnished behavior" of Clarence and Orestes, Mink's murder of Flem.

172   Flem succeeds in ridding himself and Jefferson of Byron's children without any significant cost, but the incident implies that, despite Flem's efforts throughout *The
Town* and Ratliff's mistaken comment at its end,
Snopesism is always with us. Flem's lofty isolation at the
end of *The Town* and throughout much of *The Mansion* is
not that of a deity (or devil), but that, like Shakespeare's
Richard III and Macbeth, of the dynamic impeller of
human action who cannot escape the consequences of the
evil he has committed almost as a casual by-product of
setting events in motion. Events and consequences remain with Flem as with Macbeth: they catch up to him,
they destroy him in the end. Flem is, after all, impotent in
more than one sense, and Eula is extraordinarily insightful when, in her last comment on him (and one of the few
she ever makes about him), she warns Gavin—and us:
"You've got to be careful or you'll have to pity him. You'll
have to. He couldn't bear that, and it's no use to hurt
people if you don't get anything for it" (*T*, 331). What
Eula tells us (and who has more right?) is that Flem is a
person—a striking, perhaps even exciting, notion! More-
over, as a person he deserves not to be hurt gratuitously—
not even when it's easy and obvious and feels good. This
does not, I think mitigate or trivialize Flem's evil, but it does
humanize it and afford an understandable context and
perspective. And this, if we look back over the trilogy,
emerges as one of Ratliff's main functions all along; for
despite the innumerable references to the animalism and
mechanical relentlessness of Snopesism, Ratliff (an in-
ductionist concerned with people, the ongoingness of day-
to-day life) provides us with understandable human motivation for what often seems totally inexplicable (because
not adhering to a priori assumptions) to deductive roman-
tics like Gavin.

Flem's death near the end of the trilogy effectively
completes Faulkner's pattern—and Howe's objection to
that event makes no more sense than would decrying the

neatness of, say, Macbeth's end. In one sense, Flem's death "closes" the novel, terminates the at-first mounting momentum of Flem's career and the subsequent contraction into the mansion. It is the ritualistic fulfillment of a revenge cycle, of a tragic progress; and yet it also occurs because, through *The Town* and *The Mansion*, Flem has been reduced to (or revealed to be at) the level of one who *can* die. Warren Beck puts it this way: "The impasse at which Flem has arrived illustrates him as a flat character but also contributes to his representativeness of all those whose suggestions can brave it out only so long as their victims shrink from retaliating with equal force. And that the fellow who seemed unbeatable has come to the point where he cannot even spit marks the plainest of finalities." [25]

But the novel is also "open" (as we should expect from a multi-narrative structure); Snopesism continues in all its multifarious forms: the murderous Mink heads west (literally or figuratively), perhaps to meet up with the wild, small-minded, thievish Byron: there remain the idiot Ike, Montgomery Ward the pornographer (this time in the flesh), I. O. the garrulous fool, Wat the carpenter, Wall the honest and successful grocer, and so on. This is far from the monolithic picture of Snopesism that (given only *The Hamlet*) we might have expected to end up with. It is in fact a fair sampling of the human spectrum.

In consequence, the Snopes trilogy seeks its unity against the grain of univocality, monolithic character, singleness of purpose and vision. None of its unities or movements is simple or simply directed. The novel moves forward, backward, and sideways in time; expands spatially from Frenchman's Bend to Jefferson, then contracts into Flem's parody of Monticello, and yet simultaneously comes to encompass a realm of events far beyond Mississippi. Its characters (Flem most notably, but

25 Beck, *Man in Motion*, 91.

174 Eula, Linda, and others as well) exhibit what Lawrence calls allotropic states, not the "old stable ego of character," but shifting realities that alter with the perceiver's location in time and space.[26] Further, the structures and tonal purposes of the trilogy's three parts, though they often seem askew of each other, suggest an expanding gyre of action and concern. Certainly, *The Hamlet* is the tightest and most neatly compacted of the three, but the world of Frenchman's Bend is a constricted one, one bounded by an essentially myopic vision. Thus the single viewpoint can encompass it with relative ease, and Ratliff's voice, for all its incisiveness, is as typical of Frenchman's Bend as it is uniquely his own. Jefferson is a larger, more complex world, as revealed, for instance, in the simultaneous acceptance and condemnation of Eula and De Spain, a "blend of censoriousness and indifference"[27]— followed by a tacit rewriting of eighteen years of history when Flem finally forces public acknowledgment of what the town had helped keep unexaminedly private, had in fact sanctioned. And finally, since Jefferson has been invaded not only by Flem and Snopesism but, through Gavin and Chick, by Harvard and Europe as well, *the Mansion* is the loosest and most sprawling of the trilogy because, among other things, it documents the increasing chaos of the world at large.

The greatest structural problem in *The Mansion* (perhaps in the entire trilogy) concerns Ratliff's long discursive summarizing of the past and recapitulation of the momentarily quiescent present, "a kind of Snopes doldrum" (*M*, 152), in chapters 6 and 7. What is the point of this section that adds little to what we already know from *The Hamlet* and *The Town*? For one thing, we are now made to see events, if not clear, then at least whole, from a

26 D. H. Lawrence, letter to Edward Garnett, quoted in Walter Allen, *The English Novel* (London: Penguin Books, 1963), 361. Allen adds this crucial reminder: "Any method of character-creation is a convention."

27 Beck, *Man in Motion*, 106.

single viewpoint. And in a world of anarchic larger
events this represents an affirmation of the individual
moral perspective that, among other things, allows not
only for Ratliff's subsequent elimination of Clarence
Snopes from the Senate race, but also for the relevance
and validity of his unique tall-tale way of narrating it.[28]
Ratliff's view is not entirely "clear" because he is neither
omniscient nor, ultimately, multifarious. In some ways he
knows less than we: he has not read *The Hamlet* and *The
Town* but only experienced their reality. He must sometimes "presume on a little more than jest evidence" (*M*,
139)—accurately enough when he imagines Eula asking
Gavin to marry Linda, inaccurately when he assumes that
Linda, in her senior year of high school, is avoiding Gavin
rather than vice versa. In this section, then, Ratliff displays the strengths and weaknesses—and above all, the
human significance—of his own intuitive faculties; in
addition, he offers choric commentary on the complex of
events that seems equally to fascinate all the inhabitants
of Frenchman's Bend and Jefferson. Given the opportunity, each could presumably tell a similar tale, though
doubtless with less good humor, articulateness, and
moral strength.

But most importantly, Ratliff's circuitous narration not
only reconstructs the past and helps to unify the trilogy, it
actively, organically (if momentarily) precludes the present by suspending the action which frames and structures
The Mansion: Mink's journey from Parchman to Jefferson.
The journey itself is framed by the atemporality of Mink's
life in prison and the "frozen moment" of Flem's death;

---

28 Howe gets into some difficulty when he takes Ratliff's anecdote literally
and maintains that its country humor clashes tonally with the real moral
danger that Snopesism represents. But such a view makes a number of assumptions whose invalidity I have tried to demonstrate: that Snopesism is
monolithic and simply external, that it can be confronted and defeated only by
heroic actions, that, in fact, it really *can* be defeated and eliminated, etc. See
also Brooks (pp. 234–35) for a reading of the Clarence episode that effectively
undercuts Howe's position.

176 but it gains ritual and archetypal reverberations from Ratliff's usurpation of time. Mink's journey is, among other
things, an attempt to rediscover (and therefore re-create)
time and space, but while Ratliff occupies front and
center, time is stayed. In a sense, this most moral of men
weds his two functions as teller and participant as he
"narratively acts" to forestall the moment when Mink—
freed from the timeless aridity of Parchman before Ratliff
started speaking of the past, and then freed from Ratliff's
atemporal verbiage—can move out of the past and the
verbiage long enough to shoot Flem and thus complete
his own cycle of alienation from and reunion with the
soil, and to end the book.

But no more than Snopesism is Ratliff (or Gavin or
Chick) defeated in the end—and not because either he or
his wisdom transcends the human, the immediate, but
because the opposite is true. Gavin, for one, had rejected
an ethical pattern in the rise and fall of Flem Snopes, but
as Beck insists, "Stevens's statement that 'There aren't
any morals' scarcely denies morality, for he goes on to say
people do the 'best' they can." [29] Ratliff's position is the
converse of Gavin's: for all his attempt to point a moral,
Ratliff reminds us in the end that there are no ends, no
close to the comic agony of the human cycle. Ratliff's
wisdom is real and profound not because it is oth-
erworldly but because, partaking of the intensely immediate, it can live in the most human of gestures: "Gentle and tender as a woman, Ratliff opened the car door for
Stevens to get in" (M, 433). Such a gesture symbolizes a
kind of paradoxical transcendence (the kind that never
gets off the ground), the nearest thing to omniscience in
the perspective of human mortality, and in that sense the
only kind we need. It is exactly that sort of "active" wisdom for which no disembodied "omniscient" narrator—
no matter how multifarious the roles he plays—could

29 Beck, *Man in Motion*, 116.

ever find proper expression. Ratliff never becomes a multifarious narrator because—as both teller and doer—he
remains complexly and utterly alive to the dualism that is
himself and all men.

Thus when, a quarter of the way into *The Mansion*, Ratliff offers us his version of Eula's deflowering, we know
(as he does) that it is more vital, more meaningful, than
that of the multifarious narrator who prefaces his account
with "Nobody ever knew exactly what happened" (*H*,
139–41). Similarly, though to a lesser degree, our sympathetic identification with Gavin and Chick ensures that,
for all their failings, we can never entirely view them as
objects, as simply judgable, as *other*. The multifarious
narrator of *The Mansion* seems to be attempting to regain
something of the high degree of authoritativeness he expressed in *The Hamlet*, when he had center stage pretty
much to himself. But too much has happened in the
interim to allow us to partake unequivocally of the
elegiac lyricism that (paralleling the panoramic vision of
the trilogy's opening) he offers at the end of the trilogy.
Mink's heading west, while it may link him with the im-
mortals for the narrator, doesn't really change anything
for us who—like Ratliff, Gavin, and Chick—remain behind, neither disembodied nor anonymous. We grant the
narrator, therefore, not the abstract omniscience his predecessors have claimed, but a unique impressionism of his
own. Instead of transcending our prismatic vision, he has
come to claim a facet for his own. Fortunately, the prism
itself is endlessly expandable—each additional viewer
brings yet another side to it—and this new presence
among us adds his own to the sum of understanding. We
should welcome him as "one of us."

Philip Young, Preface to *The Nick Adams Stories*

In this arrangement Nick Adams, who for a long time was not widely recognized as a consistent character at all, emerges clearly as the first in a long line of Hemingway's fictional selves. Later versions, from Jake Barnes and Frederic Henry to Richard Cantwell and Thomas Hudson, were all to have behind them part of Nick's history, and, correspondingly, part of Hemingway's.

Joseph Heller, *Something Happened*

New people are hatching inside my head always, whether I want them to or not, and become permanent residents the moment I take note of them. We are often at cross purposes.

Walt Whitman, "Song of Myself"

Do I contradict myself?
Very well then, I contradict myself,
(I am large, I contain multitudes).

6

Epilogue: Roles, Selves, and Multivalence

As I indicated in Chapter One, the subtitle for this book, "The Moral Quality of Form," comes from an essay on William Golding by Frank Kermode. Kermode is discussing the fact that the most unbearable subject and thought may become acceptable, even pleasurable, when "given the virtue of form," for to make, to shape, to posit is to affirm, to imply or assert a consciousness transcending what it seems locked into. To write passionately about the depraved, corrupt, or horrific (like Nabokov in *Lolita*, or William Goldman in his chilling *No Way to Treat a Lady*, or Fowles in *The Collector*, or even as de Sade does) is not to be monomaniacally obsessed, but rather to attempt to contextualize these negatives through ordering, juxtaposing, establishing perspectives.

There is, I think, a fundamental sense in which any creative gesture is an act of faith, of affirmation. Picasso's *Guernica*, the great statue *Despair* in the center of the rebuilt city of Rotterdam, the constricted plays of Sartre and Beckett are not the embodiments of hopelessness they may at first seem (because they depict or dramatize it), but of something approaching its opposite. They are not the aesthetic equivalents of the nihilist's bomb throwing, but an answer or alternative. As W.H. Auden puts it, "existentialists declare / That they are in complete despair, / Yet go on writing." Henry Miller speaks of *Tropic of Cancer* as a "gob of spit" rather than a book and looks forward to a world so ordered as to render artists redundant. But in the meantime, he projects, shapes, prunes—plays at both god and man as though there were value in such playing, and the wonder is that there is, even if only in the playing, even if only so long as the playing lasts. But player and playing are no more separable than Yeats's dancer and dance: this is the lesson Hamlet learns when he attempts to substitute playing for action and discovers that they are synonymous—even in their multiple meanings and puns. Yet to act (in both senses) is also to make, to achieve, to affirm—to assert a moral and aesthetic order (as do all of Shakespeare's tragedies) out of the clash and destruction of mighty opposites.

It is useful to remind ourselves that a work of art (or craft) is always broader than its ostensible subject matter and always richer than the perspectives on that subject matter that it actually depicts. And this is especially true, of course, for the fiction I have called modern and multivalent. It is also true for this book.

With this in mind, I would like to suggest that a very different slant could be given this study by an alteration in what is probably its basic metaphor: instead of "roles" one might use "selves." A recapitulation of the use of the term *roles* might be useful at this point, and will lead to a brief discussion of an alternative approach.

Throughout this book I have often used the word *roles* to suggest multiplicity. Characters, narrators, implied authors, the writers themselves, and readers as well, all appear (perceive and are perceived) in a variety of guises—a variety at times so complex that certain manifestations would seem to exclude some of the others, and yet they do not. The point of some modern novels, in fact, is to show that the apparent exclusion of possibilities is *only* apparent, and we are thus forced into a reexamination of the whole concept of possibilities. For example, a character like Fowles's Nicholas Urfe in *The Magus* shifts from playing the role of searcher (or subject) to that of victim (or object). Protean characters like Melville's Confidence Man, Woolf's Orlando, and Mann's Felix Krull may appear manifesting various sexes, ages, personalities, depths, values, and the like. Durrell's Justine "can play, in succession, the roles of *femme fatale* and sex goddess, of a rather bourgeois adulteress, of Mata Hari, of an Arab mendicant—without altering in essence."[1] Faulkner's characters—like Thomas Sutpen and Eula and Flem Snopes—are often mythologized, perceived as archetypes, and, finding such roles congenial, then play them with consummate skill for a time. Cary's Nina both hates lies and manipulates facts unendingly; Chester is a brilliant politician and a pedantic crackpot; Jim Latter asserts the validity of honesty and hard work and runs from

---

1 Alan Warren Friedman, *Lawrence Durrell and "The Alexandria Quartet": Art for Love's Sake* (Norman: University of Oklahoma Press, 1970), 177.

responsibility and destroys what he values—for all of 181
Cary's narrators seem necessarily and simultaneously to
be self-deceiving perceivers and self-perceiving de-
ceivers.

Narrators may also play roles that appear at cross purposes with themselves. Dramatized narrators may begin
as involved characters and then adopt the perspective of
distanced artists (like Faulkner's Ratliff), or as removed
commentators subsequently forced to enter the action
fully (like Conrad's Marlow and Camus' Rieux). Undramatized narrators like those in *Lord Jim*, the Snopes trilogy,
Parade's End, and *Sword of Honour* offer a broad context
within which to take the measure of human action, but
also at times enter vicariously into the acts and actions
they depict. They also both sympathize and denigrate,
seem determined both to take their protagonists at face
value and yet to trivialize them. And in the process they
force their readers similarly to adopt wildly contradictory
stances. Further, multifarious narrators are often synonymous with their implied authors, for they commonly
share breadth of outlook and purpose, a controlling and
shaping function and impulse. But in modern fiction, implied authors seem to be playing not only on us but also
against narrative personae that they both project and deny.
Thus, the third-person-subjective voice in Joyce's *Portrait*
seems at first to be that of the book's implied author; later
we come to see that it is as much victim of the implied
author's irony as is Stephen. More obviously, personal
narrators like Ford's Dowell and Nabokov's Humbert depict self-evaluations that they presume to share with their
implied authors; but the burden of their narratives is to
show us—often without realizing it—that they do not.
Even occasional multifarious narrators, like Forster's in
Passage to India, may attempt to speak for their implied
authors while saying exactly the opposite of what seems to
be the implied author's position. Similarly, Faulkner's
multifarious narrator in the trilogy seems often to identify

182 with Gavin Stevens, and yet he frames Gavin's long, introspective, and sympathetically narrated chapter with a distancing voice—the voice of a mockingbird.

D. H. Lawrence's notion of allotropic states of character
is a metaphor borrowed from chemistry. Carbon, for instance, occurs in nature in an astounding variety of
forms—from diamonds (the hardest substance known) to
graphite (a soft lubricant). More than 500,000 compounds
of carbon have been identified, and it serves as focus for
the entire complex science of organic chemistry. Lawrence's metaphor implies an unchanging core—like
carbon—and a variety of manifestations dependent on
time, place, and circumstance. This is the metaphor of
roles or personae, a metaphor that sociologists tend to
find congenial. But another and equally valid
metaphor—that of selves—seems to deny a consistent
core and, in language psychologists often employ, implies that each manifestation is the projection of its own
unique inner reality.

Is there a single Henry Miller who plays contradictory
roles—(1) I have "made a silent compact with myself not
to change a line of what I write," (2) "Every page of the
original version I went over in pen and ink, hatching and
criss-crossing until it looked like a Chinese puzzle"—
inspired by different impulses on different occasions? Or
are there multiple Henry Millers, themselves perhaps
contradictory, with each persona an accurate projection
of an otherwise unknown self? Such questions are provoked, but not answered, by Miller's blithely emitting
contrarieties as he goes—for example, that life and art
both are and are not coextensive. When Miller speaks of
something as both true and a lie, it is impossible to say
whether he is attempting to mediate between two warring
selves or is simply adopting a perverse semanticist as
persona. Probably he is doing both and our categories
will not hold. Similarly a demonized Flem Snopes finds
that monstrosity confirms and conforms to a particular
sense of self, so he plays the role thrust upon him and

plays it well. Then he is, as Faulkner puts it, bitten by the 183
bug respectability, and he plays at being De Spain for a
time. Finally, another self manifests another role—
mortal, passive, victim—and the demonizing Flem and
the De Spain Flem yield to a Flem who not only can die
but can be murdered.

One might suggest that the concept of roles is an objectification of the concept of self, and the concept of selves
an internalizing of the concept of roles: twin concepts,
then, two sides of the same coin. Since both of these notions are metaphors, ways of labeling the everyday mystery of the world we inhabit, I see nothing to be gained by
a forced choice between them. We may, I think, opt for
either, or both, as suits our needs of the moment. I have
spoken primarily of roles in this book, but the metaphor
of selves would, in many cases, serve equally well. Thus,
the critic too creates a role, projects a self. The two processes are at odds and they are one: coextensive and
mutually exclusive, they represent the vacuum that nature abhors and two different things occupying the same
space at the same time. With such reality who needs illusion? A premodern novelist who is yet one of the first
moderns suggests a synthesis; Hardy writes: "I am more
than ever convinced that persons are successively various
persons, according as each special strand in their characters is brought uppermost by circumstances."[2] "Various
persons," yet each manifests a strand of the same basic
character. Thus, the final determination of which of these
two concepts—roles or selves—is correct remains as
problematical and baffling as determining which of several appealing moral views is valid. The two concepts
that are one reflect and embody the moral qualities the
world and we would impose on each other. We and the
world are richer for yet one more validation of multivalence.

2 Thomas Hardy, *The Early Life of Thomas Hardy 1840–1891* (New York:
Macmillan, 1928), 301.

Appendix: A Galaxy of Multivolume Narration

In all sections, works are listed chronologically: in sections I–IV this is determined by initial publication of the first volume of a multivolume series. Dates cited are (1) one-volume or uniform editions (where such exist), (2) first book publication (except for stories), (3) first publication in English (for works written in other languages). Multivolume examples are followed by single-volume analogues.

Some of the works listed may seem doubtfully placed—or even doubtfully included. But given the sometime amorphous quality of narrative types and genres, subjective considerations are bound to play a role. Consequently, the novels are placed not where they indubitably belong, but where they seem to me to belong. Beyond that, I can only claim my obvious responsibility: that each placing represents a critical judgment.

I. Basic Forms

Participant Narration

Protagonist Narration: Chronological

Colette, *Claudine* (1949, 1956–1960): 4 novels (1900–1903, 1930–1935).

Siegfried Sassoon, *The Complete Memoirs of George Sherston* (1937): 3 novels (1928–1936).

186 Robert Graves, *I, Claudius* (1934), *Claudius the God* (1934); includes historical appendix.

Henry Miller, *Tropics* trilogy: *Tropic of Cancer* (1934), *Black Spring* (1936), *Tropic of Capricorn* (1939).

Pamela Hansford Johnson, Helena trilogy: *Too Dear for My Possessing* (1940), *An Avenue of Stone* (1947), *A Summer to Decide* (1948).

C. P. Snow, *Strangers and Brothers*: 11 novels (1940–1970).

Henry Miller, *The Rosy Crucifixion*: trilogy (1949–1960).

William Cooper, *Scenes from Life* (1961): trilogy (1950–1961; second novel never published).

Anthony Powell, *A Dance to the Music of Time*: 12 novels (1951–1976).

John Braine, *Room at the Top* (1957), *Life at the Top* (1962).

Mary Renault, *The King Must Die* (1958), *The Bull from the Sea* (1962).

Jan Cremer, *I, Jan Cremer* (1964, 1965), *Jan Cremer 2* (1966, 1969).

Chaim Potok, *The Chosen* (1967), *The Promise* (1969).

Philip Callow, *Another Flesh*: trilogy (1968–1971).

Brian W. Aldiss, Horatio Stubbs quartet (3 novels to date): *The Hand-Reared Boy* (1970), *A Soldier Erect* (1971), *A Rude Awakening* (1978).

Jonathan Swift, *Gulliver's Travels* (1726)

Henry James, *The Aspern Papers* (1888)

John Barth, *The Floating Opera* (1956)

Alain Robbe-Grillet, *Jealousy* (1957, 1959)

Anthony Burgess, *A Clockwork Orange* (1962)

John Fowles, *The Magus* (1966)

John Gardner, *Grendel* (1971)

Protagonist Narration: Retrospective

Marcel Proust, *Remembrance of Things Past* (1913–1927, 1934): 7 novels (1913–1927, 1922–1931).

Italo Svevo, *Confessions of Zeno* (1923, 1930; Preface by secondary character), *Further Confessions of Zeno* (1929–1949, 1969; includes a play).

J. D. Salinger, Glass family saga (8 stories to date): "Down at the Dinghy," "A Perfect Day for Bananafish," "Uncle Wiggily in Connecticut," in *Nine Stories* (1953), *Franny and Zooey*

A Galaxy of Multivolume Narration

(1961), *Raise High the Roof Beam, Carpenters and* 187
Seymour, an Introduction (1963), and "Hapworth 16,
1924" (*New Yorker*, June 19, 1965).
Lawrence Durrell, *The Revolt of Aphrodite*: 2 novels (1968–
1970).

Laurence Sterne, *Tristram Shandy* (1759–1767)
Charles Dickens, *Great Expectations* (1860–1861)
Ford Madox Ford, *The Good Soldier* (1915)
Vladimir Nabokov, *Despair* (1934, 1937)
Albert Camus, *The Plague* (1947)
Thomas Mann, *Confessions of Felix Krull, Confidence Man*
(1954, 1958)
Vladimir Nabokov, *Lolita* (1955)
Samuel Beckett, *How It Is* (1961, 1964)
William Styron, *The Confessions of Nat Turner* (1967)

Secondary Character Narration

Upton Sinclair, *Sylvia* (1913), *Sylvia's Marriage* (1914).
Christopher Isherwood, Berlin series: *Mr. Norris Changes
Trains* (1935), *Sally Bowles* (1937), *Goodbye to Berlin*
(1939)
Langston Hughes, Simple series: 4 novels (1950–1965), plus
The Best of Simple (a collection, 1961).
Andre Gide, *The Immoralist* (1902, 1930)
Joseph Conrad, *Under Western Eyes* (1911)
F. Scott Fitzgerald, *The Great Gatsby* (1925)
Claude Houghton [Oldfield], *I Am Jonathan Scrivener* (1930)
Thomas Mann, *Doctor Faustus: The Life of the German Com-
poser Adrian Leverkuhn As Told by a Friend* (1947, 1948)
Ken Kesey, *One Flew Over the Cuckoo's Nest* (1962)
Arthur A. Cohen, *In the Days of Simon Stern* (1972)

Multiple Character Narration

Joyce Cary, first trilogy (1958): *Herself Surprised* (1941), *To Be
a Pilgrim* (1942), *The Horse's Mouth* (1944).
Samuel Beckett, trilogy (1959): *Molloy* (1951, 1955), *Malone
Dies* (1951, 1956), *The Unnamable* (1953, 1958).
Joyce Cary, second trilogy: *Prisoner of Grace* (1952), *Except the
Lord* (1953), *Not Honour More* (1955).

188 Robert Gover, Kitten trilogy: *One Hundred Dollar Misun-derstanding* (1962), *Here Goes Kitten* (1964), *J. C. Saves* (1968).

Gore Vidal, *Myra Breckenridge* (1968), *Myron* (1974).

Robertson Davies, Deptford trilogy: *Fifth Business* (1970), *The Manticore* (1972), *World of Wonders* (1975).

John Hawkes, triad: *The Blood Oranges* (1971), *Death, Sleep and the Traveler* (1974), *Travesty* (1976).

Samuel Richardson, *Clarissa* (1747–1748)
Emily Bronte, *Wuthering Heights* (1847)
Wilkie Collins, *The Woman in White* (1860)
Graham Greene, *The End of the Affair* (1951)
John Fowles, *The Collector* (1963)
Larry McMurtry, *Leaving Cheyenne* (1963)
William Eastlake, *Castle Keep* (1965)
John Barth, *Giles Goat-Boy* (1966)
Mervyn Jones, *John and Mary* (1967)
B. S. Johnson, *House Mother Normal* (1971)
Nicholas Mosley, *Natalie Natalia* (1971)
Iris Murdoch, *The Black Prince* (1973)

Multifarious Narration

Single Protagonist

Joseph Conrad, Lingard trilogy: *Almayer's Folly* (1895), *An Outcast of the Islands* (1896), *The Rescue* (1920).

Ford Madox Ford, *The Fifth Queen* (1962): trilogy (1906–1908).

Henry Williamson, *The Flax of Dream*: tetralogy (1921–1928) plus *The Star-born* (1933).

Ernest Raymond, *Daphne Bruno* (1925), *The Fulfillment of Daphne Bruno* (1926).

Thomas Mann, *Joseph and His Brothers* (1948): tetralogy (1933–1943, 1934–1944).

Compton Mackenzie, *The Four Winds of Love*: tetralogy (1937–1944).

Upton Sinclair, *World's End*: 11 novels (1940–1953).

Margaret Irwin, *The Story of Elizabeth Tudor*: trilogy (1944–1953).

Henry Williamson, *A Chronicle of Ancient Sunlight*: 15 novels (1951–1969).

A Galaxy of Multivolume Narration

Doris Lessing, *Children of Violence*: 5 novels (1952–1969; includes appendix of fictional documents and letters).

Harry Kemelman, Rabbi series: 6 novels to date (1964–1976).

Yukio Mishima, *The Sea of Fertility*: tetralogy (1968–1971, 1972–1974).

Herman Melville, *Pierre or, The Ambiguities* (1852)
Oscar Wilde, *The Picture of Dorian Gray* (1891)
Virginia Woolf, *Jacob's Room* (1922)
Thomas Mann, *The Magic Mountain* (1924, 1927)
John Steinbeck, *Tortilla Flat* (1935)
Henry Green, *Loving* (1945)
Alain Robbe-Grillet, *The Erasers* (1953, 1964)

Several Protagonists

Arnold Bennett, *The Clayhanger Family* (1925): *Clayhanger* (1910), *Hilda Lessways* (1911), *These Twain* (1916).

Wyndham Lewis, *The Human Age*: tetralogy (1928–1955; vol. 4 unfinished).

Margaret Irwin, seventeenth-century series: tetralogy (1932–1939).

J. R. R. Tolkien, *The Hobbit* (1937), plus *Lord of the Rings* (1969): trilogy (1954–1955).

Olivia Manning, Balkan trilogy: *The Great Fortune* (1960), *The Spoilt City* (1962), *Friends and Heroes* (1965).

J. B. Priestley, *The Image Men* (1969): 2 novels (1968).

Joseph Conrad, *The Secret Agent* (1908)
E. M. Forster, *Passage to India*, (1924)
John Dos Passos, *Manhattan Transfer* (1925)
Henry Green, *Living* (1929)
John Fowles, *The French Lieutenant's Woman* (1969)
Walter Abish, *Alphabetical Africa* (1974)

Family / Social Chronicle

John Galsworthy, Forsyte Chronicles: *The Forsyte Saga* (1922): trilogy (1906–1921); *On Forsyte' Change* (1930); *A Modern Comedy* (1929): trilogy (1924–1928); *End of the Chapter* (1934): trilogy (1931–1933).

Sigrid Undset, *Kristin Lavransdatter* (1920–1922, 1963): trilogy (1966–1968, 1923–1927).

190 Roger Martin du Gard, *The Thibaults* (11 vols. in French,
1922–1940): *The Thibaults* (1939), *Summer 1914* (1941).
Mazo de la Roche, *Chronicles of the Whiteoak Family*: 16
novels (1927–1960).
Mikhail Sholokhov, *The Silent Don*: 2 novels (1928–1939,
1934–1940).
————, *Virgin Soil Upturned*: 2 novels (1941–1960, 1932–
1960).
Sholem Asch, *Three Cities, a trilogy* (?, 1933).
John Cheever, *The Wapshot Chronicle* (1957), *The Wapshot
Scandal* (1964).
R. F. Delderfield, *The Avenue*: 5 novels (1958–1969).
————, *A Horseman Riding By*: trilogy (1966–1968).
————, *The Swann Saga*: trilogy (1970–1973).
Alexander Solzhenitsyn, World War I trilogy (1 novel to date):
August 1914 (1971, 1972).
Leo Tolstoy, *War and Peace* (1963–1869, 1886)
Gabriel García Márquez, *One Hundred Years of Solitude*
(1967, 1970)

Third-Person-Subjective Narration

Univocal

Romain Rolland, *Jean Christophe* (1905–1912, 1910–1913): 3
novels (10 vols. in French: 1904–1912, 1910–1913).
Booth Tarkington, *Penrod* (1931): trilogy (1914–1929).
Dorothy Richardson, *Pilgrimage* (1967): 13 novels (1915–1967).
Compton Mackenzie, *The Adventures of Sylvia Scarlett* (1950):
two novels (1918–1919).
Colette, *Cheri* (1949, 1951): 2 novels (1920–1926, 1930–1933).
James T. Farrell, *Studs Lonigan* (1935): trilogy (1932–1935).
Ford Madox Ford, *The Rash Act* (1933), *Henry for Hugh* (1934).
James T. Farrell, Danny O'Neill series: *A World I Never Made*
(1936), *No Star Is Lost* (1938), *Father and Son* (1940), *My
Days of Anger* (1943), *The Face of Time* (1953).
————, Bernard Carr trilogy: *Bernard Clare* (1946), *The Road
Between* (1949), *Yet Other Waters* (1952).
Roger Peyrefitte, *Diplomatic Diversions* (1953, 1953), *Diplomatic Conclusions* (1954, 1954).

James T. Farrell, *A Universe of Time*: 7 novels (1963–1970).
  Henry James, *The Ambassadors* (1903)
  ———, *The Beast in the Jungle* (1903)
  Dalton Trumbo, *Johnny Got His Gun* (1939)
  Saul Bellow, *Herzog* (1967)

Multiple

Ford Madox Ford, *Parade's End* (1961): tetralogy (1924–1928).
L. P. Hartley, *Eustace and Hilda* (1958): trilogy (1944–1947).
  Gertrude Stein, *Three Lives* (1909)
  Virginia Woolf, *Mrs. Dalloway* (1925)
  Irwin Shaw, *The Young Lions* (1948)
  Nathalie Sarraute, *The Planetarium* (1959, 1961)
  Uwe Johnson, *Two Views* (1965, 1966)
  David Lodge, *The British Museum Is Falling Down* (1965)
  Paul Bowles, *Up Above the World* (1966)
  Larry McMurtry, *Moving On* (1970)
  Wilfrid Sheed, *Max Jamison* (1970)

II. HYBRID NARRATION

Multifarious Plus Participant

R. H. Mottram, *The Spanish Farm Trilogy, 1914–1918* (1927): 1924–1927.
Aldous Huxley, *Brave New World* (1932), *Brave New World Revisited* (1959; nonfiction), *Island* (1962).
Charles Nordhoff and James Hall, *The "Bounty" Trilogy* (1932–1934).
Georges Duhamel, *The Pasquier Chronicles*: 10 novels (1933–1945, 1934–1946).
James Branch Cabell, *It Happened in Florida*: trilogy (1943–1949; vol. I nonfiction, written with A. J. Hanna).
Simon Raven, *Alms for Oblivion*: 8 of 10 novels to date (1964–1972).

  Samuel Richardson, *Pamela, or Virtue Rewarded* (1740–1741)
  Joseph Conrad, *The Nigger of the "Narcissus"* (1897)
  Virginia Woolf, *The Waves* (1931)

Samuel Beckett, *Watt* (1953)
Alain Robbe-Grillet, *In the Labyrinth* (1959, 1967)
Vladimir Nabokov, *Ada, or Ardor: A Family Chronicle* (1969)
John Barth, *Chimera* (1972)
Francine Prose, *Judah the Pious* (1973)
Philip Roth, *The Great American Novel* (1973)
Kurt Vonnegut, Jr., *Breakfast of Champions* (1973)

Participant Plus Third-Person-Subjective

Peter De Vries, *Comfort Me With Apples* (1952), *The Tents of Wickedness* (1959).
Lawrence Durrell, *The Alexandria Quartet* (1962): 1957–1960.
Anthony Burgess, Enderby trilogy: *Inside Mr. Enderby* (1963), *Enderby Outside* (1968), *The Clockwork Testament, or Enderby's End* (1974).
Lawrence Durrell, *Monsieur* (1974)

Multifarious Plus Third-Person-Subjective

Theodore Dreiser, Frank Cowperwood trilogy: *The Financier* (1912), *The Titan* (1914), *The Stoic* (1947).
D. H. Lawrence, *The Rainbow* (1915), *Women in Love* (1920).
Thomas Wolfe, *Look Homeward, Angel* (1929), *Of Time and the River* (1935), *The Web and the Rock* (1939), *You Can't Go Home Again* (1940).
John Dos Passos, *U.S.A.* (1937): trilogy (1930–1936).
Pearl Buck, *House of Earth* (1935): trilogy (1931–1935).
Vardis Fisher, Idaho tetralogy: *In Tragic Life* (1932), *Passions Spin the Plot* (1934), *We Are Betrayed* (1935), *No Villain Need Be* (1936).
James Branch Cabell, *Heirs and Assigns*: trilogy (1938–1942).
John Dos Passos, *District of Columbia* (1952): trilogy (1939–1949).
Conrad Richter, Ohio trilogy: *The Trees* (1940), *The Fields* (1946), *The Town* (1950).
Jean-Paul Sartre, *The Roads to Freedom*: trilogy (1945–1949, 1947–1950).
Frederick Manfred, *Wanderlust* (1962): trilogy (1949–1951).
Evelyn Waugh, *Sword of Honour* (1965): trilogy (1952–1961).
John Updike, *Rabbit, Run* (1960), *Rabbit Redux* (1971).

A Galaxy of Multivolume Narration

Richard Hughes, *The Human Predicament*: 2 of 3 projected
   novels (1961–1973).
Edward Fisher, *The Silver Falcon*: trilogy (1962–1965).
William Goldman, *The Thing of It Is . . .* (1967), *Father's Day*
   (1971).
Jane Austen, *Emma* (1816)
Henry James, *Daisy Miller* (1878)
———, *What Maisie Knew* (1897)
Joseph Conrad, *Nostromo* (1904)
John Dos Passos, *Three Soldiers* (1921)
Virginia Woolf, *To the Lighthouse* (1927)
Vladimir Nabokov, *King, Queen, Knave* (1928, 1968)
Virginia Woolf, *Orlando* (1928)
———, *The Years* (1937)
———, *Between the Acts* (1941)
Malcolm Lowry, *Under the Volcano* (1947)
William Golding, *Lord of the Flies* (1954)
———, *The Inheritors* (1955)
———, *Pincher Martin* (1956)
Joseph Heller, *Catch-22* (1961)
Thomas Pynchon, *The Crying of Lot 49* (1966)
Nicholas Mosley, *Impossible Object* (1968)
Nathalie Sarraute, *Between Life and Death* (1968, 1969)
John Gardner, *The Sunlight Dialogues* (1972)

Participant Plus Multifarious Plus Third-Person-Subjective

Joseph Conrad, Marlovian tales (1923–1928): *Youth* (1898),
   Heart of Darkness (1899), *Lord Jim* (1900), *Chance* (1913).
James Branch Cabell, *The Biography of the Life of Manuel*
   (1927–1930); 21 vols. (1905–1924, includes vols. of short
   stories and poetry).
James Joyce, *A Portrait of the Artist as a Young Man* (1916),
   Ulysses (1922).
Hermann Broch, *The Sleepwalkers: A Trilogy* (1928–1931,
   1947).
William Faulkner, The Yoknapatawpha cycle (14 novels): *Sar-*
   toris (1929), *The Sound and the Fury* (1929), *As I Lay*
   Dying (1930), *Sanctuary* (1931), *Light in August* (1932),
   Absalom Absalom! (1936), *The Unvanquished* (1938), *The*

194   *Hamlet* (1940), *Go Down, Moses* (1942), *Intruder in the Dust* (1948), *Requiem for a Nun* (1951), *The Town* (1957), *The Mansion* (1959), *The Reivers* (1962).
Anthony Burgess, *The Long Day Wanes* (1965): trilogy (1956–1959).
Paul Scott, *The Raj Quartet* (1966–1975).

Herman Melville, *Moby-Dick* (1851)
Charles Dickens, *Bleak House* (1853)
James Joyce, *Finnegans Wake* (1939)
Juan Rulfo, *Pedro Paramo* (1955, 1959)
Peter De Vries, *Reuben, Reuben* (1956)
Brian Moore, *An Answer from Limbo* (1962)
Mario Vargas Llosa, *The Time of the Hero* (1962, 1966)
John Updike, *The Centaur* (1962)
Julio Cortázar, *Hopscotch* (1963, 1966)
Mario Vargas Llosa, *The Green House* (1966, 1968)
Donald Barthelme, *Snow White* (1967)
Joyce Carol Oates, *Do With Me What You Will* (1973)
Wilfrid Sheed, *People Will Always Be Kind* (1973)

III. PRE-TWENTIETH-CENTURY MULTIVOLUME NOVELS

Chronicle or Roman Fleuve

Wang Shih-chen [?], *The Golden Lotus*: tetralogy (17th century, 1939).
Sir Walter Scott, Waverley novels (1892): 5 novels (1814–1818).
James Fenimore Cooper, *Leather-Stocking Tales* (1850): 5 novels (1823–1841).
Honoré de Balzac, *The Human Comedy* (1855–1863, 1895–1900): *ca.* 83 novels (1829–1850).
Leopold von Sacher-Masoch, *The Heritage of Cain*: 2 of 6 projected novels (1870–1874, ?).
Alexandre Dumas, the elder, The Valois romances (?, 1893): trilogy (1843–1846, 1845–1857).
Benjamin Disraeli, trilogy (1870): *Coningsby* (1844), *Sybil* (1845), *Tancred* (1847).

Alexandre Dumas, the elder, Three Musketeers series: 5 novels
(1844–1851, 1846–1851).
———, Marie Antoinette romances: 5 novels (1846–1860, 1862–1878).
William Makepeace Thackeray, trilogy: *The History of Pendennis* (1849–1850), *The Newcomes* (1854–1855), *The Adventures of Philip* (1862).
Anthony Trollope, Barsetshire novels: 6 vols. (1855–1867).
Alexandre Dumas, the elder, Napoleon romances: trilogy (1859–1872, 1894–1897).
Anthony Trollope, Palliser novels: 6 vols. (1864–1880).
Mark Twain, Tom Sawyer series: 3 novels (1876–1896).

Counterpointed

Francois Rabelais, *Gargantua and Pantagruel* (1533–1564, 1653–1694).
Miguel de Cervantes, *Don Quixote* (1863, 1901–1903): 2 parts (1605–1615, 1612–1620).
John Bunyan, *The Pilgrim's Progress* (1780): 2 parts (1678–1681).
Daniel Defoe, *Robinson Crusoe*: 3 parts (1719–1720).
John Cleland, *Fanny Hill: Memoirs of a Woman of Pleasure* (1749), *Memoirs of a Coxcomb* (1760).
Marquis de Sade, *Justine; or, The Misfortunes of Virtue* (1787, 1953), *Juliette; or, Vice Amply Rewarded* (1797, 1958–1959).
Johann Wolfgang von Goethe, *Wilhelm Meister's Apprenticeship* (1795, 1824), *Wilhelm Meister's Travels* (1819–1821, 1824).
Stendahl [Marie-Henri Beyle], *Lucien Leuwen*: 2 novels (1837, 1951).
Thomas Hughes, *Tom Brown's Schooldays* (1857), *Tom Brown at Oxford* (1861).
Lewis Carroll, Alice books (1936): 2 novels (1866–1872).
Samuel Butler, *Erewhon* books: 2 novels (1872–1901).
Mark Twain, *The Adventures of Tom Sawyer* (1876), *The Adventures of Huckleberry Finn* (1884).
———, *A Tramp Abroad* (1880), *More Tramps Abroad* (1897).
Robert Louis Stevenson, *Kidnapped* (1886), *Catriona* (1893).

IV. SOME VARIATIONS

Fictional Manuscript

Plus Participant Narration

Gore Vidal, *Burr* (1973), *1876* (1976)

Nicholas Meyer, *The Seven-Per-Cent-Solution* (1974), *The West End Horror* (1976).

Mihail Lermontov, *A Hero of Our Time* (1840, 1854)

Mark Twain, *A Connecticut Yankee in King Arthur's Court* (1889)

Henry James, *The Turn of the Screw* (1898)

Hermann Hesse, *Steppenwolf* (1927, 1929)

Aldous Huxley, *Ape and Essence* (1949)

A. M. Klein, *The Second Scroll* (1951)

Vladimir Nabokov, *Pale Fire* (1962)

Thomas Berger, *Little Big Man* (1964)

Kurt Vonnegut, Jr., *Mother Night* (1966)

Frederick Prokosch, *The Missolonghi Manuscript* (1968)

Kurt Vonnegut, Jr., *Slaughterhouse Five* (1969)

Gore Vidal, *Two Sisters* (1970)

Peter De Vries, *Mrs. Wallop* (1970)

Philip Roth, *My Life as a Man* (1974)

Plus Multifarious Narration

George M. Fraser, *The Flashman Papers*: 5 novels to date (1969–1975).

Charles Dickens, *The Pickwick Papers* (1838)

Andre Gide, *The Counterfeiters* (1925, 1927)

James Purdy, *Cabot Wright Begins* (1964)

Plus Third-Person-Subjective

John Barth, *The Sot-Weed Factor* (1961)

THE SHORT STORY AS MULTIVALENT NOVEL

O. Henry, *The Four Million* (1902)

James Joyce, *Dubliners* (1916)

Sherwood Anderson, *Winesburg, Ohio* (1919)

A Galaxy of Multivolume Narration

Ernest Hemingway, *In Our Time* (1925)
Samuel Beckett, *More Pricks than Kicks* (1934)
F. Scott Fitzgerald, *The Pat Hobby Stories* (1962, 1940–1941)
Malcolm Lowry, *Hear Us O Lord from Heaven Thy Dwelling Place* (1961)
John Updike, *Olinger Stories* (1964)
John Barth, *Lost in the Funhouse: Fiction for Print, Tape, Live Voice* (1969)
Bernard Malamud, *Pictures of Fidelman: An Exhibition* (1969)
John Updike, *Bech: A Book* (1970)
Ernest Hemingway, *The Nick Adams Stories* (1972, 1927–1972)

THE POEM AS MULTIVALENT NOVEL

Chronicle

Dante, *The Divine Comedy* (1300–1321)
Geoffrey Chaucer, *The Canterbury Tales* (late 14th century)
Walt Whitman, *Leaves of Grass* (1855)
Robert Browning, *The Ring and the Book* (1868–1869)
Alfred, Lord Tennyson, *The Idylls of the King* (1874)
Edgar Lee Masters, *Spoon River Anthology* (1915)
Edwin Arlington Robinson, Arthurian trilogy (1917–1927)
Carl Sandburg, *The People, Yes* (1936)
Ted Hughes, *Crow* (1970)

Counterpointed

Homer, *The Iliad* and *The Odyssey* (ca. 10th century B.C.)
John Milton, *Paradise Lost* (1667), *Paradise Regained* (1671)
William Blake (1794): *Songs of Innocence* (1789), *Songs of Experience* (1794)

Bibliography

MULTIVALENT NOVELISTS ON THE ART OF FICTION

Allott, Miriam, ed. *Novelists on the Novel*. New York: Columbia University Press, 1959.

Beckett, Samuel, *Proust*. New York: Grove Press, 1931.

Block, Haskell M., and Herman Salinger, eds. *The Creative Vision: Modern European Writers on their Art*. New York: Grove Press, 1960.

Burgess, Anthony. *The Novel Now*. New York: Norton, 1967.

Cary, Joyce. *Art and Reality*. New York: Anchor Books, 1961 (1958).

Conrad, Joseph. *Joseph Conrad on Fiction*. Edited by Walter F. Wright. Lincoln: University of Nebraska Press, 1964.

Cooper, William. "Reflections on Some Aspects of the Experimental Novel." *International Literary Annual*, II (1959), 29–36.

Cowley, Malcolm, ed. *Writers at Work: The "Paris Review" Interviews*. New York: Viking, 1959; second series, intro. Van Wyck Brooks. New York: Viking, 1965.

Durrell, Lawrence. *A Key to Modern British Poetry*. Norman: University of Oklahoma Press, 1952.

Farrell, James T. "Some Observations on Naturalism, So Called, in Fiction." *Antioch Review*, X (June, 1950), 247–64.

Bibliography

200 Ford, Ford Madox. *Henry James: A Critical Study*. London: Martin Secker, 1913.

———. *Joseph Conrad: A Personal Remembrance*. London: Duckworth, 1924.

———. *The English Novel from the Earliest Days to the Death of Joseph Conrad*. London: Constable, 1930.

———. *Portraits from Life*. Chicago: Henry Regnery, 1937.

———. *Critical Writings of Ford Madox Ford*. Edited by Frank MacShane. Lincoln: University of Nebraska Press, 1964.

Gide, Andre. *Pretexts: Reflections on Literature and Morality*. Edited by Justin O'Brien. New York: Meridian, 1959.

Gwynn, Frederick L., and Joseph L. Blotner, eds. *Faulkner in the University*. Charlottesville: University of Virginia Press, 1959.

Hartley, L. P. "The Novelist's Responsibility." *Essays and Studies*, XV, n.s. (1962), 88–100.

James, Henry. *The Art of the Novel*. New York: Scribner's, 1934.

———. *The Future of the Novel: Essays on the Art of Fiction*. New York: Vintage, 1956.

Lawrence, D. H. *Selected Literary Criticism*. Edited by Anthony Beal. New York: Viking, 1956.

Proust, Marcel. *Marcel Proust on Art and Literature, 1896–1919*. Translated by Sylvia Townsend Warner. New York: Meridian, 1958.

Robbe-Grillet, Alain. *For a New Novel: Essays on Fiction*. Translated by Richard Harris. New York: Grove Press, 1965.

Sarraute, Nathalie. *The Age of Suspicion: Essays on the Novel*. Translated by Maria Jolas. New York: G. Braziller, 1963.

Sartre, Jean-Paul. *What is Literature?* Translated by Bernard Frechtman. New York: Philosophical Library, 1949.

Snow, C. P. "Science, Politics, and the Novelist." *Kenyon Review*, XXIII (1961), 1–17.

Stein, Gertrude. *Narration*. Chicago: University of Chicago Press, 1935.

Wolfe, Thomas. *The Story of a Novel*. New York: Scribner's, 1936.

Woolf, Virginia. *The Common Reader*. New York: Harvest Books, 1953 (1925).

————. *The Second Common Reader.* New York: Harvest
  Books, 1960 (1932).

————. *The Captain's Death Bed and Other Essays.* New York:
  Harvest Books, 1950.

CRITICISM OF AUTHORS DISCUSSED

Joyce Cary

Adam International Review (London), Nos. 212–13,
  November–December 1950 (special number on Cary).

Adams, Hazard. "Joyce Cary's Three Speakers." *Modern Fiction Studies,* V (Summer, 1959), 108–120.

Bloom, Robert. *The Indeterminate World: A Study of the
  Novels of Joyce Cary.* Philadelphia: University of Pennsylvania Press, 1962.

Foster, Malcolm. *Joyce Cary: A Biography.* London: Michael
  Joseph, 1969.

Hardy, Barbara. "Form in Joyce Cary's Novels." *Essays in Criticism,* IV (April, 1954), 180–90.

Hoffmann, Charles G. "The Genesis and Development of Joyce
  Cary's First Trilogy." *PMLA,* LXXVIII (September, 1963),
  431–39.

————. "'They Want to be Happy': Joyce Cary's Unfinished
  Castle Corner Series." *Modern Fiction Studies,* IX (Autumn, 1963), 217–25.

————. *Joyce Cary: The Comedy of Freedom.* Pittsburgh: University of Pittsburgh Press, 1964.

Kerr, Elizabeth M. "Joyce Cary's Second Trilogy." *University of
  Toronto Quarterly,* XXIX (April, 1960), 310–25.

Mahood, M. M. *Joyce Cary's Africa.* London: Methuen, 1964.

Mitchell, Giles. "Joyce Cary's *Prisoner of Grace.*" *Modern Fiction Studies,* IX (Autumn, 1963), 263–75.

Stockholder, Fred. "The Triple Vision in Joyce Cary's First
  Trilogy." *Modern Fiction Studies,* IX (Autumn, 1963),
  231–44.

Teeling, John, S. J. "Joyce Cary's Moral World." *Modern Fiction
  Studies,* IX (Autumn, 1963), 276–83.

Wolkenfeld, Jack. *Joyce Cary: The Developing Style.* New York
  and London: New York University Press and University of
  London Press, 1968.

Bibliography

202 Wright, Andrew. *Joyce Cary: A Preface to His Novels.* New York: Harper and Brothers, 1958.

Joseph Conrad

Baines, Jocelyn. *Joseph Conrad: A Critical Biography.* New York: McGraw-Hill, 1967.

Fleishman, Avrom. *Conrad's Politics: Community and Anarchy in the Fiction of Joseph Conrad.* Baltimore: Johns Hopkins University Press, 1967.

Guerard, Albert J. *Conrad the Novelist.* New York: Atheneum, 1967.

Hay, Eloise Knapp. *The Political Novels of Joseph Conrad.* Chicago: Chicago University Press, 1963.

Jean-Aubry, G. *Joseph Conrad: Life and Letters.* Garden City, New York: Doubleday, 1927.

Johnson, Bruce. *Conrad's Models of Mind.* Minneapolis: University of Minnesota Press, 1971.

Leavis, F. R. *The Great Tradition.* New York: Anchor Books, 1951.

Miller, J. Hillis. *Poets of Reality* (New York: Atheneum, 1969), 13–67.

Modern Fiction Studies, I, 1955 (special number on Conrad).

Moser, Thomas. *Joseph Conrad: Achievement and Decline.* Cambridge: Harvard University Press, 1957.

Sherry, Norman. *Conrad's Eastern World.* Cambridge: Cambridge University Press, 1966.

———. *Conrad's Western World.* Cambridge: Cambridge University Press, 1971.

Teets, Bruce E., and Helmut E. Gerber, eds. *Joseph Conrad: An Annotated Bibliography of Writings about Him.* DeKalb: Northern Illinois University Press, 1971.

Thomas, Claude, ed. *Studies in Joseph Conrad.* Montpellier: Université Paul-Valéry, 1975.

Tindall, William York. "Apology for Marlow." *From Jane Austen to Joseph Conrad.* Edited by Robert C. Rathburn and Martin Steinmann, Jr. (Minneapolis: University of Minnesota Press, 1958), 274–85.

Wiley, Paul L. *Conrad's Measure of Man.* Madison: University of Wisconsin Press, 1954.

Bibliography

Zyla, W. T., and Wendell M. Aycock, eds. *Joseph Conrad:*
Theory and World Fiction. Lubbock: Texas Tech University Press, 1974.

William Faulkner

Adams, Richard P. *Faulkner: Myth and Motion.* Princeton: Princeton University Press, 1968.

Beck, Warren. *Man in Motion: Faulkner's Trilogy.* Madison: University of Wisconsin Press, 1961.

Brooks, Cleanth. *William Faulkner: The Yoknapatawpha Country.* New Haven and London: Yale University Press, 1963.

Hoffman, Frederick J., *William Faulkner.* New York: Twayne, 1961.

Hoffman, Frederick J., and Olga W. Vickery, eds. *William Faulkner: Three Decades of Criticism.* East Lansing: Michigan State University Press, 1960.

Howe, Irving. *William Faulkner: A Critical Study.* New York: Vintage, 1962.

Kirk, Robert W., and Marvin Klotz. *Faulkner's People.* Berkeley and Los Angeles: University of California Press, 1963.

Malin, Irving. *William Faulkner: An Interpretation.* Stanford: Stanford University Press, 1957.

Millgate, Michael. *The Achievement of William Faulkner.* New York: Random House, 1966.

O'Connor, William Van. *The Tangled Fire of William Faulkner.* Minneapolis: University of Minnesota Press, 1959.

Petesch, Donald A. "Theme and Characterization in Faulkner's Snopes Trilogy." Ph.D. dissertation, University of Texas, 1969.

Southern Review, No. 11, Autumn, 1970 (contains five essays on Faulkner).

Thompson, Lawrance. *William Faulkner: An Introduction and Interpretation.* New York: Holt, Rinehart and Winston, 1963.

Vickery, Olga W. *The Novels of William Faulkner: A Critical Interpretation.* Baton Rouge: Louisiana State University Press, 1959.

Volpe, Edmund L. *A Reader's Guide to William Faulkner.* New York: Farrar, Straus, 1964.

Bibliography

204 Watson, James Gray. *The Snopes Dilemma: Faulkner's Trilogy*. Coral Gables: University of Miami Press, 1968.

Ford Madox Ford

Cassell, Richard A. *Ford Madox Ford: A Study of His Novels*. Baltimore: Johns Hopkins University Press, 1961.

Goldring, Douglas. *The Last Pre-Raphaelite: The Life and Writings of Ford Madox Ford*. London: MacDonald, 1948.

Gordon, Ambrose, Jr. *The Invisible Tent: The War Novels of Ford Madox Ford*. Austin: University of Texas Press, 1964.

Hafley, James. "The Moral Structure of *The Good Soldier*." *Modern Fiction Studies*, V (Summer, 1959), 121–28.

Harvey, David Dow. *Ford Madox Ford, 1873–1939: A Bibliography of Works and Criticism*. Princeton: Princeton University Press, 1962.

Meixner, John A. *Ford Madox Ford's Novels: A Critical Study*. Minneapolis: University of Minnesota Press, 1962.

Mizener, Arthur. *The Saddest Story: A Biography of Ford Madox Ford*. New York and Cleveland: World, 1971.

Ohmann, Carol. *Ford Madox Ford: From Apprentice to Craftsman*. Middletown: Wesleyan University Press, 1964.

Schorer, Mark. "The Good Novelist in *The Good Soldier*." *Horizon*, XX (August, 1949), 132–38.

Wiley, Paul L. *Novelist of Three Worlds: Ford Madox Ford*. Syracuse: University of Syracuse Press, 1962.

Young, Kenneth. *Ford Madox Ford*. London: Longmans, Green, 1956.

Henry Miller

Baxter, Annette Kar. *Henry Miller Expatriate*. Pittsburgh: University of Pittsburgh Press, 1961.

DeMott, Benjamin. "Henry Miller: Rebel-Clown at Eighty." *Saturday Review*, December 11, 1971, pp. 29–32.

Durrell, Lawrence. "Studies in Genius: Henry Miller." *Horizon*, XX (July, 1949), 45–61.

Durrell, Lawrence, Alfred Perles, and Henry Miller. *Art and Outrage*. New York: Dutton, 1961.

Gordon, William A. *The Mind and Art of Henry Miller*. Baton Rouge: Louisiana State University Press, 1968.

Hassan, Ihab. *The Literature of Silence: Henry Miller and Samuel Beckett*. New York: Alfred A. Knopf, 1967.

Mitchell, Edward B., ed. *Henry Miller: Three Decades of Criti-* 205
cism. New York: New York University Press, 1971.

Moore, Thomas H., ed. *Bibliography of Henry Miller.* Minneapolis: Henry Miller Literary Society, 1961.

Perles, Alfred. *My Friend Henry Miller.* Toronto: Longmans,
1956.

Porter, Bern, ed. *Happy Rock: A Book About Henry Miller.* Berkeley: Bern Porter, 1945.

Rexroth, Kenneth. *Bird in the Bush, Obvious Essays.* New York:
New Directions, 1959.

Wickes, George, ed. *Henry Miller and The Critics.* Carbondale:
Southern Illinois University Press, 1964.

———, ed. *Lawrence Durrell and Henry Miller: A Private Cor-
respondence.* New York: Dutton, 1964.

Widmer, Kingsley. *Henry Miller.* New York: Twayne, 1963.

Evelyn Waugh

Bergonzi, Bernard. "Evelyn Waugh's Gentlemen." *Critical
Quarterly,* V (Spring, 1963), 23–36.

Bradbury, Malcolm. *Evelyn Waugh.* Edinburgh and London:
Oliver and Boyd, 1964.

Carens, James F. *The Satiric Art of Evelyn Waugh.* Seattle and
London: University of Washington Press, 1966.

Doyle, Paul A. "Evelyn Waugh: A Bibliography (1926–1956),"
Bulletin of Bibliography, XXII (May–August, 1957).

Hollis, Christopher. *Evelyn Waugh* (Writers and Their Work,
No. 46). London: Longmans, Green, 1954.

Stopp, Frederick J. *Evelyn Waugh: Portrait of an Artist.* London:
Chapman and Hall, 1958.

Voorhees, R. J. "Evelyn Waugh's War Novels." *Queens Quarterly,* LXV (Spring, 1958), 53–63.

CRITICISM RELEVANT TO THE MODERN NOVEL

Aldridge, John W., ed. *Critiques and Essays on Modern Fiction:
1920–1951.* New York: Ronald Press, 1952.

Allen, Walter. *The Modern Novel in Britain and the United
States.* New York: Dutton, 1965.

Alter, Robert. *Rogue's Progress: Studies in the Picaresque
Novel.* Cambridge: Harvard University Press, 1964.

Bibliography

206 ———. *Partial Magic: The Novel as a Self-Conscious Genre*. Berkeley: University of California Press, 1975.

Auerbach, Erich. *Mimesis: The Representation of Reality in Western Literature*. New York: Anchor Books, 1957.

Barthes, Roland. *Writing Degree Zero*. New York: Hill & Wang, 1968(1953).

———. *S/Z*. New York: Hill & Wang, 1975 (1970).

———. *The Pleasure of the Text*. New York: Hill & Wang, 1975 (1973).

Beach, Joseph Warren. *The Twentieth Century Novel: Studies in Technique*. New York: Century, 1932.

Bergonzi, Bernard. *The Situation of the Novel*. Pittsburgh: University of Pittsburgh Press, 1971.

Booth, Wayne C. *The Rhetoric of Fiction*. Chicago and London: University of Chicago Press, 1961.

Braudy, Leo. *Narrative Form in History and Fiction*. Princeton: Princeton University Press, 1970.

Brown, E. K. *Rhythm in the Novel*. Toronto: University of Toronto Press, 1950.

Burke, Kenneth. *The Philosophy of Literary Form*. Rev.ed. New York: Vintage, 1957 (1941).

Church, Margaret. *Time and Reality: Studies in Contemporary Fiction*. Chapel Hill: University of North Carolina Press, 1963.

Edel, Leon. *The Modern Psychological Novel*. New York: Universal Library, 1964.

Forster, E. M. *Aspects of the Novel*. New York: Harcourt, Brace, 1927.

Foucault, Michel. *The Order of Things*. New York: Pantheon, 1971.

Frank, Joseph. *The Widening Gyre: Crisis and Mastery in Modern Literature*. New Brunswick: Rutgers University Press, 1963.

Freedman, Ralph. *The Lyrical Novel*. Princeton: Princeton University Press, 1963.

Friedman, Alan. *The Turn of the Novel*. New York: Oxford University Press, 1966.

Friedman, Alan Warren, ed. *Forms of Modern British Fiction*. Austin: University of Texas Press, 1975.

Friedman, Melvin. *Stream of Consciousness: A Study in Literary Method*. New Haven: Yale University Press, 1955.

Friedman, Norman. "Point of View in Fiction: The Development of a Critical Concept." *PMLA*, LXX (December, 1955), 1160–84.

————. *Form and Meaning in Fiction*. Athens: University of Georgia Press, 1976.

Gardner, John. *On Moral Fiction*. New York: Basic Books, 1978.

Glicksberg, Charles I. *The Self in Modern Literature*. University Park: Pennsylvania State University Press, 1963.

Gregor, Ian, and Brian Nicholas. *The Moral and the Story*. London: Faber and Faber, 1962.

Hardy, Barbara. *The Appropriate Form: An Essay on the Novel*. London: University of London, Athlone Press, 1964.

Harvey, W. J. *Character and the Novel*. London: Chatto and Windus, 1965.

Humphrey, Robert. *Stream of Consciousness in the Modern Novel*. Berkeley and Los Angeles: University of California Press, 1965.

Iser, Wolfgang. *The Implied Reader: Patterns of Communication in Prose Fiction from Bunyan to Beckett*. Baltimore: Johns Hopkins University Press, 1974.

Kennedy, Alan. *The Protean Self: Dramatic Action in Contemporary Fiction*. New York: Columbia University Press, 1974.

Kermode, Frank. *The Sense of an Ending*. New York: Oxford University Press, 1967.

Kostelanetz, Richard, ed. *On Contemporary Literature*. New York: Avon, 1969.

Kumar, Shiv K. *Bergson and the Stream of Consciousness Novel*. New York: New York University Press, 1963.

Lemon, Lee T., and Marion J. Reis, trans. and eds. *Russian Formalist Criticism: Four Essays*. Lincoln: University of Nebraska Press, 1965.

Lewis, R. W. B. *The Picaresque Saint*. Philadelphia and New York: Lippincott, 1959.

Lodge, David. *Language of Fiction: Essays in Criticism and Verbal Analysis of the English Novel*. New York: Columbia University Press, 1966.

Bibliography

208 Lubbock, Percy. *The Craft of Fiction*. New York: Viking, 1957 (1921).

Mack, Maynard, and Ian Gregor, eds. *Imagined Worlds: Essays on Some English Novels and Novelists in Honour of John Butt*. London: Methuen, 1968.

Mendilow, A. A. *Time and the Novel*. New York: Humanities Press, 1965 (1952).

Miller, J. Hillis, ed. *Aspects of Narrative*. New York: Columbia University Press, 1971.

Muir, Edwin. *The Structure of the Novel*. London: Hogarth Press, 1949.

O'Connor, William Van, ed. *Forms of Modern Fiction*. Bloomington: Indiana University Press, 1964.

Poirier, Richard. *The Performing Self*. New York: Oxford University Press, 1971.

Poulet, Georges. *Studies in Human Time*. New York: Harper and Brothers, 1956.

Preston, John. *The Created Self: The Reader's Role in Eighteenth-Century Fiction*. London: Heinemann, 1970.

Ramsey, Roger. "The Available and Unavailable 'I': Conrad and James." *English Literature in Transition*, XIV, No. 2 (1971), 137–45.

Scholes, Robert. *The Fabulators*. New York: Oxford University Press, 1967.

———, ed. *Approaches to the Novel: Materials for a Poetics*. San Francisco: Chandler, 1966.

Scholes, Robert, and Robert Kellogg. *The Nature of Narrative*. New York: Oxford University Press, 1966.

Sherbo, Arthur. *Studies in the Eighteenth Century English Novel*. East Lansing: Michigan State University Press, 1969.

Speirs, John. *Poetry Towards Novel*. New York: New York University Press, 1971.

Spencer, Sharon. *Space, Time and Structure in the Modern Novel*. New York: New York University Press, 1971.

Stevick, Philip, ed. *The Theory of the Novel*. New York: Free Press, 1967.

Tillyard, E. M. W. *The Epic Strain in the English Novel*. London: Chatto and Windus, 1958.

Van Ghent, Dorothy. *The English Novel: Form and Function.* 209
New York: Harper and Brothers, 1953.

Weinberg, Helen. *The New Novel in America.* Ithaca: Cornell
University Press, 1970.

Wilson, Edmund. *Axel's Castle: A Study in the Imaginative
Literature of 1870–1930.* London: Fontana Library, 1961
(1931).

Zabel, Morton Dauwen. *Craft and Character in Modern Fiction.*
London: Victor Gollancz, 1957.

Index

Index